Looking Back on President Barack Obama's Legacy

Wilbur C. Rich
Editor

Looking Back on President Barack Obama's Legacy

Hope and Change

Editor
Wilbur C. Rich
Department of Political Science
Wellesley College
Wellesley, MA, USA

ISBN 978-3-030-01544-2   ISBN 978-3-030-01545-9   (eBook)
https://doi.org/10.1007/978-3-030-01545-9

Library of Congress Control Number: 2018962971

Cover illustration: White House Photo / Alamy Stock Photo

This Palgrave Macmillan imprint is published by the registered company Springer Nature
Switzerland AG
The registered company address is: Gewerbestrasse 11, 6330 Cham, Switzerland

*To Professor Charles V. Hamilton, scholar, mentor, and friend,
whom I met as his student at Tuskegee Institute. Thank you
for the advice, insights, and opportunities that you have provided
to me in my career and for writing the foreword for this book.*

FOREWORD

Obviously, there are and will be many books on the legacy of President Barack Obama. This book will be one of the most interesting and useful one. It presents the views of twelve scholars with varying analytical interpretations on varying policy topics: foreign policy, global warming, health care, budget crises, and so on. Obama, from the beginning of his two terms had to cope with all these issues.

Thus, his "legacy" (at this early stage of his "post-presidency") is still in the making. In fact, in a sense, precisely because of his dynamic two terms and the clear opposite nature (policy-wise and otherwise) of his successor, Obama's legacy is still being formed. This is a good thing. This book is an excellent guide to all the analytical factors to follow. It presents different views of Obama's presidency from different sharp perspectives that ought to be part of any serious presidency. Integrity and intelligence ought to be part of the calculus.

Obama's presidency is a good one to study.

Whatever it was, it was a "first." All "firsts" have a special place in American narratives. AMERICANS LIKE FIRSTS. The first to go to the moon, to discover a health vaccine, to be the first black Supreme Court Justice, the first woman astronaut.

Obama was America's first Black President.

From that point, all political analysis began with a new chapter.

What did it mean?

The title of this book is appropriate: Hope and Change.

What did this pretend? What would this change? This is the analytical task of this book. It should be studied (not just read) slowly and seriously. Something like the "legacy" of the man who so admirably is its subject.

Columbia University   Charles V. Hamilton
New York, NY, USA

CONTENTS

NOTES ON CONTRIBUTORS

Meena Bose is Executive Dean for Public Policy and Public Service Programs, Peter S. Kalikow School of Government, Public Policy and International Affairs, and Director of the Peter S. Kalikow Center for the Study of the American Presidency, at Hofstra University, USA. She is the author of *Shaping and Signaling Presidential Policy: The National Security Decision Making of Eisenhower and Kennedy* (Texas A&M University Press, 1998), and the editor of several volumes in presidential studies. She is an author of the *American Government: Institutions and Policies* textbook (16th edition, 2019) and of *The Paradoxes of the American Presidency* textbook (5th edition, Oxford University Press, 2018).

George A. Gonzalez is Professor of Political Science at University of Miami, USA. His books include *Energy and Empire: The Politics of Nuclear and Solar Power in the United States, Energy and the Politics of the North Atlantic and American Empire and the Canadian Oil Sands*. He has written extensively on issues of environmental policy and ethics.

Charles V. Hamilton is a former Professor of Political Science at Columbia University, USA, where he served as the Wallace S. Sayre Professor of Political Science. He published several books and articles including a famous book entitled *Black Power* with Stokely Carmichael.

Kimberley S. Johnson is a Professor in the Department of Social and Cultural Analysis at New York University, USA. She has published *Governing the American State* and *Reforming Jim Crow*.

Daniel Lanford is a Postdoctoral Research Fellow at the Scholars Strategy Network. Daniel coordinates the SSN in Georgia and holds affiliations at Emory University with the department of sociology and at Georgia State University with the departments of sociology, political science, and public management. His current research focuses on racialized political sentiments, democratic theory, health policy, and population health. As an SSN fellow, Daniel spends half his time on research and half his time helping scholars connects their research to the policy process.

Ruth Milkman is Distinguished Professor of Sociology at City University of New York Graduate Center, USA, and Research Director at City University of New York's Murphy Institute for Labor Studies, USA. Her sole-authored books include *Gender at Work, Farewell to the Factory, L.A. Story* and most recently, *On Gender, Labor and Inequality.*

Jill Quadagno is Professor Emerita of Sociology at Florida State University, USA, where she held the Mildred and Claude Pepper Eminent Scholar Chair in Social Gerontology. She has published 12 books and more than 80 articles on aging, health and social policy issues. Among her books are *One Nation, Uninsured: Why the US Has No National Health Insurance, The Color of Welfare: How Racism Undermined the War on Poverty* and *Aging and the Life Course.* Her areas of specialization include social security reform, health policy, long-term care, and public attitudes toward social programs.

Lyn Ragsdale is the Radoslav A. Tsanoff Professor of Public Affairs and Professor of Political Science at Rice University, USA. She has published several books including The *American Nonvoter*, with Jerrold G. Rusk and *Vital Statistics on the Presidency, 4th ed.* and numerous articles on the American presidency and elections.

Stanley Renshon is Professor of Political Science at the City University of New York Graduate Center, USA, and also a certified psychoanalyst in private practice.

He is the author of over 100 professional articles and 16 books in the areas of presidential psychology and leadership, Immigration and American National Identity, and American Foreign Policy. His most recent book is entitled *Barack Obama and the Politics of Redemption.* His psychological biography of the Clinton presidency—*High Hopes: The Clinton Presidency and the Politics of Ambition* won Political Science Association's Richard

E. Neustadt Award for the best book published on the presidency and the National Association for the Advancement of Psychoanalysis' Gradiva Award for the best published work in the category of biography. He is at work on his fourth psychologically framed analysis of a sitting president—Donald Trump—entitled: *Disruption by Design: The Trump Presidency and the Politics of American Restoration*.

Wilbur C. Rich is William R. Kenan Jr. Emeritus Professor of Political Science at Wellesley College, USA. His books include *Coleman Young and Detroit Politics, David Dinkins and New York City Politics* and *The Post-Racial Society Is Here*. He has also written extensively on political leadership and issues of race relations.

Kristoffer Smemo is Historian and Visiting Fellow at the Center for Work, Labor, and Democracy at the University of California, Santa Barbara, USA. He is completing a book on how urban social movements shaped the emergence of the "liberal" wing of the mid-century Republican Party.

Isaac Unah is Associate Professor of Political Science at University of North Carolina at Chapel Hill. Professor Unah is the former Chair of the Law and Courts Section of the American Political Science Association and former Director of the Law and Social Sciences Program at the National Science Foundation. His first book, *The Courts of International Trade: Judicial Specialization, Expertise, and Bureaucratic Policymaking* examined the role of specialized courts in US trade policy implementation. His second book, *The Supreme Court in American Politics*, uses an evolutionary perspective to give readers a firm understanding of the US Supreme Court. He has also published articles in the *American Journal of Political Science, Political Research Quarterly, Law & Policy, Business and Politics, Social Sciences*, and several major law reviews.

Ryan Williams is a PhD candidate in the Department of Political Science at the University of North Carolina at Chapel Hill. His primary research area is in American judicial politics and political institutions, and his research focuses on specialized American courts and the interaction between the US Supreme Court and other American political institutions. He is currently researching the nature of expertise in American specialized courts and the role specialization plays in altering judicial outcomes. His research has been published in *Justice System Journal* and *The Routledge Handbook of Judicial Behavior*.

LIST OF FIGURES

List of Tables

The Obama Legacy in American Electoral Participation

The Legacy of President Obama in the U.S. Supreme Court

Introduction: Barack Obama and the Transformational Impulse

Wilbur C. Rich

American presidential history is full of commended political firsts—first military general to serve in the office, the first father/son to serve as presidents, the first Catholic president, and so on. The celebrated honor of being the first person to achieve the historical breakthrough carries with it an incredible amount of triumphalism and a high burden of expectations. When Barack Hussein Obama became the first African American president of the United States, his election represented a sharp turn in America's racial history as well as a fascinating self-actualization of political ambitions. He inherited a venerated office with a job description that had a 221-year history. It is also an office that continues to change.

After President Obama finished taking the Oath of Office, remained questions about whether he was up to the job. Granted this is true for all new presidents but Obama was so unlike any of his predecessors. Barack Obama was born in Hawaii, worked as community organizer, served in the Illinois state senate, taught law at University of Chicago, and served in the US Senate for three years. Against many odds he became the 44th president of the United States.

W. C. Rich (✉)
Department of Political Science, Wellesley College, Wellesley, MA, USA
e-mail: wrich@wellesley.edu

© The Author(s) 2019
W. C. Rich (ed.), *Looking Back on President Barack Obama's Legacy*,
https://doi.org/10.1007/978-3-030-01545-9_1

1

The eighteenth-century Framers of the United States Constitution enumerated an intriguing set of qualifications for the presidency. For them, the newly elected president would be a statesman who could command the respect of the citizenry. Ideally the president should be a literate property-owning man with experience in public affairs. They assumed that more statesmen like George Washington, the prototype, would emerge. The Framers of the Constitution certainly could not have predicted that a black man named Barack Hussein Obama II would be the 44th president of the United States and that his overall political impetus would be to fundamentally change the American establishment. Nor could they have expected the office of the presidency to be a vehicle for socio-economic change as it has emerged. The men who served in the office after President Washington expanded the roles of the office and Congress added the statutory modifications to make the president responsible for the economy and awaited respondent for catastrophes, that is, chief comforter. The Framers would not recognize the modern presidency. With each expansion of the presidency, new contradictions and paradoxes are introduced for the incumbents. Political scientists Thomas E. Cronin and Michael A. Genovese observed,

> We admire presidential power, yet fear it. We yearn for inspiration, idealism and optimism, yet know the need for realism. We yearn for the heroic, yet are also inherently suspicious of it. We demand dynamic leadership, yet grant only limited power to the president. We want presidents to be dispassionate leaders and listeners, yet they must also be decisive. We are impressed with presidents who have calm and even fearless self-confidence, yet we dislike arrogance and respect those who express reasonable self-doubt. We want leaders to be bold and innovative, yet we allow presidents to take us only where we want to go. In a sense, we want presidents to be representative of us, yet not too representative.[1]

Did President Obama meet these conflicting demands, cross-pressures, and contradictions in his term? The chapters in this book examine President Barack Obama's transformational impulse to make America a different and "better" nation. The underline premise was that the nation was not living up to its creedal obligations, economic potential, and moral responsibilities. Obama thought he could be a catalyst for fundamental change in America. In his 2009 Inaugural Address he proclaimed

On this day, we gather because we have chosen hope over fear, unity of purpose over conflict and discord. On this day, we come to proclaim an end to the petty grievances and false promises, the recriminations and worn-out dogmas that for far too long have strangled our politics… The time has come to reaffirm our enduring spirit; to choose our better history; to carry forward that precious gift, that noble idea passed on from generation to generation: the God-given promise that all are equal, all are free, and all deserve a chance to pursue their full measure of happiness.[2]

"Yes we can" was one of the themes of his campaign. Indeed, changing America had been a recurrent theme for many modern American presidential campaigns. The question was what type of change and what type of leadership was appropriate for the task. In 2008 Barack Obama ran a campaign that promised to make fundamental change in America. In his book *The Audacity of Hope*, Obama made a commitment to economic democracy. The book emphasizes opportunity, fairness, and accountability.[3] In his travel around the nation he thought that he had encountered a yearning for "Hope and Change." From his perspective, America was a nation that needed to make major changes to make it an even greater nation than it is. Otherwise why would he, a serious change agent, apply for the job? In that historical election Obama won 52.9% of the popular vote and 365 electoral votes. Obviously, he received support from a variety of groups including 95% of African American voters.[4] His election suggested that the American people wanted a transformational presidency and that Obama concluded that he was such a leader. Obama told his audience

I'm the one who brings change. It is my vision. It is my agenda. I believe deeply that we cannot solve the challenges of our time … unless we perfect our union by understanding that we may have different stories, but we hold common hopes; that we may not look the same and we may not have come from the same place, but we all want to move in the same direction. This belief comes from my unyielding faith in the decency and generosity of the American people. But it also comes from my own American story.[5]

The Framers of the Constitution would be stunned at this statement. Not only would that statement offend their eighteenth-century social sensibilities but it was not what they wanted to the presidency to be. Rereading this statement tells us how Barack Obama interpreted his transformational role. The quote contains an incredible amount of self-referencing and pro-jections about the motives of the American people. As we shall see in this book, self-referencing and projections did present problems for President Obama as it does for presidential leadership in general.

TYPES OF PRESIDENTIAL LEADERSHIP

Some president watchers and historians claim they can immediately iden-tify what type of leaders a new president will be. Political scientist James McGregor Burns is credited with making a critical distinction about the nature of leadership. His simple typology-transformational and transac-tional leadership can be applied to most American presidents. Presidents who are transactional leaders seek political solutions for the given moment but do not try to fundamentally change existing political and economic arrangements. Such leaders just want to get through the day; make what-ever political compromises needed to keep the government functioning and to keep those around him (the public, staff, and family) satisfied. American voters elected such presidents to continue existing policies of the government; Dwight Eisenhower, George H.W. Bush, and George W. Bush were also examples of such leadership. This is not to suggest that all Republican presidents were transactional. Lincoln and Reagan were definitely transformational. Republican voters in the post-Reagan era apparently wanted candidates to continue to reflect Reaganism. The potential transactional leaders have campaigned as such. Such presidents understand that they were not elected to do anything radical or to change how the nation is organized.

Presidents who believed they are transformational leaders, by contrast, seek to radically and permanently change the nation's politics and econ-omy. They are most successful during crises. For such a president changing the nation is a personal sojourn for them and in the process all Americans will benefit. These types of presidents argue for new ways to deal with economic and social problems. During their campaigns they tell voters that the nation is in a crisis and their welfare is at stake, therefore electing them can alleviate their situations. Robert Kuttner, author of *Obama's Challenge*, suggested that the then Senator Barack Obama had the skills to be a transformational president in the mode of Presidents Lincoln and Roosevelt.[6] Such candidates view their election as averring confirmation and a mandate for fundamental change.

Granted the typology categories are not mutual exclusive, but it allows us to appreciate presidential behavior in the office. History shows that presidents can be a mix of both transactional and transformational styles. President Lyndon Johnson comes to mind as synthesis of both types.

Yet political scientist Stephen Skowronek believes actual transformational presidents are those that completely changed how government works. He called them "Reconstruction Presidents," since they seek to repudiate the old ways of doing and thinking about politics.[7] Such presidents appear at certain junctions in American history as a response to a collapse of governing consensus or at times of economic dislocation. Abraham Lincoln and Franklin Roosevelt are often cited as examples of transformational presidents. Lincoln won the Civil War, emancipated slaves in the Confederate States, and expanded the transcontinental railroad. In the process he expanded the prerogatives of the presidency. Roosevelt took the nation away from the Great Depression, instituted a mixed economic system, established a social security system, and promoted a new workfare program called the New Deal. Indeed, Barack Obama regarded President Lincoln as one of his role models. He may have been channeling Lincoln, but his statement above suggested deeper sources of motivation.[8] If one reads the Obama statement slowly one gets the sense of secondary motivations that includes a personal and consecrated journey.

BARACK OBAMA AS TRANSFORMATIONAL CANDIDATE

Several contributors in this book commented on Barack Obama's campaign to be a transformational figure. In his first national political speech at the 2004 National Democratic Convention, he asserted that there were no blue states or red states in America but rather a United States of America. To some the speech was spellbinding and uplifting because of its hyper-optimistic tone and promise. Journalist Ta-Nehisi Coates recalled, "Obama's DNC speech is the key. It does not belong to the literature of 'struggle'; it belongs to the literature of prospective presidents-men (as it turned out) who speak not to gravity and reality, but to aspirations and dreams."[9] Four years later the junior senator from Illinois was running for president of the United States. Obama was Ivy League educated, with a bi-racial ancestry, an international childhood, great oratory skills, and his family was picture perfect. Still people were asking silly questions. Was he black enough? Could a community organizer handle the job of being

president? Could he tear himself away from his Chicago political moor-
ing? Would whites vote for him? In his 2008 campaign Obama presented
himself as an uplifting and change-oriented candidate. Indeed, he suggested that the Obama administration would be a post-partisan and race-
neutral one. America, under his tutelage, would emerge as a very different
nation in substance and spirit. He asserted that "Hope and Change"
would replace the Washington partisan bickering and ideological joust-
ing. American voters who voted for him understood what they were voted
for: fundamental change.

Obama saw as his purpose as transforming American politics. He was
not just going to be the first African American president but his approach
to the presidency that would be entirely different. His strategy was to
appeal to the fair and good aspirational qualities of the American people.
The President flattered and challenged them. "You, the American people
elected me [Barack Obama] to do something radical, now let's do it."
Obama said as much in his 2016 interview with Coates. "At some level
what the people want to feel is that the person leading them sees the best
in them."[10] Although Obama did not offer an overall policy theme such as
the New Deal or the Great Society, he sought to make America more
inclusive socially and economically. He sought to make Americans more
aware of the economic dislocation problems associated with a globalized
economy.

When Obama became president in 2008 the media characterized his
election as a major breakthrough (read race relations) in American politics.
He was such an elegant speaker and had a likable personality. Journalists
used adjectives like *thoughtful, deliberate, rational,* and *professorial* to
describe his style. More importantly, he embraced this image and apparently regarded it as an indissoluble faith in the goodness of the American
people. He repeated that faith on several occasions. His speeches were of
full optimism and assurances that the world could be a better place. His
election was greeted by the world as new American beginning. Barack
Obama was both a leader and a teacher. In many ways he taught us a lot
about ourselves. His stint in the White House was "no ordinary times."
For that reason, the Obama presidency will remain an intriguing part of
our nation's political history. The world took notice of this prospect. In
2009 President Obama was given the Nobel Peace Prize for inspiring
peace in the world. He had not been in office a year.

OBAMA AS AN EFFECTIVE PRESIDENT

One of the first things a new president realizes is that being elected president is not the same as being president. Becoming an effective president requires even more skills because the choices are more complicated. An entire research literature devotes itself to analyzing effectiveness of presidents. Political scientist Fred Greenstein, one of the leading experts on presidential leadership, outlined six qualities for an effective president.[11] An effective president must be, first of all, proficient as a public communicator. Greenstein found that many presidents have been failures as communicators. Obama was a great communicator. He was what Greenstein called a "shining exception" in the history of poor presidential communicators.[12] Because President Obama was such a great communicator he was clearly the face of his administration. He stood foursquare on his agenda that was to make improvements in the quality of life and the nation more inclusive. Obama mastered the teleprompter, phrase making, and extemporaneous assertions. The nation had not seen anything like his rhetorical performance since the presidency of John F. Kennedy. Some contributors for this book conceded that President Obama was a good communicator but question his effectiveness as a change agent.

The second quality for effectiveness is presidential organizational capacity. Greenstein describes this as the ability to create "a team and get the most out of it."[13] A president must be able to rally his colleagues and "create an effective institutional arrangement." Before deciding, Obama gained a reputation of "exposing himself to vigorous give and take."[14] Selecting the right staff members is critical to making an effective interactive process work. According to the media, Obama staff meeting resembled university seminars with the president and staff debating issues before making decisions. Political scientist James P. Pfiffner agreed that White House staffs reflect the incumbent values. He described Obama's White House staff as an organization engaging in "Careful, and sometimes lengthy, deliberations [that] marked Obama's style of decision making. He insisted on multiple advocacy by requiring his staffers to argue their cases in front of him, as when he demanded that dissenting perspectives on economic and military policy be aired in person."[15] Describing Obama leadership style with those adjectives may be only an impression made from a distance. We will have wait for Obama staff members to write their books to inform us about what is like to work for the former president.

Retrospectively, one could question Obama's selections for key staff positions, but these choices were made to help him achieve his agenda. Presidents Lincoln and Obama were seen as similar in that they selected a team of rivals or former opponents as members of their staff (e.g. Hillary Clinton and Joe Biden).[16] Indeed at the time of their appointments, the staff choices seemed reasonable. There were turnovers but no major blow-ups or scandals. Managing presidential staff is by nature idiosyncratic. Greenstein admired Eisenhower procedural presidency with clearly defined staff roles. Obama was not inclined to organize the White House in a military manner.

Greenstein's third quality for presidential effectiveness was political skill. Presidents need great political skill to get elected and to govern. Governing requires dealing with Congress, recurrent national crises, and the world leaders. This book will discuss what happened when Obama policies began navigating the labyrinth of Congress. All presidents learn early that espousing a policy is easy but getting it thorough Congress and having it legitimated by the Supreme Court is another matter. What the post-partisan policymaking Obama espoused did not always happen. Despite overall agreement that the Great Recession put the nation on the precipice, none of Republicans in the House and only three in the Senate voted for 2009 American Recovery and Reinvestment Act. Congressional leaders unashamedly defended their ideological positions. Increasingly throughout his presidency Obama resorted to using budget reconciliations and executive orders to get things done.

Political scientist Richard Neustadt has argued that the presidency works when the president can persuade Washington establishment to join him in policymaking.[17] Failure to persuade can lead to legislative repudiation and even gridlock. Obama's Neustadt's moment came as he tried to get his initial agenda through the Congress. The Republican Party leaders balked. They dismissed his rhetoric as plain election talk and made a political calculation if the president legislation was stalled it could lead to increase Republican seats in Congress. Retrospectively the tactic was a prescient one. Republicans opposed his proposals, especially the Affordable Care Act. Although he attempted to consult Republicans, he did not get a single Republican vote in support of the bill. Republican leaders predicted that Obama would be a one-termer like Jimmy Carter. Mitch McConnell stated that his job was to make sure that Obama was a one-term president. This strategy worked in the 2010 congressional elections. However Republican leaders made tactical errors in the run-up to the

2012 elections and nominated the wrong candidate, Mitt Romney, to oppose the President.[18] Obama won reelection.

As I stated earlier President Obama did meet his Neustadt moment, that is, making an unpersuasive policy proposal, with the Congress and the Washington establishment. For example, he was not able to use the office to generate public support for gun control legislature. Despite having public support, the National Rifle Association (NRA) proved to be an effective opposition group to even a small policy change. The president did not use threats, subterfuge, or extra-constitutional means to defeat NRA. In other words, Obama was no Machiavelli or President Lyndon Johnson.

The fourth quality for presidential effectiveness was a vision for public policy. For Greenstein, vision was defined as consistency of viewpoint.[19,20] Obama espoused a progressive agenda and practiced it where possible. Because Obama was a "rhetorically gifted president," his vision for equality, fairness, and unlimited opportunity for Americans seemed clear and elegant. Obama continually tried to convince Americans that a nation would be better off if its economic policies adhered to inclusiveness and uplifted the less fortunate.

Greenstein's fifth quality for presidential effectiveness was a cognitive style that easily processes a large amount of information. Presidents receive a lot of information. Some presidents are able to digest more of it than other. Because some problems are so complex, understanding them doesn't always provide ways of solving them. Granted an effective president must have an open and discerning mind. Here President Obama stood out. He had a professorial propensity to read and analyze information provided to him before making decisions. His intellectual curiosity was never questioned. He may not have read every memo that came to his desk, but he seemed well informed about public issues.

The sixth quality of presidential effectiveness is emotional intelligence. Presidents must be able to manage their emotions and turning them into constructive purposes. One never got the impression that Obama was dominated by his emotions and that they undermined his performance as president. Other than reporters referencing to his race in their reporting, there did not seem to be a "distracting emotional perturbations."[21] Although the Constitution does not require the president to be the nation's comforter, it is now a role expectation. Obama had a penchant for being the great comforter at times of extreme national trauma (e.g. gun violence and murder in Newtown and Charleston).

In view of Greenstein's definitions of presidential effectiveness, did Obama have the qualities of an effective president? It depends whether one shares Greenstein's definition of presidential effectiveness. Some contributors in this book raised questions about whether Obama was an effective president. Indeed, historical evaluations of Obama's achievements and the appropriateness will be varied. As most presidents discover, and as Obama's memoir may reveal, the job of president kept changing and as did expectations. Nevertheless, what happens during his watch will be a part of Obama's legacy.

OBAMA LEGACY: HOPE AND CHANGE?

There is a no general theory of presidential legacy. As mentioned at the outset, the presidency has evolved beyond the Framers' notion of the chief executive. Some presidents have expanded the reach of the office. What a president does now is more important than what the presidency was originally designed to be. Our nation's politics are now centered on the presidency. Television has changed the image and activity of the presidency. Obama followed his predecessors in attracting the stargazing attention once reserved for celebrities. Yet the public often associates presidential legacy with notable events. In his 2013 inauguration address, President Obama got several bursts of applauses when he stated

> This generation of Americans has been tested by crises that steeled our resolve and proved our resilience. A decade of war is now ending. An economic recovery has begun. America's possibilities are limitless, for we possess all the qualities that this world without boundaries demands: youth and drive; diversity and openness; an endless capacity for risk and a gift for reinvention. My fellow Americans, we are made for this moment, and we will seize it—so long as we seize it together.[22]

President Obama's legacy had become associated his rescue of the economy after the Great Recession. He also negotiated a nuclear deal with Iran, participated in the 2015 Paris Climate Agreement, reduced combat in Iraq and Afghanistan, supported extending civil rights to the LGBTQ community, and passed fair sentencing laws among many other accomplishments.

Coming to the presidency in the midst of the 2008 Great Recession, Obama took Rooseveltian posture by "digging the economy out of the ditch," that is, a phrase the president used when describing how Republican policies had put the economy in danger. Rescuing Wall Street, General Motors, and struggling homeowners simultaneously was no minor feat. Apparently, the president's early successes encouraged him to double down on his initial inspiring message. It is perhaps too cynical to say that Obama believed his own rally speeches. Yet the majority of voters approved of the way Obama conducted the first four years of his presidency and reelected him to office.

Obama will probably be remembered as not being adept at the transactional aspects of the presidency. He was not a Washington community smoother, a convivial personality that enjoyed socially interacting with the power brokers. He was more of an executive president than a legislative one. Since his legislative agenda lagged, Congress forced him to make a series of singular Executive Orders. In a 2007 essay on presidential potential for racial progress, I made a distinction between policies that were Situational Improvement Policies and those that could be classified as Racial Adjustment Gestures.[23] The former policies could be identified as improving the socio-economic situation of African Americans. The latter were symbolic changes that made people feel better about a given event or a political slight but did little to change the overall economic conditions of African Americans. I was surprised that President Obama used the latter policies as much as he did. In my 2011 essay in Dirk C. VanRaemdonck et al.'s *The Obama Presidency: Change and Continuity*, I pointed out that the president's commendable reactions to Professor Henry Gates's arrest and the Shirley Sherrod's wrongful firing from the US Department of Agriculture were individual-specific and mainly symbolic.[24] The media made much of these events, but they had little impact on the daily lives of African Americans.

THE SHORT LEASH OF EXPECTATIONS

The 2008 candidate Barack Obama was a different man than the President Barack Obama. Candidate Obama could attack the Congress for not doing its job. President Obama had to work with Congress and their allies in the lobby community. A president alienates them at his peril. Soliciting them can be fruitful and rewarding. It did not take long for Obama to publicly admit his Neustadt moment (i.e. gradual realization that to get things done in government, one needs to persuade the Washington establishment to support one's policies). Obama acknowledged that his presidential powers were limited. In addition, the tug of his ambition and public expectations were omnipresent. Three years into his presidency, James T. Kloppenberg and Joseph Peschek separately expressed disappointments about the direction of Obama economic policies.[25] They argued that the president had emerged as an economic centrist, business supporters, and not a progressive. For them the forces of neoliberalism had won.

Political scientist George C. Edwards concluded in *Overreach: Leadership in Obama Presidency* that the president had simply overreached the limits of presidential power. Accordingly, to this presidential scholar, success in this job did not come from creating new opportunities but rather identifying openings and capitalizing on existing opportunities. As a result of his having proposed an expensive and polarizing agenda, Obama undermined his own presidency and helped to bring about the 2010 midterm congressional results, losses the president referred to a "shellacking."

In retrospect Obama's first term had a series of successful policies. After less than a month in office he was able to sign a $787 billion economic stimulus package into law. The new law contained $50 billion in funds to prevent foreclosure for Americans who were in danger of losing their homes. Additionally, he also supported loans for near-bankrupt American automakers. The measure also contained monies for the development of so-called "green jobs" and public schools reform. Aside from the economic turnaround of the Great Recession, the President moved to promote a policy to alleviate climate change and reform health care.

Entering its second term, the Obama administration found itself responding to a series of political events rather than creating new programs and establishing a new narrative. Obama's analytical style impressed the chattering media pundits and African Americans who saw him as a role model for them and a leader for new racial beginning.

Michael Genovese and Todd Belt's *The Post-Heroic Presidency* claimed that since 1970 the United States can only exercise minimalist hegemony in world affairs; that is, it can no longer act as the dominant military and economic power. This is due to the rise of other countries and the decline of American power. Accordingly, presidents have limited domestic and international powers. Simply put, because of lack of the resources, American presidents are minimalist leaders.[26] For President Obama, the controversial Iran nuclear deal was considered a successful diplomatic triumph. He received kudos for the successful Osama bin Laden raid and for the restoration of diplomatic relations with Cuba. There were also some problematic missteps and policies. His rhetoric about drawing a red line over the use of possible poison gas by the Syrian government turned out to be a miscalculation. However, when the President asked Congress for support, they did not give him the authority to make unlimited bombing strike. Moreover, President Obama should be applauded for not laying waste to Syria's infrastructure to punish the Syrian leaders. Yet Genovese and Belt labeled Obama a "defensive minimalist."[27]

During the campaign and while in office, President Obama expressed concern about the quality of American public schools. Teachers' unions and state education officials, who were Obama supporters, had condemned the Bush school reform policy, that is, No Child Left Behind Act.

The president first tried to address school reform with his Race-to-Top funds from the 2009 Recovery Act. This program was designed to assist states in reforming their local districts. The administration also supported a new law entitled Every Student Succeeds Act that let the states to continue to decide education policy. There were fewer mandates for accountability. This decision repudiated George W. Bush's school reform policies.

Changing Bush policies on a variety of issues was a way of showing contrast with the previous administration and to begin the consolidation of the nascent Obama legacy. Obama's tenure in office can loosely be organized as preferential and referential legacies. The matrix in Fig. 1 shows calculated and inadvertent.

	Calculated	Inadvertent
Preferential	Economic Rescue Health Care Reform (ACA), Nuclear Agreement with Iran, Diplomatic recognition of Cuba	Elimination of Osama Bin Laden Increased presidential role as Chief Comforter
Referential	Reduced Military presence in Iraq Repeal of Don't Ask, Don't Tell policy in the Military	Unaccompanied children immigrants Failure of the Arab Spring Movement

Fig. 1   Obama legacies

Preferential legacies are those policy objectives presidents strive to achieve. Presidents want to make policy achievements that historians will underscore as a colophon of the presidency. Some such achievements are calculated/planned and other just happen; that is, they are inadvertent. The outrageous shooting of school children in Newtown, Connecticut, and shooting of church members in Charleston, South Carolina, provided the president with an opportunity to express the nation's profound sympathy. He did so well that future presidents might follow his lead as chief comforter. Referential legacies are reputational, that is, what the general public remembers about a particular presidency. Often presidents will promote policies that solve an ongoing situation. Some policies are deliberate, and others are often out of control of the president. The failure of the Arab Spring protests in the Middle East countries after President Obama's 2009 uplifting speech at Cairo University can be traced to a variety of explanations. The immigration problem preceded President Obama but his reactions to it changed how future presidents will react to the problem. Few people could have predicted an influx of unaccompanied children crossing the nation's southern borders. Neither did anyone expect the drone technology would change the way terrorism is fought. Genovese and Belt called Obama the "drone president." They stated, "The use of drones as a tool of policy underscores Obama's approach to foreign policy."[28] They claimed Obama was "extraordinary risk averse when dealing with day-to-day mechanism of the war on terror."[29]

Obviously, these legacy categories are not mutually exclusive. Too often quick judgments about legacy are made before a president leaves office.

QUICK JUDGMENTS ABOUT PRESIDENTS

Several books and articles have been written about the presidency of Barack Obama. Journalists and academics are trying to discern what just happened. Before evaluating him, we should consider Bruce Miroff's *Pragmatic Illusions,* one of the best works on the *Kennedy* legacy. Miroff defined Kennedy as a conservative force that protected business interest at home and abroad. Kennedy's conservative deeds were in contrast to his highly inflated progressive image. In effect the American people brought into the myth of Camelot and the carefully framed Kennedy image.

Is it possible that some Americans invested themselves psychologically in President Obama in hope that he would be the true source of progressive change in America? Or was it just simple cases of irrational projections on the part of his supporters and reading his speeches as a Rorschach test run amok? The president recognized this possibility. In an interview, he stated, "I serve as a blank screen on which people project their own views. As such, I am bound to disappoint some, if not all, of them."[30] Despite having a longer tenure than President Kennedy and arriving in power during the Great Recession, did Obama do more to "preserve existing patterns of power and wealth than alter it"?[31] Were we overtaken by his novelty, style, and charisma? Were we misled by prospects of benevolent presidentialism?[32] Were his limitations those of the presidency in general as Charles O. Jones's *The Presidency in a Separated System* has taught us?[33] Can any president succeed legislatively in times of hyper-change and hyper-partisanship?

If Miroff and Jones are correct, then who was Barack Obama? And what did he do to us? What did we, the public, do to him? Will he become the liberal Democrat's version of Ronald Reagan, an icon for future presidential candidates? Over the next 10 years, will the rose-colored glasses with which we viewed Barack Obama fade? The Obama story may be troubling on a different level. Carlos Lazada raised interesting questions about self-referencing the Obama story.

> Obama called himself "a prisoner of my own biography," yet throughout his presidency, biography would also empower him. Whether in foreign policy, race relations, electoral politics, or even in the meaning of the hope and change he promised, Obama has turned to his life and symbolism as a default reference and all-purpose governing tool.
>
> The personalized presidency can be inspiring. It can also feel arrogant. And it can bypass some of the very norms and institutions Obama rhapsodizes about so frequently—a dangerous proposition as the country braces for an unpredictable, unmoored successor.[34]

President Obama's farewell speech returned to the flattening theme discussed in this chapter. The president supposedly had 55% approval rating and, like Eisenhower, enjoyed keeping that positive image.

> After my election, there was talk of a post-racial America. Such a vision, however well-intended, was never realistic. For race remains a potent and often divisive force in our society. Now, I've lived long enough to know that race relations are better than they were 10, or 20, or 30 years ago—you can see it not just in statistics, but in the attitudes of young Americans across the political spectrum. But we're not where we need to be. And all of us have more work to do.[35]

In *The Post Racial Society Is Here*, I made a similar observation but did African Americans expect too much?[36] Should the president have explained what the future goals of race relations were and strategies to achieving full equality? In his farewell address there was absence of information about being president; rather, it was about how proud he was of the American people and the fact that they elected him. Through eloquent prose, Barack Obama urged Americans to become more politically active.

Some writers in this volume will conclude that President Obama did great things and believe more could be done if the Republican-dominated Congress had made greater bipartisan efforts. Others will conclude his legacy will be modest. Certainly, his signature legislative legacy may be the Affordable Care Act (aka Obamacare). His second legacy is the restarting the economy and restoring faith in the people who run the financial-oriented economy. The authorizing of the elimination of Bin Laden is also significant. Restoring diplomatic relations with Cuba helps the Cuban people and ends a dubious 50-year-old isolation policy.

Given this brief overview of his term, we return to an earlier question. Was Obama an effective president? This is a difficult question to answer because the presidency keeps changing.

THE CHANGING NATURE OF THE PRESIDENCY

The emergence of the age of "hyper-change" did alter the character of the office.[37] Indeed, being president is an incredibly difficult job to master. The Framers of the Constitution had only a vague idea about what they were creating and how the office would evolve over time. Some of the occupants in the office may have not completely understood what the job encompassed. In other words, one could become president and not know what the job is and leave it not knowing what the job was. History is full of men who held the office with a seemingly naive understanding of the job (e.g. James Buchanan). Just dealing with what comes to one's desk is not the entire job (Jimmy Carter).

What complicates things further is that the job changes with each generation. Presidents are forced to engage in what political scientist Victor Thompson calls dramaturgy.[38] They have to pretend that they know what they are doing to make everyone else comfortable. The American presidency is a social construction that permits an incredible amount of self-referencing and expectations. President George Washington's constituency did not know what to expect. He was relatively free to improvise.

This led to problems for future presidents. Constituencies expected the president to make up the description as long as they stayed within the boundaries of the US Constitution. President Andrew Jackson's constituency expected more from the office and President Franklin Roosevelt's even more. Stretching the presidency is not the same as understanding the job. Discerning which part of the job is real and which is just a performance is perhaps the conundrum that faces each president in the morning. Anything can happen and then again nothing can happen.

One of the new stresses on the president is the trend toward centering the moral authority of the nation on the presidency. Franklin Roosevelt was the first president to publicly proclaim himself as a moral leader. There is no constitutional basis for this assertion. The presidency was not designed to perform moral leadership. Besides this generation of Americans is more secular than the generations of political elites that wrote the Constitution. The moral agenda of Framers, if there were ever one, was never written down. If there is a glaring moral vacuum in twenty-first century America, there is no reference in the Constitution or American social tradition for an individual to assume the role; therefore, presidents who attempt to assume that role do so because of what they perceived as role expectations.

This moral role was very difficult for President Obama to assume. He said things that had moral content, but he did have the necessary social authority to get people to accept this view of the world, but he was not Martin Luther King and he had not been to the mountaintop. One of the persistent problems for Obama was the fact that he was an African American. Obama's election had less to do with creating a post-racial America and more to do with validating the fact that Americans elect presidents based on merit rather than race. Obama's election represented a type of collective triumphalism, yet it carried with it an unspoken dread. The American people in general, and African Americans in particular, had projected unprecedented expectations on the Obama presidency (a president with his unfailing optimism) and something had to go wrong. Something did go wrong. Coates's essay on the Obama presidency hints at this notion. "I still want Obama to be right. I still would like to fold myself into the dream. This will not be possible."[39] Ian Reifowitz disagreed and proclaimed that Obama truly transformed the national identity.[40] And John Kenneth White is even more optimistic about Obama's impact. He proclaimed that the Obama presidency aided four revolutions: racial, family, gay rights, and religion. In effect, we now live in an era of "moral libertarianism."[41] Fewer Americans publicly question how other people lead their lives.

Obviously, the chapters in this book do not cover all of the successes and failures of the Obama administration but the authors do analyze key aspects of his policies. At best this is a preliminary evaluation. As more data is accumulated and documents are declassified, we may have a clearer understanding of what happened during the Obama administration. Obviously, all presidential legacies are comparative in nature. But the contributors in the volume tried to look critically at Obama years.

Overview of This Book

In the chapter "The Obama Legacy in American Electoral Participation," Lyn Ragsdale examines the 2016 election of Donald Trump as president and voting behavior and the nature of the turnout during the Obama years, 2008, 2010, 2012, and 2014. The election of the first black president represented an historical sharp turn in American politics and race relations but what it does say about his electoral legacy? She asserted that turnout in American elections is often considered to be low but during the 2008, 2010, 2012, and 2014 elections, it hit levels last seen in the 1960s. This chapter examined the nature of turnout during the Obama years. It considers how a high degree of uncertainty in the national campaign context pushed turnout higher. It also examines which groups in America were most responsible for the increased participation. Despite exhortations from President Obama, turnout in 2016 among people of color went down and turnout among whites went up. What is somewhat ironic is that some of the people who supported Obama also supported Donald Trump.

In the chapter "Managing a Regime in Crisis: The Twilight of Neoliberalism and the Politics of Economic Recovery During the First Year of the Obama Administration" Kristoffer Smemo provides a historical overview of flawed economic policies that led up to the Great Recession. The Great Recession is presented as an economic regime on the verge of collapse. For Smemo "Privatized Keynesiansm," that is private sector advocacy of monetary and fiscal policies to increase employment and spending, led to the meltdown of the economy. His analysis brings together the nexus of business and political party politics. He questions the leadership of Obama during the Great Recession. Instead of trying to reform the overall economic system, Obama policies abetted Wall Street investors, banks and automobile makers. In effect, he emboldened past economic policies. This chapter linked President Obama to his predecessors' economic policies.

In the chapter "The Obama Health Care Legacy: The Origins, Implementation, and Effort to Repeal the Affordable Care Act of 2010" Jill Quadagno and Daniel Lanford review the history and impact of the Affordable Care Act (the ACA) or Obamacare. The construction of this historical breakthrough in public policy came in the first two years of the President Obama term. Although the Republican Party opposed the act and no Republican Congressperson voted for it, the law changed the national narrative about whether health is an appropriate entitlement. The chapter explains the provisions of the Patient Protection and Affordable Care Act of 2010. It provided medical care for millions of uninsured Americans by expanding Medicaid and providing subsidies. The chapter also reviews the implementation of ACA and the regulatory reform. Finally, the chapter examines why the Republican attempt to repeal Obamacare has failed. And why the current Trump administration's repeal of the individual mandate is part of a continuing effort to undermine Obamacare.

In the chapter "Appraising the Foreign Policy Legacy of the Obama Presidency," Meena Bose assesses Obama's national security strategy and his overall management of foreign policy. In the 2008 presidential campaign, Obama indicated that he would be a very different type of president than his predecessor, George W. Bush. As a campaigner, Obama had opposed the Iraq War and the USA Patriot Act. He broke with Bush's unilateral approach to foreign policy and pursued a multilateral one. Obama emphasized diplomacy and appointed two former Democratic senators (Hillary Clinton and John Kerry) as Secretary of State. Bose examines Obama's military policies in Afghanistan, Iraq, Libya, and Syria. Her appraisal of Obama's foreign policy examines the difference between Obama's promise and his performance. Obama's foreign policy achievements included signing the Paris Agreement on Climate Change and the Trans-Pacific Partnership. His establishment of diplomatic relations with Cuba was one of the most dramatic changes in US policy toward Latin America. But Obama also had foreign policy disappointments; for example, he pledged to close the Guantanamo Bay detention center but was unsuccessful, due to largely (though not exclusively) partisan congressional opposition.

In the chapter "The World We Have Lost: US Labor in the Obama Years" Ruth Milkman discusses Obama's labor policy. Organized labor was among the strongest support of President Obama's campaign election. In his book *The Audacity of Hope* Obama had supported key aspects of the Employee Free Choice Act. Many thought he would be a pro-labor president but he was unable to deliver lost gains of organized labor. Union organizing rates continued their long decline in the Obama years. Obama was an administrative president rather than a legislative president. He did use executive orders to promote pro-labor interest and for low-wage workers; most of what he did was challenged in courts and the Trump administration have undone most of the regulation. Yet Wall Street loyalists dominated the team that he put together to lead the nation out of the Great Recession. Labor leaders were disappointed the American Recovery and Reinvestment Act did not produce more jobs. There was no New Deal–style jobs program.

In the chapter "Swimming the Multiple Currents: The Political and Racial Time of Barack Obama's Presidency" Kimberley Johnson examines the idea of political and racial time to scrutinize Obama's civil rights record. Obama was a black president inhabiting both political time and racial time. According to Stephen Skowronek, political time is represented in the interplay of between the institutional ordering (constitutional, organizational and political) of the presidency. Obama, like all presidents, was shaped by these political orderings, and can fitted with identified types of presidencies. The racial time of Obama was the hope for a post-racial society. Was Obama what Skowronek would call a Reconstruction President—repudiating the old regime, building a new governing coalition, and introducing a new way of problem solving? Johnson reviews a variety of policy issues and explains why Obama failed to become a reconstructive president. Johnson explains why Obama appears to be a disjunctive president. Such presidents are unsuccessful in neither shoring up a faltering socio-economic system nor repudiating it.

In the chapter "The Legacy of President Obama in the US Supreme Court" Isaac Unah and Ryan Williams evaluates the Obama administration and its relations with the US Supreme Court. With the advice and consent of the US Senate, President Obama appointed two justices for the Supreme Court and several lower federal court judges. This chapter examines Obama's legacy in the Supreme Court and the critical cases (e.g. campaign finance, health care, voting rights, same-sex marriage) that faced the Roberts Court. They argue that Obama's presidency was transformative for the institution and politics of the Court. President Obama experienced both successes and failures in attempting to shape the Court in his own image, but he largely succeeded in using the Supreme Court to secure some of his biggest victories as president. At the end of the tenure, Obama was only partially successful in slowing down the aggressive rightward shift of the Court. Obama appointed two relatively liberal/progressive-minded women justices (Justices Sonia Sotomayor and Elena Kagan) to the Court. They are a counterweight to the current Court's conservative majority. The liberal minority has only slowed the Court from moving dramatically to the right. The chapter makes that conclusion after examining the voting behavior of the Obama appointed justices.

In the chapter "The Obama Administration's Global Warming Legacy: Going with the Flow and the Politics of Failure" George A. Gonzalez analyzes Obama's program for attacking the problem of greenhouse gas emissions from the nation's power plants. Gonzales uncovers a flaw in this 2014 policy. The flaw is that implementation of the policy relies on state governments who are less interested in reducing emission than in economic growth. This federalism requirement was a part of the history of the Environment Protection Agency. Accordingly, Obama's greenhouse emission policy is more symbolic than a real reform. The dominant figure in the making of environmental policy has been the business community. Allowing the states to implement said environment policy undermined the policy. Firstly, the 30% target reduction from power plants was meager as utilities are switching to natural gas and will likely achieve this target without government intervention. Secondly, the Obama administration's reliance on the states to achieve even this modest goal communicates that the administration was not interested in reducing greenhouse gasses, but in managing, assuaging the public's concerns over climate change. Thus, the administration's policies on global warming were symbolic, not substantive.

In the chapter "Unfulfilled Hopes: President Obama's Legacy" Stanley Renshon explores Obama as both a candidate and as a president. Obama campaigned as a thoughtful pragmatist with populist overtones. The president said he wanted to move beyond the divisive politics of Washington. Yet, Obama also wanted to be a "great" and "transformational" president and modeled himself after those predecessors he thought had been. In doing so he committed what Renshon characterizes as basic political faults—hiding his true ambition behind his moderate persona and campaign rhetoric. As a result, he allowed himself to contribute to the decades-long decline in trust in government. The public wanted Obama to concentrate on the economy. Yet, he was focused on being a great, transformative president. The Democratic majority in Congress gave him a significant victory in the Affordable Care Act but his legislature successes slowed considerably when the Republicans took over the House and then the Senate. Accordingly, Obama then sought national transformation through the use of executive orders. These efforts are a cautionary tale of how personal ambitions, however necessary or benevolent they appear to a president, can be interpreted differently by the American people, especially if that was not what they voted for or wanted.

Finally, Stanley Renshon examined President Obama the man, his psychology and his presidential ambitions. Obama's presidential record was a mixed one. Renshon believes that the ultimate source of his modest record was Obama's burning desire to be a "great," "transformative" president. Obama attempted to achieve a presidency worthy of a spot on Mt. Rushmore. Yet many Americans wanted him only to govern as he had promised—moderately and focusing on the economic issues that worried them.

In the end, Mr. Obama's enormous personal skills and his political opportunity to be a president of the first rank were undone by his determination to give Americans a "transformational" presidency they didn't want.

In the concluding chapter "Conclusion: Who Was President Barack Obama?," I will reevaluate the issues and observations made in the prior chapters and revisit the overall issues of the Obama presidential legacy. I will return to the point made in the introduction regarding the two types of legacy: preferential and referential. I will emphasize how different historians may make different assessment of whether Obama met the demands of hope and change. I will discuss why some writers were prepared to dismiss his claims of a transformational president two years into his presidency. And he dealt with the contradictions and paradoxes implicit in the presidency itself. I also cite Professor Scacco and Coe's notion of an "ubiquitous presidency" as a way to explain Obama's challenges. The modern presidency communicates with an increasing number of groups and is involved with a variety of issues. Finally, I will discuss how institutionalizing presidential libraries and the pressure for former presidents to write quick memoirs about their tenure changed how scholars look at their legacy.

Notes

1. Thomas E. Cronin and Michael A. Genovese, *The Paradoxes of the American Presidency* (New York: Oxford University Press, 2013) p. 1.
2. "President Barack Obama's Inaugural Address," January 21, 2009. www. Obamawhitehouse.archives.gov
3. See Barack Obama *The Audacity of Hope: Thoughts on Reclaiming the American Dream* (New York: Three River Press, 2006) Chapter 5.

4. For an interpretation of the election, see Michael Tesler and David O. Sears *Obama's Race: The 2008 Election and Dreams of a Post Racial Society* (Chicago: University of Chicago Press, 2010).

5. "President Barack Obama's Inaugural Address," January 21, 2009. www. Obamawhitehouse.archives.gov

6. See Robert Kuttner *Obama's Challenge: America's Economic Crisis and the Power of a Transformative Presidency* (White River Junction, VT: Chelsea Green, 2008).

7. Stephen Skowronek *The Politics Presidents Make: Leadership from John Adams to George Bush* (Cambridge, MA: Belknap Press, 1993).

8. Wilbur C. Rich "The Lincoln and Obama Legacies: The perils of channeling" unpublished paper delivered at UI Springfield).

9. Ta-Nehisi Coates "My President Was Black" *The Atlantic* (January/February, 2017) p. 52.

10. Coates, op.cit p. 60.

11. Fred Greenstein, "The Qualities of Effective Presidents: An Overview from FDR to Bill Clinton," *Presidential Studies Quarterly* Vol. 30, No. 1 (March, 2000). pp. 178–185.

12. Ibid., 180.

13. Ibid., 181.

14. Ibid., 181.

15. James P. Pfiffner "Decision Making in the Obama White House" *Presidential Studies Quarterly* Vol. 41, No. 2 (June, 2011), p. 260.

16. See Doris Kearns Goodwin, *Team of Rivals: The Political Genius of Abraham Lincoln,* (New York: Simon & Schuster, 2006).

17. See Richard Neustadt *Presidential Power* (Free Press, New York, 1991).

18. Former Massachusetts Governor Romney had signed a similar health care reform bill in his state that made his criticisms of Obamacare hollow. During his time in Massachusetts Romney had a reputation of being a moderate and therefore he had to appeal to very conservative party base. He spent a lot of time and energy reassuring the base he was a serious conservative. He also made an insensitive remark about 47% of Americans. He claimed that they pay no income taxes and that he was not worrying about these people.

19. Neustadt, p. 183.

20. Ibid.

21. Ibid., p. 184.

22. "Inaugural Address by President Obama" January 21, 2013. www. Obamawhitehouse.archives.gov

23. See Wilbur C. Rich, "Presidential Leadership and the Politics of Race: Stereotypes, Symbols and Scholarship," in Wilbur C. Rich ed. *African American Perspective on Political Science,* (Philadelphia: Temple University Press, 2007), pp. 232–250.

24. See Wilbur C. Rich, "Making Race Go Away: President Obama and the Promise of a Post-Racial Society," in Andrew J. Dowdle, Dirk C. Van Raemdonck and Robert Maranto, ed. *The Obama Presidency: Change and Continuity,* (New York: Routledge, 2011), pp. 17–29.

25. James T. Kloppenberg, *Reading Obama: Dreams, Hope, and the American Political Tradition* (Princeton, NJ: Princeton University Press, 2011), and Joseph Perschek "The Obama Presidency and the Recession: Political Economy, Ideology, and Policy" *New Political Science,* Vol. 33, No. 4 (December, 2011) pp. 429–444.

26. See Michael A. Genovese and Todd L. Belt *The Post-Heroic Presidency: Leveraged Leadership in an Age of Limits* (Santa Barbara, CA: Praeger, 2016).

27. Ibid., p. 196.

28. Ibid., p. 197.

29. Ibid.

30. Quoted in "Explaining the Riddle" *Economist* (August 23, 2008) p. 20.

31. Bruce Miroff, *Pragmatic Illusions* (New York: David McKay Company, Inc., 1976). p. 294.

32. See Benjamin Ginsberg *Presidential Government* (New Haven, Ct: Yale University Press, 2016).

33. Charles O. Jones *The Presidency in a Separated System* (Washington, D. C.: Brookings Institution Press, 2005).

34. Carlos Lazada "The Self-Referential Presidency of Barack Obama" *Washington Post* (December 15, 2016) Lozada, Carlos. "Essay: The self-referential presidency of Barack Obama." *Washington Post,* 15 Dec. 2016. *Science In Context,* http://link.galegroup.com.librarylink.uncc.edu/apps/doc/A473994620/SCIC?u=char69915&sid=SCIC&xid=3cdd9030. Accessed 15 June 2018.

35. "Remarks by the President in Farewell Address." January 10, 2017. http://Obamawhitehouse.archives.gov/the-press-office/

36. See Wilbur C. Rich, *The Post-Racial Society is Here* (New York: Routledge, 2013).

37. See Michael A. Genovese and Todd Belt, op cit, p. 219.

38. See Victor Thompson, *Modern Organization,* (New York: Knopf, 1961).

39. Ta-Nehisi Coates "My President Was Black" *The Atlantic* (January/February, 2017).

40. Ian Reifowitz. *Obama's America: A Transformative Vision of National Identity,* (Washington DC: Potomac Books, 2012).

41. John Kenneth White *Barack Obama's America: How New Conceptions of Race, Family, and Religion ended the Reagan Era* (Ann Arbor: University of Michigan Press, 2009) p. 152.

The Obama Legacy in American Electoral Participation

Lyn Ragsdale

Speaking at the 2016 Congressional Black Caucus gala, Barack Obama extolled the power of voting to ensure his legacy as president:

> If I hear anybody saying their vote does not matter, that it doesn't matter who we elect—read up on your history. It matters. We've got to get people to vote. I will consider it a personal insult—an insult to my legacy—if this community lets down its guard and fails to activate itself in this election. You want to give me a good sendoff? Go vote.[1]

Regardless of how presidents hope to be remembered, their legacies are an important part of how they are judged in history and in direct comparison to each other. One of the central features of Obama's legacy is not about what he accomplished or the tough decisions he made, but it is about being the first black to be elected president of the United States. This is one undeniable aspect of his legacy that is not subject to interpretation or revision by commentators. This chapter considers that electoral legacy, how it was shaped, and what it means in the future of the office.

L. Ragsdale (✉)
Rice University, Houston, TX, USA
e-mail: lkragsdale@rice.edu

© The Author(s) 2019   25
W. C. Rich (ed.), *Looking Back on President Barack Obama's Legacy*,
https://doi.org/10.1007/978-3-030-01545-9_2

STUDYING PRESIDENTIAL LEGACIES

A presidential legacy can be considered in two ways. Most often analysts focus on the major policy or political accomplishments a president achieved that had implications for Americans' lives long after the president left the White House. Franklin Roosevelt's creation of Social Security, Dwight Eisenhower's conception of the federal highway system, and Lyndon Johnson's establishment of Medicare come quickly to mind. But there is another type of legacy that involves a historic benchmark being reached, a precedent being set, or a political barrier being broken during the president's tenure. A central part of George Washington's legacy was establishing a two-term norm for future presidents. Until Franklin Roosevelt violated, it was unthinkable that anyone would seek a third term. Lyndon Johnson left not only policy legacies but also a political one—he was the first southerner elected to the presidency since the Civil War. His victory in 1964 demonstrated that the South was no longer an isolated region of the country and paved the way for southerners Jimmy Carter, George H.W. Bush, Bill Clinton, and George W. Bush to win the White House. As another example, Jimmy Carter appointed more women to positions in his administration than had any previous president. His efforts created an expectation for future presidents to have significant numbers of women.[2] This kind of legacy is about political "firsts" that lay the groundwork for future expectations, opportunities, or changes in the political system. These firsts do not necessarily create an immediate permanent shift in political patterns. It may take years for the "second" instance to occur or for a pattern to emerge. But the fact that the barrier has been broken or a landmark has been achieved is the cornerstone of the legacy.

At the same time, it is important to understand that there are pitfalls in exploring presidential legacies. First, not every policy victory or political first is part of a legacy. Legacies are functions of the future. They are based on comparisons with what happens next over a long period of time. In this vein, legacies are distinct from exceptional events—events that are historic in nature but happen once and are not repeated. These events are truly the exception that proves the rule. One of the most vivid electoral events of this kind was Theodore Roosevelt's run for the White House in 1912 as a member of the Progressive Party. Roosevelt had been president as a Republican from 1901 through 1908, but decided not to run again deferring to his Vice President William Howard Taft to be his successor. By 1912, Roosevelt had second thoughts and he directly challenged Taft with

Roosevelt's Bull Moose third-party bid permitting the Democrat, Woodrow Wilson, to win the race. The sheer number of complicated personal and political turns that occurred in Roosevelt's run in 1912 demonstrates how exceptional events are just that—exceptional—and not part of any legacy or pattern.

Second, it is also possible to too quickly dismiss the prospect of a legacy because a president's key achievements are undercut by his successor. New presidents often come into office bent on dismantling what the previous president did, even when they are of the same party. George H.W. Bush campaigned explicitly on the theme of a "kinder, gentler America," a not so subtle acknowledgment that some of the harshest policies of the Reagan years on the environment and social welfare should be rethought. Yet years later the Reagan legacy of conservatism and strong defense is far more vivid than its kinder Bush replacement. While the Trump administration has gone to great lengths to dismantle many policies of the Obama presidency, it is not yet clear which direction will prevail. So, we cannot say there is an Obama legacy on, say, immigration as the Trump White House drafted successive travel bans. But we also cannot say that there is not.

Third, it is important not to paint any legacy too vividly too soon after a president leaves office. Discerning a legacy of either the first type about policy or the second type about political firsts requires patience and an eye for predicting future events. And analysts are often not especially good at making such predictions. Based on the immediate results of the 2016 election, it appears that there was actually little to the Obama electoral legacy. The turnout went down among people of color. The turnout among whites went up. Some of the key groups who supported Obama especially in 2008 supported Trump in 2016. Many including Trump himself suggested that his election victory was a direct repudiation of Obama's presidency. Whether the Trump candidacy was in some ways a backlash against the Obama legacy as the first black elected to the presidency will not be clear for years to come.

With these cautions in mind, this chapter examines the electoral dimension of the legacy that Barack Obama may leave. This electoral dimension is considered in three parts. First, while the size and shape of that legacy will not be known for several decades, what we do know is that Barack Obama's election as the first black president will be a pivotal part of his legacy. It is a legacy wrapped around a political first that immediately provides a different way of thinking about who can become president. Even if years go by before a second person of color is elected president, the barrier has been broken and cannot easily be rebuilt. Second, participation among people of color in 2008 and 2012 was a substantial ingredient in the election of the first black president and it adds to the legacy. Finally, there was considerable discussion of the so-called "Obama coalition" throughout his presidency. This was an association of people of color, the young, the highly educated, and white working-class voters outside the South. Commentators were quick to point out that in 2016 Hillary Clinton was unable to keep together the Obama coalition. But, is there any reason to expect that a presidential candidate's winning coalition is anything but specific to that candidate?

ELECTING THE FIRST BLACK PRESIDENT

The old adage that "anyone can grow up to be president" has always been a very problematic saying in American politics. It suggests that democracy in America permits anyone from the most humble background to rise to the highest office in the land. And indeed, this is true when counting Abraham Lincoln, a country lawyer; Harry Truman, the owner of men's clothing store; and Richard Nixon, the son of a grocer, among American presidents. But, it tends to ring hollow to women, people of color, religious minorities, and non-heterosexuals.

Until John Kennedy in 1960, no Catholic had been elected president. Al Smith, the first Catholic to run for president in 1928, faced considerable anti-Catholic sentiment. Campaign attacks suggested that Smith's allegiance would be to the Vatican and not the Constitution. Rumors insinuated that Smith had miraculously dug a tunnel under the ocean from New York to Rome for quicker access to the pope. A cartoon appearing in a New Jersey church publication showed the pope blowing up a balloon with Smith's likeness on it. When Kennedy ran in 1960 his Catholicism was also a major issue. The Kennedy campaign handled the matter with considerable skill and finesse. In May, Kennedy entered the West Virginia primary—a state with a small Catholic population—to demonstrate that he could win even in heavily Protestant communities. When polls showed him running behind by 20 percentage points, he made an impassioned speech before the American Society of Newspaper Editors:

> Are we going to admit to the world that a Jew can be elected Mayor of Dublin, a Protestant can be chosen Foreign Minister of France, a Moslem can be elected to the Israeli Parliament—but a Catholic cannot be President

of the United States? Are we going to admit to the world—worse still, are we going to admit to ourselves—that one-third of the American people is forever barred from the White House?[3]

In September, 1960 Kennedy met the issue head on in a speech before Protestant ministers in Houston saying, "I believe in an America where the separation of church and state is absolute, where no Catholic prelate would tell the president (should he be Catholic) how to act."[4] Thereafter the intensity of the issue dissipated and the Nixon campaign never brought it up. Today it would be impossible to imagine that a Catholic would be stopped from running for or winning the White House. John Kerry, a Catholic, ran as the Democratic nominee in 2004. A large number of Republican primary candidates in 2016 were Catholic, including Jeb Bush, Marco Rubio, Rick Santorum, Chris Christie, Bobby Jindal, and George Pataki. Joseph Biden, a Catholic, served as Obama's Vice President. Thus, a lasting part of the Kennedy legacy is that there is no question that a Catholic can run for president. Even though no Catholic has won since Kennedy it is a settled political matter that a Catholic can occupy the White House without fear that images of the pope running the United States will reemerge.

Forty-eight years after Kennedy, Barack Obama was the next presidential nominee of a major party to challenge the norms surrounding who can be president. From the beginning of the republic, these norms suggested that the two most critical characteristics for someone to be president were being white and being male. In a country with a long and violent history of slavery, segregation, and racism, the barriers to a black becoming president were dramatic. Obama had prophetically asserted that "Societies don't, overnight, completely erase everything that happened 200 to 300 years prior."[5] While blacks including Shirley Chisholm, a New York congresswoman; Jesse Jackson, a Chicago civil rights activist; Herman Cain, a Detroit businessman; and Ben Carson, a Baltimore neurosurgeon, had run in both Democratic and Republican primaries, none had achieved much success.

Because the initial front-runner in the Democratic primaries in 2008 was a woman, former First Lady and New York senator, Hillary Clinton, Obama faced a somewhat easier task on race than Kennedy had faced on religion. No matter who won the nomination, one of the two "requirements" to be a presidential nominee—whiteness and maleness—was going to fall.

However, in March 2008, ABC News released a story highlighting controversial sermons that Obama's long-time pastor, Jeremiah Wright, had delivered from the pulpit at Chicago's Trinity United Church of Christ. In a 2003 sermon, Wright proclaimed, "The government gives them the drugs, builds bigger prisons, passes a three-strike law and then wants us to sing 'God Bless America.' No, no, no, not God bless America. God damn America." The Obama campaign initially tried to downplay Wright's remarks; Obama likened Wright to "an old uncle who says things I don't always agree with."[6] But more Wright sermons surfaced dogging the candidate.

Obama then confronted the matter head on in a major address on race at the National Constitution Center in Philadelphia on March 18, 2008. Obama set up guideposts "Toward a More Perfect Union": "For the African-American community, that path means embracing the burdens of our past without becoming victims of our past... In the white community, the path to a more perfect union means acknowledging that what ails the African-American community does not just exist in the minds of black people; that the legacy of discrimination—and current incidents of discrimination, while less overt than in the past—are real and must be addressed."[7] The speech helped Obama move past Wright's remarks and marked a turning point in the campaign against Clinton. Like Kennedy's address about Catholicism to Protestant ministers in Houston, Obama made an impassioned case for why the norm of "whites only" should no longer apply to the presidency. By late May, Obama had secured a small lead in the delegate count against Clinton but a lead big enough that it did not leave Clinton sufficient time to catch up. On August 27, 2008, Barack Obama became the first black to become a major party presidential nominee.

Although Obama toppled the race barrier associated with the American presidency, his candidacy did not profoundly change attitudes about race. While it might seem that the victory of the first black president would mean more tolerant political views or more favorable views toward blacks by other racial and ethnic groups, this is not the case. Table 1 examines how racial and ethnic groups perceived each other from 1980 to 2016. The table reveals a fair amount of consistency of each group's views toward the other groups. In addition, when there is variation, the 2008 and 2012 elections are not especially noteworthy. For example, the table shows that whites had the greatest degree of favorability for blacks in 2000 (71 percent favorable) and 2004 (73 percent favorable), not in 2008 (69 percent) and 2012 (65 percent).

Table 1 Favorability toward other racial and ethnic groups by race, 1980–2016

	White views of blacks	White views of Hispanics	White views of whites	White views of Asians	Black views of blacks	Black views of Hispanics	Blacks views of whites	Black views of Asians
1980	66.5	65.9	80.0	–	90.6	77.7	81.5	–
1984	68.1	66.2	78.2	–	81.8	72.7	76.6	–
1988	63.3	61.4	76.7	–	86.0	74.5	76.1	–
1992	65.3	63.6	73.8	63.3	87.7	72.6	74.6	68.3
1996	67.2	65.9	74.0	–	85.8	77.4	79.3	–
2000	70.5	68.7	76.6	71.1	85.5	75.5	80.4	75.0
2004	72.9	70.6	76.7	71.7	87.6	73.5	75.7	68.5
2008	69.4	66.3	75.3	67.9	86.4	73.1	78.5	73.1
2012	65.1	64.1	77.1	67.5	84.6	71.5	71.5	69.8
2016	66.5	66.4	73.5	68.5	84.0	71.0	67.5	68.2
Mean	67.5	65.9	76.2	68.3	86.0	73.9	76.2	70.5

	Asian views of blacks	Asian views of Hispanics	Asian views of whites	Asian views of Asians	Hispanic views of blacks	Hispanic views of Hispanics	Hispanic views of whites	Hispanic views of Asians
1980	52.5	59.8	63.8	–	74.7	80.5	83.2	–
1984	61.2	71.1	68.7	–	74.1	81.6	79.4	–
1988	61.3	65.8	75.2	–	74.6	83.0	78.2	–
1992	65.7	62.4	69.4	75.1	74.8	81.5	76.4	70.9
1996	71.2	68.8	75.1	–	75.6	80.3	76.4	–
2000	77.6	75.0	73.1	81.2	78.4	83.4	82.6	76.6
2004	76.5	75.0	75.0	73.5	77.6	81.5	77.7	70.3
2008	64.9	66.2	66.2	71.4	74.0	83.3	74.5	70.9
2012	64.9	67.1	70.6	77.9	70.2	81.5	73.0	68.1
2016	61.9	63.9	66.4	76.8	68.1	79.1	68.2	68.6
Mean	65.8	67.5	70.3	76.0	74.2	81.6	77.0	70.9

Note: Entries are "feeling thermometer" ratings on a scale from 0 to 100, asking the respondent how coolly (0) or warmly (100) they feel toward the group

Table 2 examines the prospect of Obama's candidacy reducing racial resentment. From 2000 through 2016, the table considers how racial and ethnic groups responded to the question "Do you think blacks have received less than they deserve in recent years?" The final column in each year block calculates the difference between whites and blacks in answering the question. The results in that column show that Obama's victories

Table 2 Racial and ethnic group attitudes toward blacks' treatment, 2000–2016

	Whites	Blacks	Asians	Hispanics	White-black difference
2000					
Strongly agree	3.8	35.3	11.5	6.7	−31.5
Agree	21.5	33.3	26.9	26.0	−11.8
Neutral	17.6	12.7	23.1	26.0	4.9
Disagree	32.2	12.7	30.8	22.1	19.5
Strongly disagree	24.1	6.0	7.7	19.2	18.1
2004					
Strongly agree	3.9	24.5	10.5	6.5	−20.6
Agree	17.3	39.1	21.1	19.6	−21.8
Neutral	23.3	19.9	36.8	30.4	3.4
Disagree	33.7	11.3	26.3	20.7	22.4
Strongly disagree	21.8	5.3	5.3	22.8	16.5
2008					
Strongly agree	4.4	25.2	6.5	8.7	−20.8
Agree	14.6	32.7	29.0	20.3	−18.1
Neutral	23.4	21.2	36.1	26.8	2.2
Disagree	30.8	12.7	25.8	25.1	18.1
Strongly disagree	26.8	8.3	10.6	19.2	18.5
2012					
Strongly agree	2.4	25.9	2.4	4.3	−23.5
Agree	9.7	29.2	3.7	15.4	−19.5
Neutral	23.7	23.5	41.5	28.3	0.2
Disagree	31.1	14.4	39.3	25.3	16.7
Strongly disagree	33.1	7.0	13.2	26.8	26.1
2016					
Strongly agree	8.0	36.4	7.0	11.1	−28.4
Agree	17.2	27.0	19.3	26.7	−9.8
Neutral	25.6	21.4	32.5	25.3	4.2
Disagree	21.4	9.1	24.6	16.4	12.3
Strongly disagree	27.7	6.2	16.7	20.5	21.5

Note: Entries are in response to the question: "Do you believe blacks have received less than they deserve in recent years"

did not dampen the gap between white and black perceptions of the black experience in the United States. For example, there is a net white-black difference of 21 percentage points in 2004 and a similar gap in 2008. In other words, in both 2004 and 2008, whites were 21 percentage points less likely to believe that blacks have been mistreated than did blacks. So, the Obama legacy does not extend to altering public opinions about race.

Participation and an Obama Electoral Legacy

The first sentence of any future description of Barack Obama will be that he was the first black elected president. That legacy rests in part on a surge in turnout among people of color during the Obama years. It is important to put that participation in a longer historical perspective. Commentators have lamented that the United States is a "low turnout society."[8] Yet during the 2008 and 2012 presidential elections Americans went to the polls in high numbers to elect and then reelect the first black president. More specifically, in both elections diverse populations of citizens participated in ways that had not been true in the past. In 2012, for the first time in history, a higher percentage of black Americans participated in a presidential election than did white Americans. In addition, Hispanic and Asian-Americans, long lagging behind other groups in participation rates, voted in their highest numbers ever.

Table 3 offers a view of turnout in American elections since World War II. Examining the "Nation Turnout" column, in the immediate post-war

Table 3   US turnout by region, 1948–2016

Year	Nation turnout	South turnout	Non-South turnout	West turnout	Midwest turnout	East turnout
1948	53	34	62	62	63	62
1952	64	46	72	70	73	74
1956	61	44	70	68	71	71
1960	66	49	74	71	76	76
1964	64	51	70	69	71	71
1968	63	55	67	64	68	68
1972	57	48	62	60	64	61
1976	54	48	57	53	62	57
1980	56	50	59	58	63	57
1984	57	52	59	58	62	58
1988	54	49	57	55	59	56
1992	60	54	63	61	65	62
1996	54	49	56	55	58	55
2000	55	51	56	56	55	59
2004	64	60	66	64	68	66
2008	63	60	64	62	66	65
2012	60	57	61	58	63	62
2016	62	59	63	60	64	66

Source: Lyn Ragsdale and Jerrold Rusk, *The American Nonvoter.* Oxford: Oxford University Press, 2017, updated by the author

election of 1948, the turnout was quite low at 53 percent as many service-men and servicewomen returning to civilian life did not immediately register to vote. But beginning in 1952 and continuing through 1968 the turnout increased to its highest levels since women entered the electorate in 1920.[9] Indeed, the turnout in the 1960 election was the highest of any election since 1900—66 percent of voting-eligible Americans voted. This occurred amid the backdrop of the single closest race since 1880 when John Kennedy won against Richard Nixon by just 0.17 percent of the vote. The turnout then dropped in the 1970s and 1980s, rebounded in 1992 but returned to the levels last seen in the 1960s beginning with the 2004 election.

The unpopularity of the Iraq War, concerns about the economy, and the closeness of the 2000 race drew people to the polls in 2004. Despite Bush's reelection in 2004, many people reported that they voted to ensure that the result did not hinge on some 537 votes in Florida on which the results of the 2000 race rested. The turnout increased from 55 percent in 2000 to 64 percent in 2004, a level last seen 40 years earlier in 1964. The increase was sustained in 2008 and 2012 as national turnout continued at high levels—63 percent in 2008 and 60 percent in 2012. It remained high in 2016 at 62 percent. Table 3 also makes clear that this national picture is reflected regionally. There was a spike in turnout across all regions of the country in 2004 and this was sustained in 2008, 2012, and 2016.

A DIVERSE VOTING POPULATION

A comparison of the 2004 and 2008 elections reveals that the increased turnout in the two election years occurred with very different demographic profiles. Figure 1 examines how racial and ethnic groups among the eligible citizen population voted in presidential elections from 1980 to 2016. The increase in turnout in 2004 was partly an upswing in participation among whites. From 2000 to 2004, white turnout increased by five percentage points from 62 percent in 2000 to 67 percent in 2004. Only in 1992 did whites vote in higher numbers when 70 percent participated. Black turnout, too, went up from 2000 to 2004 but at a slower rate of three percentage points—from 57 percent to 60 percent. This increase in black turnout was part of a longer trend upward that began in 1996. Asian turnout increased slightly by one percentage point from 2000 to 2004 and Hispanic turnout increased by two percentage points. Yet turnout among Asian-Americans and Hispanic-Americans has been historically low. For example, in 2000, Hispanic turnout was at 45 percent, some 17

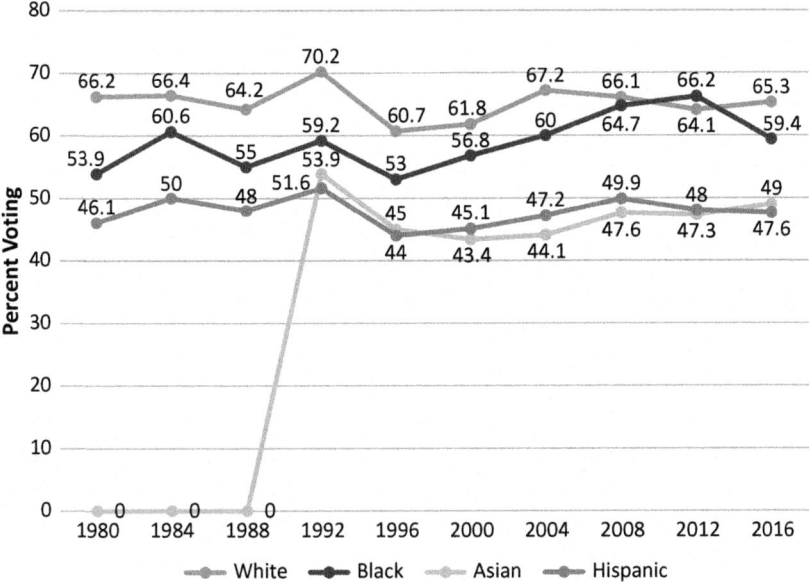

Fig. 1   Turnout by race and ethnicity, 1980–2016

percentage points lower than white turnout and 12 percentage points lower than black turnout. Similarly, in 2000, turnout among Asian-Americans was 43 percent, fully 19 percentage points lower than white turnout and 14 percentage points lower than black turnout.

From 2004 to 2008 and continuing to 2012, the turnout picture changed. As seen in Fig. 1, black turnout increased by five percentage points from 60 percent in 2004 to 65 percent in 2008. It increased slightly again to 66 percent from 2008 to 2012. From 2004 to 2008, Hispanic turnout increased three percentage points from 47 percent to 50 percent. This is the first time since 1992 that Hispanic turnout reached the 50 percent mark. It dropped back to 48 percent in 2012. Asian-American turnout increased by four percentage points from 44 percent in 2004 to 48 percent in 2008 and declined slightly to 47 percent in 2012. To complete the 2004–2008–2012 comparisons, white turnout declined slightly by one percentage point from 67 percent to 66 percent from 2004 to 2008 and then dropped further to 64 percent in 2012. Remarkably, this meant that in 2012 black turnout exceeded white turnout for the first time ever.

These benchmarks for people of color were not fully sustained in 2016. Most significantly, black turnout fell six percentage points nationwide from 66 percent 2012 to 59 percent in 2016. Yet Asian turnout nudged up by a point to 49 percent and Hispanic turnout remained steady at 49 percent. White turnout increased slightly by one percentage point from 64 percent in 2012 to 65 percent in 2016. Nevertheless, the fact that black turnout was nearly equal to white turnout in 2004 and exceeded it in 2008 is an historic part of the Obama legacy. To understand this legacy fully, it is critical to look back at previous elections in greater detail and then make some assessments about future elections.

Obama's Legacy for Black Turnout

It is hard to overstate the significance of the two milestones in black turnout of 2008 and 2012 in American political history. Prior to the Obama candidacy, black turnout had always lagged behind white turnout reflecting broad patterns of discrimination across the country and pointed attempts at disenfranchisement especially in the South. From 1968 to 2004, the race gap between white and blacks in presidential races was on average nine percentage points in favor of whites. From 2008 through 2016, the average race gap was one percentage point in favor of blacks.

Thus, a key part of the Obama legacy is how the barrier to black voting, present in many presidential elections before his candidacy, was broken during the Obama elections. And although black turnout declined in 2016, it is unclear whether that decline will continue in 2020. To understand how black turnout increased with Obama it is important to understand the depths of the historical problems associated with black voting.

There is no amendment to the Constitution with less effect than the 15th Amendment from the time of its ratification in 1870 to the early 1960s.[10] The amendment assured that "The right of citizens of the United States to vote shall not be denied or abridged by the United States or by any State on account of race, color, or previous condition of servitude." Yet throughout the South, few, if any, blacks were registered to vote because an array of literacy tests, poll taxes, and residency requirements blocked them from doing so.[11] Federal remedies were limited and difficult to enforce under the existing Civil Rights Acts of 1957 and 1960 passed during the Eisenhower administration. Even though the 1957 law created a new Civil Rights Division in the Justice Department and the 1960 law provided for federal inspection of local registration rolls and penalties for obstructing someone's attempt to register or vote, the laws were structured reactively, permitting the Justice Department to enjoin injustices after they had been committed, one registrar, sheriff, and county at a time. The Civil Rights Act of 1964 toughened language against the unequal application of voter registration requirements, but still offered no direct enforcement mechanisms against voter intimidation.

This meant that the problem of black voter registration was vast. Table 4 compares voter registration in southern states before and after the passage of the Voting Rights Act of 1966. The pre-passage entries are taken from the 1964 elections, with the exceptions of Arkansas (October 1963) and Georgia (December 1962). So even with the many registration efforts that began in 1961 and continued through the 1964 elections, voter registration among African-Americans in the South remained very low, with Tennessee being the only state where African-American registration was similar to white registration. As one example, under Alabama law, prospective voters had to fill out a complicated form, answer a 20-page questionnaire on constitutional topics, and have a registered voter sponsor them. Little wonder that in Lowndes County Alabama in 1965, with an African-American adult population of 12,000 and a white adult population of 3000, no African-Americans were registered to vote, while three-quarters of whites were. Commented one of the members of the Board of Registrars, "I don't know of any Negro registration here, but there is a better relationship between whites and niggers here than any place I know of."[12]

Figure 2 continues this examination by considering the difference between black and white voting in presidential elections from 1968 through 2016 in the South and outside the South. The figures show that in the early elections, there were substantially more white voters than black voters, especially in the South, but the number of black voters rapidly increased. Beginning in 1992 a key pattern emerged in which black voting in the South was consistently higher than that in the Non-South. This is true for each of the 12 elections through 2016. Overall, the rate of African-American voting in the South continued to be higher than it was outside the South. Indeed, with Obama on the ballot, white southern voting fell behind black southern nonvoting from 2008 through 2012.

Figure 3 elaborates on the differences between black and white voting with a breakdown by sex. Black women were much more likely to be voters than black men.[13] Indeed, in every election from 1964 through 2012, more black women voted than did black men.[14] Beginning in 1982, black women and white women participated at similar levels. Indeed, from 2008

Table 4 Voter registration by race, before and after the passage of the Voting Rights Act of 1965

State	Pre-act registration	Post-act registration	Pre-act percent registered	Post-act percent registered
Alabama				
African-American	92,737	248,432	19.3	51.6
White	935,695	1,212,317	69.2	89.6
Arkansas				
African-American	77,714	121,000	40.4	62.8
White	555,944	616,000	65.5	72.4
Florida				
African-American	240,616	299,033	51.2	63.6
White	1,938,499	2,131,105	74.8	81.4
Georgia				
African-American	167,663	332,496	27.4	52.6
White	1,124,415	1,443,730	62.6	80.3
Louisiana				
African-American	164,601	303,148	31.6	58.9
White	1,037,184	1,200,517	80.5	93.1
Mississippi				
African-American	28,500	263,754	6.7	59.8
White	525,000	665,176	69.9	91.5
North Carolina				
African-American	258,000	277,404	46.8	51.3
White	1,942,000	1,602,980	96.8	83
South Carolina				
African-American	138,544	190,017	37.3	51.2
White	677,914	731,096	75.7	81.7
Tennessee				
African-American	218,000	225,000	69.5	71.7
White	1,297,000	1,434,000	72.9	80.6
Texas				
African-American	2,939,555	400,000	53.1	61.6
White		2,600,000		53.3
Virginia				
African-American	144,259	243,000	38.3	55.6
White	1,070,168	1,190,000	61.1	63.4

Source: United States Commission on Civil Rights, Political Participation: A Study of the *Participation by Negroes in the Electoral and Political Processes in 10 Southern States since Passage of the Voting Rights Act of 1965, May 1968, pp. 12–13*

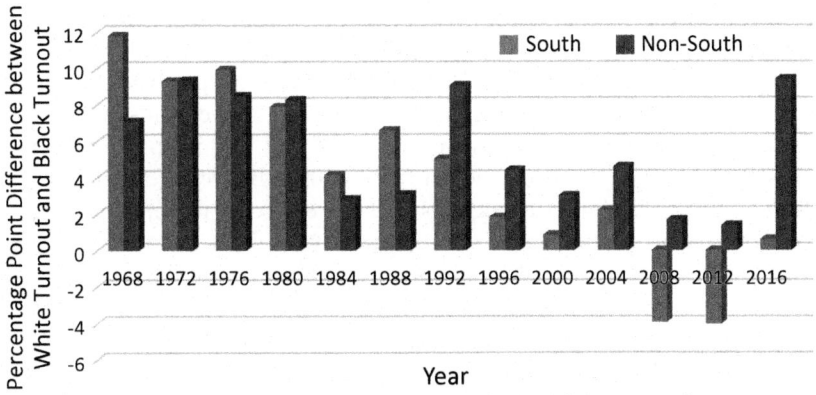

Note: Bar above 0 indicates greater white voting; bar below 0 indicates greater black voting.

Fig. 2 Difference between white and black voting, 1968–2016

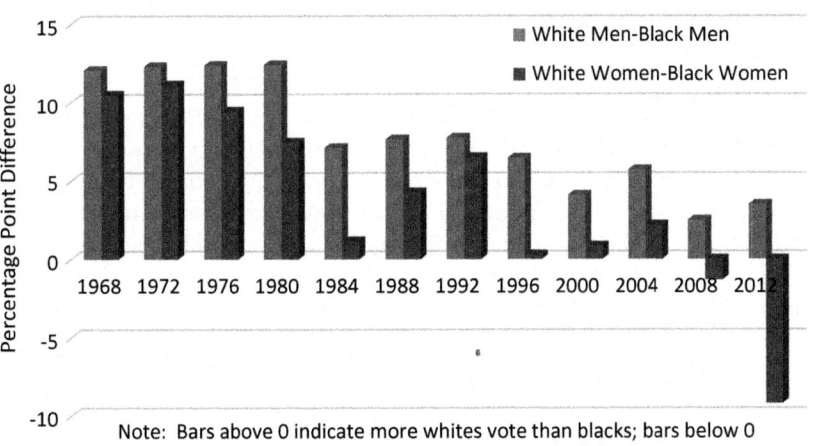

Note: Bars above 0 indicate more whites vote than blacks; bars below 0 indicate more blacks vote than whites

Fig. 3 Difference in voting by race and sex, 1968–2012

through 2012, black women exceeded white women as voters. Overall, the long-term impact of the Voting Rights Act of 1965 has been as profound as were the earlier opposing efforts to leave the 15th Amendment unenforced. But the Obama effect was also historic as a final color barrier was broken with more blacks than whites voting.

Although turnout among people of color fell slightly in 2016, this does not likely reflect that their voting in 2008 and 2012 were exceptions that will not reoccur. In the South, 2016 black turnout dropped below white turnout by a scant 0.6 percentage points. It was in the Non-South that black voting was substantially down in 2016 not just from the Obama years but from many election cycles prior to 2008. But research on participation patterns in America suggests that once a cohort of people enters the electorate in a particular election year, they are likely to continue to be active. Research indicates that people are not necessarily active in every election cycle, but come and go in and out of the electorate over a series of elections.[15] But, they do not exit in a particular election and then never return. It would appear that 2016 was one of those elections that found blacks outside the South temporarily on the sidelines. But the fact that black voting, especially in the South, is well established and broke records during the Obama elections suggest that black voting is not likely to move permanently downward over the next several election cycles. Black voting in 2016, while lower, nevertheless was at its average for the period from 1980 to 2012. So, milestones achieved cannot be easily erased from the American political scene.

Thus, one element of the Obama legacy is reflected in an upswing in participation rates for people of color. Their future participation is not likely to require a person of color to bring them back to the polls. Public opinion data throughout Donald Trump's first year in office consistently showed that high numbers of blacks and Hispanics strongly disapproved of Trump's handling of his job in office. If these intensely negative views continue in 2020, this will drive the turnout up among people of color no matter who Trump's Democratic opponent is.[16]

An Obama Legacy in Party Politics?

The first aspect of Barack Obama's electoral legacy is clear: he is the first black to be elected president. The second aspect of his electoral legacy—the upswing in participation among people of color—seems apparent but it awaits future elections to determine the breadth and historical extent of the legacy. The third aspect of Obama's electoral legacy pertains to the so-called "Obama coalition"—people of color, the young, the highly educated, and the white working class outside the South—who assembled to support him in 2008 and 2012. Throughout his presidency, much was made of this coalition. And many pundits noted that the Clinton campaign of 2016 left the Obama coalition in tatters.

Yet in an era of structural polarization when parties have a lock on key regions of the country but are not competitive in others, it is unlikely that the "Obama coalition" or any candidate's coalition will survive the person's own elections or time in office.[17] When presidential races are closely competitive, the candidates can build a coalition for only a specific election with little confidence that it will be repeated in the next election. Table 5 provides information about the absence of any meaningfully stable "Obama coalition." One key example is young voters (18–29 years old) who were touted as a pivotal group of Obama supporters. In 2008, 66 percent of young voters voted Democratic but in 2012, that number dropped to 60 percent. Although Hillary Clinton received only 55 percent of the youth vote, this was nevertheless eight percentage points higher than the average youth vote of 47 percent received by Democratic candidates from 1980 through 2004. While 63 percent of people without high school degrees voted for Obama in 2008, only 51 percent did so in 2012. Blacks were the most stable supporters across the two elections but even with them fewer voted for Obama in 2012 (93 percent) than they had done so in 2008 (95 percent). So the Obama coalition itself was not fully stable from 2008 to 2012. More broadly, the era in which the Obama elections occurred does not speak to a party legacy left by Obama or any other candidate.

Part of the difficulty of sustaining a party coalition from one election to the next is the strong national competition in presidential elections since 1992. Table 6 presents the net difference between the Democratic percent of the vote and the Republican percent of the vote in elections since 1920. The table shows how parties were dominant in the early elections after women won the right to vote in 1920. The Republican coalition dominated the elections from 1920 through 1928 with a 13 percentage point advantage for Republicans across those three elections. And this was despite the "solid Democratic South." The Democratic coalition transformed elections in 1932 and this continued with an average 20 percentage point advantage through 1948.

But the table also reveals the highly competitive races for president beginning in 1992. From 1992 through 2016, the average victory margin is −0.24 percentage points, indicating that at the national level the parties are, in effect, tied. Thus, since 1992, there actually is very little one can point to as a dominant party or candidate-based coalition that leaves a legacy for

Table 5   Party voting among Demographic groups, 1980–2016

		1980	1984	1988	1992	1996	2000	2004	2008	2012	2016
Race											
White	Democrat	36	35	40	39	43	42	41	43	41	37
	Republican	56	64	59	40	46	54	58	55	59	58
	Independent	7	–	–	20	9	3	–	–	–	–
	D–R difference	−20	−29	−19	−1	−3	−12	−17	−12	−18	−21
Black	Democrat	85	90	86	83	84	90	88	95	93	88
	Republican	11	9	12	10	12	8	11	4	7	8
	Independent	3	–	–	7	4	1	–	–	–	–
	D–R difference	74	81	74	73	72	82	77	91	86	80
Asian	Democrat	–	–	–	31	43	54	56	62	73	65
	Republican	–	–	–	55	48	41	44	35	27	29
	Independent	–	–	–	15	8	4	–	–	–	–
	D–R difference				−24	−5	13	12	27	46	36
Hispanic	Democrat	56	62	69	61	72	62	53	67	71	65
	Republican	35	37	30	25	21	35	44	31	29	29
	Independent	8	–	–	14	6	2	–	–	–	–
	D–R difference	21	25	39	36	51	27	9	36	42	36
Age											
18- to 29-year-olds	Democrat	44	40	47	43	53	48	54	66	60	55
	Republican	43	59	52	34	34	46	45	32	40	37
	Independent	11	–	–	22	10	5	–	–	–	–
	D–R difference	1	−19	−5	9	19	2	9	34	20	18
30- to 44-year-olds	Democrat	36	42	45	41	48	48	46	52	52	50
	Republican	55	57	54	38	41	49	53	46	48	42
	Independent	8	–	–	21	9	2	–	–	–	–
	D–R difference	−19	−15	−9	3	7	−1	−7	6	4	8
45- to 59-year-olds	Democrat	39	40	42	41	48	48	48	49	49	44
	Republican	55	60	57	40	41	49	51	49	51	53
	Independent	5	–	–	19	9	2	–	–	–	–
	D–R difference	−16	−20	−15	1	7	−1	−3	0	−2	−9
60 and older	Democrat	41	39	49	50	48	51	46	47	44	45
	Republican	54	60	50	38	44	47	54	51	56	53
	Independent	4	–	–	12	7	2	–	–	–	–
	D–R difference	−13	−21	−1	12	4	4	−8	−4	−12	−8

(*continued*)

Table 5   (continued)

		1980	1984	1988	1992	1996	2000	2004	2008	2012	2016
Education											
Not a high school graduate	Democrat	51	50	56	54	59	59	50	63	51	51
	Republican	46	50	43	28	28	39	49	35	47	45
	Independent	2	–	–	18	11	1	–	–	–	–
	D–R difference	5	0	13	26	31	20	1	28	4	6
High school graduate	Democrat	43	39	49	43	51	48	47	53	51	51
	Republican	51	60	50	36	35	49	52	46	47	43
	Independent	4	–	–	21	13	1	–	–	–	–
	D–R difference	–8	–21	–1	7	16	–1	–5	7	4	8
Some college education	Democrat	35	38	42	41	48	45	46	51	49	43
	Republican	55	61	57	37	40	51	54	47	48	52
	Independent	8	–	–	21	10	3	–	–	–	–
	D–R difference	–20	–23	–15	4	8	–6	–8	4	1	–9
College graduate	Democrat	–	–	37	39	44	45	46	50	49	49
	Republican	–	–	62	41	46	51	52	48	51	45
	Independent	–	–	–	20	8	3	–	–	–	–
	D–R difference	–	–	–25	–2	–2	–6	–6	2	–2	4
Post graduate education	Democrat	–	–	48	50	52	52	55	58	55	58
	Republican	–	–	50	36	40	44	44	40	45	37
	Independent	–	–	–	14	5	3	–	–	–	–
	D–R difference			–2	14	12	8	11	18	10	21

Source: *New York Times* exit polls from 1980 to 2016
For 2012, see https://www.nytimes.com/elections/2012/results/president/exit-polls.html
For 1980–2008, see https://www.nytimes.com/elections/2008/results/president/national-exit-polls.html
For 2016, see https://www.nytimes.com/interactive/2016/11/08/us/politics/election-exit-polls.html

future candidates of that party. So, when analysts discuss the demise of the Obama coalition, they are actually pointing to something we would expect to happen and not be surprised by in today's political climate. One need look no further than the change in Obama's own regional support from 2008 to 2012. While he held a four percentage point advantage over John McCain nationally in 2008 this was 0.7 percentage points in 2012. The advantage he had in the Non-South, which was ten percentage points in 2008, dropped to six percentage points in 2012. So even though Obama was reelected, the Obama coalition shifted between 2008 and 2012.

Table 6   Party victory in presidential elections, 1920–2016

Year	Nation	South	Non-South
1920	−14.8	22.2	−33.3
1924	−11.6	30.8	−23.8
1928	−12.6	5.9	−21.8
1932	27.8	54.5	14.5
1936	31.8	53.5	21.0
1940	18.8	46.8	4.9
1944	13.9	38.2	28.0
1948	6.4	17.5	0.9
1952	−11.9	4.3	−19.9
1956	−13.9	0.5	−21.1
1960	−1.5	3.9	−4.0
1964	18.3	1.5	26.0
1968	−2.4	−2.9	−2.1
1972	−25.8	−38.8	−19.9
1976	1.2	10.0	−2.9
1980	−11.5	−4.2	−14.8
1984	−20.4	−22.4	−19.4
1988	−8.6	−14.2	−6.0
1992	4.3	4.6	5.6
1996	6.6	2.3	8.6
2000	−3.6	−9.4	−1.0
2004	−5.7	−14.0	−2.0
2008	4.3	−8.8	10.2
2012	0.7	−9.9	5.5
2016	−3.7	−15.4	1.7

Note: Entries are the Republican percent of the vote subtracted from the Democratic percent of the vote. So, positive entries denote a Democratic advantage. Negative entries denote a Republican advantage

CONCLUSION

Some presidents leave more well-defined electoral legacies than others. Among modern presidents, Franklin Roosevelt stands out as someone who defined American politics and the presidency for years to come. It did not hurt that Roosevelt ran for election four times and served for 12 years. Because he was such a dominant figure during both the Great Depression and World War II, public opinion polls showed it was hard for voters to imagine another person in the White House. For other reasons, Richard Nixon also stands out as a president with a strong electoral legacy. In 1968, Nixon developed a carefully honed image that was all about being "presidential" which many candidates followed thereafter. While the "new

Nixon" was an image designed to overcome shortcomings of his 1960 campaign, it had long-term consequences for how candidates appeared on television and how a scripted campaign became the order of the day.[18] Of course Nixon's electoral legacy was also more nefariously tied to the Watergate break-in and doing anything to win, including breaking the law.

Other presidents leave little trace in the electoral realm. While there may be moments in their campaigns that stand out and keenly capture the era within which they ran, it is unlikely that this carries forward to influence future campaigns and elections. Despite Lyndon Johnson's landslide victory in 1964, his election provided little in the way of precedents because of the Goldwater candidacy against him. Since many perceived Goldwater as outside the mainstream, Johnson did not need to build a strong coalition of supporters that could have helped him in 1968. Indeed, his decision not to run in 1968 rested not just on the fate of the Vietnam War, but also on the lack of a strong base from which to run. Gerald Ford too left few traces after his election bid in 1976 when he had little to run on except his highly unpopular pardon of Richard Nixon. Thus, there have been presidential candidates who come and go even though they served in the White House.

Barack Obama's electoral legacy will become clearer in the years to come. It is certainly not as forgettable as Johnson's or Ford's, but it is also not likely to be as dramatic and sweeping as Roosevelt's. There is no doubt that being the first black person elected president will be the focal point of the legacy. It is also clear that breaking this barrier is more dramatic than Kennedy's toppling the Catholic barrier. But how much Obama's election and reelection will serve to encourage future generations of people of color to be active in politics and vote in presidential elections will be questions answered in the coming decade.[19]

NOTES

1. M.J. Lee, Dan Merica, and Jeff Zelny, "Obama: Would be a 'personal insult' to legacy of black voters don't back Clinton," CNN, September 17, 2016, found at http://www.cnn.com/2016/09/17/politics/obama-black-congressional-caucus/index.html
2. Gary King and Lyn Ragsdale, *The Elusive Executive* Washington, D.C.: CQ Press, 1988, p. 236.
3. "John F. Kennedy and Religion," John F. Kennedy Presidential Library and Museum, found at https://www.jfklibrary.org/JFK/JFK-in-History/JFK-and-Religion.aspx

4. "Transcript: JFK Speech on His Religion," National Public Radio, found at https://www.npr.org/templates/story/story.php?storyId=16920600

5. Zeba Blay, "11 Times Barack Obama Talked Openly and Honestly About Race," *Huffington Post,* January 9, 2017 found at https://www.huffingtonpost.com/entry/11-times-barack-obama-talked-openly-about-race_us_586d6ae6e4b0c4be0af2c0ab

6. Brian Ross and Rehab El-Buri, "Obama's Pastor: God Damn America, U.S. to Blame for 9–11," ABC News, March 13, 2008, found at http://abcnews.go.com/Blotter/DemocraticDebate/story?id=4443788

7. Barack Obama, "Toward a More Perfect Union," National Constitution Center, Philadelphia, March 18, 2008 found at https://constitutioncenter.org/amoreperfectunion/

8. Ruy Teixeira, *The Disappearing American Voter* (Washington, D.C.: Brookings Institution, 1992), p. 24.

9. Lyn Ragsdale and Jerrold Rusk, *The American Nonvoter.* Oxford: Oxford University Press, 2017.

10. A complete discussion of this is found in Ragsdale and Rusk, 2017, Chapter 6.

11. Jerrold G. Rusk and John Stucker, "The Effect of the Southern System of Election Laws on Voting Participation," in Joel Silbey, Allan Bogue, and William Flanigan, eds., *The History of American Voting Behavior* (Princeton: Princeton University Press, 1978), 198–250.

12. John Herbers, "Black Belt of Alabama is a Stronghold of 19th Century Racism," *New York Times,* February 14, 1965, 70 found at http://search.proquest.com

13. The relationship is also generational. In data not shown, older African-American men are much more likely not to vote than younger African-American men.

14. 2016 results are not available by race and sex in US Census, "Voting and Registration in the Election of 2016." found at https://www.census.gov/data/tables/time-series/demo/voting-and-registration/p20-580.html

15. Lee Sigelman, Philip Roeder, Malcolm Jewell, and Michael Baer, "Voting and Nonvoting: A Multi-election Perspective," *American Journal of Political Science* 29 (November 1985): 749–765.

16. See Ragsdale and Rusk, 2017. A Quinnipiac Poll taken in November 2017 showed that 86 percent of black strongly disapproved and 62 percent of Hispanics strongly disapproved of Trump's job performance. An additional 5 percent of blacks and 8 percent of Hispanics disapproved of his job in office. Found at https://poll.qu.edu/national/release-detail?ReleaseID=2500

17. Merle Black and Earl Black, *Divided America: The Ferocious Power Struggle in American Politics.* New York: Simon and Schuster, 2007.

18. Joe McGinnis, *The Selling of the President* New York: Penguin Press, 1969.

19. Ragsdale and Rusk, 2017; Bernarnd Fraga, *The Turnout Gap* Cambridge: Cambridge University Press, 2018.

Managing a Regime in Crisis: The Twilight of Neoliberalism and the Politics of Economic Recovery During the First Year of the Obama Administration

Kristoffer Smemo

To mark Barack Obama's victory in the 2008 presidential election, *Time* magazine famously featured an illustration of the president-elect striking the same pose a triumphant Franklin Roosevelt had some 70 years earlier. Driving an open-top car along a packed parade route and with FDR's trademark cigarette-holder protruding from a supremely confident grin, Obama stood poised to tackle the most catastrophic economic breakdown since the Great Depression. The unfolding economic crisis had shifted the political center of gravity in the United States to the left after decades of rightwing drift. Journalist Peter Beinart's cover story situated Obama and the Democrats' big wins that November as the final break with almost three decades of Republican austerity and intense free marketeering. To Beinart, it seemed obvious that a Democratic White House and Congress

K. Smemo (✉)
Center for Work, Labor, and Democracy, University of California, Santa Barbara, Santa Barbara, CA, USA
e-mail: ksmemo@umail.ucsb.edu

© The Author(s) 2019
W. C. Rich (ed.), *Looking Back on President Barack Obama's Legacy*,
https://doi.org/10.1007/978-3-030-01545-9_3

47

would implement a sweeping set of reforms modeled on Roosevelt's New Deal. "If he can do what F.D.R. did—make American capitalism stabler and less savage—he will establish a Democratic majority that dominates U.S. politics for a generation."[1] It became very clear, very quickly, that Obama and his administration would not, and could not, follow this course of action.

Historians have already noted that making an analogy between the political responses to the "Great Recession" and the "Great Depression" is misleading.[2] The unemployment figure of 2008 stood at only a little over 7 percent, compared to the staggering jobless rate 25 percent in 1930. In addition, manufacturing had declined in significance as a low-skilled job creator. By 2008, finance, real estate, and the service sectors drove the US economy. As a result, the very structure of the American political economy looked dramatically different than when Franklin Roosevelt took office.

No president possesses an absolute authority to manage the economy under conditions of democratic capitalism. The strict separation of powers enumerated in the Constitution creates steep barriers for any policymaker to intervene in the supposedly sacrosanct rights of private property. Even as the New Deal developed a more sophisticated and intensive regulatory apparatus, its operation remained tightly constrained by hostile forces in Congress and the Court. As a result, the political common sense of the New Deal era came marked by an ambitious—yet very limited—program to reform a manufacturing-based economy. In contrast, the common sense of the early twenty-first century reflected decades of Republican (and Democratic) efforts to dismantle much of the New Deal. That process dovetailed with a larger structural transformation of the United States from an industrial to a postindustrial economy. When President Obama entered office, he inherited much of his recovery program from the Bush administration, particularly the Troubled Asset Relief Program (TARP) and its controversial "bailouts" of banks and automakers, both dependent on consumer debt.[3] More than that, he inherited an institutional and intellectual framework premised on recovering an economy completely different than that of President Roosevelt's day.

As a result, there could be no return to New Deal-style Keynesianism after 2008. Nor could Obama and his administration chart a more expansive set of reforms to those already on offer. In effect, any alternative set of financial reforms foundered on the shoals of neoliberalism. While often invoked as an epithet, neoliberalism holds a very compelling economic explanation for the crisis of capitalism. David Harvey's classic formulation of neoliberalism asserts "that human well-being can best be advanced by liberating individual entrepreneurial freedoms and skills within an institutional framework characterized by strong property rights, free markets, and free trade."[4] The neoliberal turn to the markets began as escalating class struggles of the 1960s wracked the New Deal and its postwar, Fordist welfare state. This once-obscure ideological worldview soon became the center of policymaking discourses for parties of the right and left. At base, the rise of a durable neoliberal regime depended on unleashing a new mode of capital accumulation.

This came principally by unleashing the productive capacities of financial capital through a trifecta of deregulation, privatization, and austerity. Governing an increasingly "financialized" capitalist economy required a transformation of government's obligation to its citizens. No longer would government ensure high aggregate demand through classic Keynesian public spending on entitlements, regulation of international capital flows, or the protection of collective bargaining rights. Neoliberalism promised to preserve economic stability and growth through a massive extension of consumer credit (and personal debt) to working and impoverished peoples, all the while opening investment opportunities in derivatives and futures markets for the wealthy. According to political scientist Colin Crouch, this system of "privatized Keynesianism" became neoliberalism's overriding social and economic policy for three decades.

The operating logic of privatized Keynesianism sowed the seeds of its own destruction. The financial meltdown of 2007–2008 began with the implosion of the housing market pumped up by subprime mortgages. The collapse of housing prices, and a wave of defaults and foreclosures, threatened major banks and financial institutions, not to mention hastened the impending bankruptcy of major auto manufacturers. Thus, when President Obama entered office in January of 2009, he faced a neoliberal regime on the verge of national, if not global, collapse. His sense of political possibilities, however, remained firmly bounded by the worldview of neoliberalism. Backed by solid Democratic majorities in Congress, Obama's ambitious recovery agenda adopted a single-minded focus on saving the crumbling structures of the neoliberal regime. Obama did not advance radical new reforms to confront a regime in collapse. Rather, he and the administration, with the assistance of Congress, struggled only to resuscitate neoliberalism through the orthodoxies of neoliberalism itself.

Obama's approach took two, interconnected forms. First, the president sought to address the immediate crisis of accumulation threatening neoliberal capitalism. The administration marshaled the tremendous resources and expertise of the federal government to rescue and rebuild the structures of privatized Keynesianism. That required some measure of continuity with the outgoing Bush administration. He did not keep Hank Paulson on as Secretary of Treasury, for instance, but he did hire one of his lieutenants, Timothy Geithner, for the job.

Second, Obama still needed to respond to the deepening crisis of legitimacy facing the neoliberal regime. To do so, the president framed the government's "bailout" of Wall Street finance and corporate capital as absolutely essential to staving off a truly catastrophic breakdown of the entire economy.[5] The president and congressional Democrats advanced a mix of stimulus spending and regulatory policy with the American Recovery and Reinvestment Act (ARRA), the Public-Private Investments Program, and the government-engineered bailouts of the auto industry. Each piece of this recovery program sought to restore and relegitimize the essential functions of privatized Keynesianism. In short, Obama presented a host of neoliberal, market-based solutions to resolve a crisis wrought by the remarkable failure of neoliberalism's market-based policies.

The Obama administration successfully revived the neoliberal regime, but perhaps only for a moment. Like Roosevelt's mid-century successors, Obama could not bring back to life a regime that never actually fulfilled its promise of boundless growth. Neither New Deal Keynesianism nor neoliberalism ever fully harnessed the alleged magic of the market. Just as the 1960s exposed the deep, and ultimately irresolvable, contradictions of New Deal Keynesianism, so too did the 2007–2008 lay bare the impending crisis of the neoliberal regime. At best, the administration's recovery program papered over the staggering inequalities created by neoliberal economic management at the dawn of the twenty-first century. The course of the recovery, as expected, continued to concentrate more and more wealth in fewer and fewer hands, while doing little to address stagnating wages or the precariousness of working people. We know well how the era of New Deal Keynesianism came to an end, but the crisis of neoliberalism continues to unfold. This leaves us with a pressing question: was the Obama administration's management of the crisis only signaling the twilight of neoliberalism?

MAKING THE NEOLIBERAL REGIME

Neoliberalism emerged as the *sui generis* product of an interlocking set of intellectual, bureaucratic, and political "faces" across the Western capitalist democracies.[5] The first intellectual face came from a cadre of rightwing Anglo-American thinkers who detested the regulations and negotiations of the so-called "postwar settlement."[6] Their ideological commitment to "free" markets dovetailed with the material interests of capitalists and their representatives in conservative parties. This directly informed neoliberalism's second, bureaucratic face. Neoliberalism's bureaucratic imperative focused on compelling government to abandon any "interference" in the operation of the market, principally through the deregulation of finance, and the recommodification of such public goods as housing, education, and healthcare. Finally, the political face of neoliberalism struggled to make such market-centric politics the prevailing "common sense" of government policymaking. Taken as a whole, the three faces of neoliberalism emerged as a historically specific set of alternatives to the postwar Keynesian welfare national state (KWNS) of the Fordist manufacturing economy.[7]

In the United States, the KWNS took shape through the New Deal regime, and thus carried the marks of the New Deal order's internal contradictions.[8] Each of its core reforms (e.g. encouraging near-full employment, promoting collective bargaining, and providing a baseline of social welfare entitlements) stabilized capitalism after the 1929 crash and during World War II. The postwar KWNS, therefore, operated according to a market logic. As John Maynard Keynes concluded 30 years earlier, preserving long-term capitalist stability required some governing body to publicly manage private investment. Market forces alone do not ensure an adequate source of countercyclical spending to arrest an economic downturn and stimulate economic recovery.[9]

Yet, as Keynes's colleague Michael Kalecki accurately foresaw, capitalists and rentiers quickly banded together to block the creation of any such body.[10] In the United States, organized business joined forces with southern segregationists in the 1940s to ensure that final authority over investment, pricing, and production remained squarely in private hands.[11] But capitalists by and large could never embrace this compromise precisely because encouraging high aggregate demand made labor costlier and much less pliable. It also recognized labor as a political subject in own right, and placed the onus for aggregate demand on workers' power to bargain for higher wages. In this largely depoliticized system, the federal government lacked adequate institutional capacity to actually plan for economic stability, much less resolve its endemic social conflicts.

The crisis of "stagflation" in the late 1960s crystalized the institutional inability of American Keynesianism to satisfy popular demands for better wages and public goods while maintaining a positive climate for continued capitalist investment. American Keynesianism relied on a potentially endless inflation of the money supply (whether through wage increases or deficit spending) to keep consumer demand high. But for employers and creditors, inflation ate away at the value of their money and investments and weakened their pricing power. According to economic sociologist Greta Krippner, the market offered a way out of this mounting fiscal crisis without creating the government institutions to manage private investments that capitalists hated.[12] Postwar policymakers assumed that the economy was capital-scarce and credit-short. Their job focused on arbitrating how to best allocate such limited resources to ensure social stability and prosperity. But by deregulating financial markets and loosening the flow of credit, policymakers could cede politically difficult questions of resource allocation to supposedly impartial market forces. This dovetailed with policies designed to loosen capital controls (sparked by Nixon's abandonment of the Bretton Woods agreement) and stimulate the infusion of foreign capital. Stimulating international and domestic investment required first creating "a high-interest rate regime" to discipline labor's wage demands and any other popular demands for public goods. When the Federal Reserve ratcheted interest rates up to 20 percent in 1979, the planned recession wiped out inflation with a huge spike in unemployment, and with it the productive and social basis of New Deal variation of the KWNS. From the wreckage, a competing neoliberal mode of production with its own social relations and political institutions began to take shape.

The resulting "financialization" of the US economy can be traced to the rising tide of anti-Keynesian political logic in Washington, DC. But, as Krippner concludes, its emergence was haphazard. Policymakers eager to combat inflation also took aim at the taxes used to fund the entitlement spending that sought to put more money in more consumers' pockets. The supply-side tax cuts advanced by monetarists in the Reagan administration promised to spur a renewed surge of investment. The nagging recession that continued into the early 1980s, though, challenged their grand claims of recovery. In reaction, Reagan's White House continued on policies begun in the 1970s. Republicans eagerly pursued the deregulation of the financial sector. The hope was that ready access to capital could energize rapid growth in the high-tech and service industries, thereby supplanting once and for all the manufacturing industries that had sustained the postwar KWNS. The steady destruction of the "tax state" in the 1980s gave way to what sociologist Wolfgang Streeck calls the "debt state" of the late twentieth and early twenty-first centuries.[13] For policymakers, the free flow of capital across the globe offered the potential to use market mechanisms to replace the government provision of public goods and compensate for deteriorating wages and the disappearance of entitlements.

Here lay the material basis of what Colin Crouch calls "privatized Keynesianism." The logic was simple, and seductive to politicians anxious to bury the compromises and conflicts of the Fordist welfare state. "Instead of governments taking on debt to stimulate the economy," Crouch writes, "individuals did so."[14] Through an incredible extension of consumer credit (and growing personal debt), the market could effectively plug the holes left by gutted entitlement spending and the destruction of collective bargaining. Privatized Keynesianism also offered tremendous profits for the financial sector by aggressively recommodifying home ownership, healthcare, and education. Thus, this financialized solution to the distributional crisis of the 1970s became the centerpiece of the neoliberal mode of accumulation. It also transformed the political imaginations and governing logics of both major American political parties for the next three decades.

No Alternative

In the United States, as elsewhere, this neoliberal regime emerged as part of a broad and durable bipartisan consensus. Conservative parties, of course, eagerly used the stagflation crisis of the 1970s to assault the foundations of the postwar settlement. But the crisis of the postwar KWNS proved especially troubling for the parties that actually built that regime in the 1940s and 1950s. Given that this system set only to manage—and not overthrow—capitalism, social democratic and labor parties remained bound to the social relationships of capitalist democracy. This trapped left parties in a party system compelled to privilege the general needs of business. Specifically, this meant the privatized Keynesianism that became the prime neoliberal mode of accumulation. Under an increasingly financialized economy this demanded that parties reorient themselves to reproduce the overall conditions needed for finance capital to profit.[15] By the end of the 1970s, so-called "third way" party advocates brought neoliberal discourses and practices into the social democratic mainstream across

Western Europe. From the United Kingdom to Sweden, privatization, deregulation, labor market "flexibility," and the retrenchment of welfare entitlements became hallmarks of the left's governing platforms.[16] There would be no alternative to neoliberal capitalism, just as the Conservative Prime Minister Margaret Thatcher insisted.

Though not exactly a party of the left in terms of European socialism, the American Democratic Party adopted the same ideological posture as its transatlantic counterparts. While the collapse of the party's segregationist wing in the mid-1960s offered a tangible moment to transform the Democrats into a social democratic party, the unfolding crises of KWNS dashed any such realignment. Coupled with the landslide defeat of left-leaning George McGovern's presidential bid in 1972, the Democratic leadership strata became increasingly convinced that the party's own working-class base was as an electoral liability. During the internal party reform moment of the 1970s, a growing "neoliberal" Democratic bloc refused to commit to a robust program to expand the KWNS, one demanded by the trade unions, civil rights organizations, and other insurgent social movements.[17] Thus, when the Democrats reclaimed the White House under Jimmy Carter in 1976, the party focused on the deregulation of trucking, airlines, and especially banking. Meanwhile, the president sidelined pro-union labor law reform, and pushed for a hopelessly watered down full employment bill despite Democratic majorities in Congress. Furthermore, Paul Volcker, Carter's appointee to chair the Federal Reserve, administered the "shock" that sharply raised interest rates to dramatically spike unemployment in order to throttle inflation.[18]

Carter's concessions to the financialized economy arguably cost him the White House in a race against Ronald Reagan (who ultimately doubled down on the very economic policies begun under Carter). Nonetheless, his administration's program still convinced a young cadre of Democrats to accept that the New Deal regime was dead. In its place, the discursive and material politics neoliberalism became the new orthodoxy. Whereas the KWNS relied on mass parties that incorporated an organized working class into politics as never before, the turn to neoliberalism dramatically narrowed the electoral constituency. Affluent, white-collar professionals who lived in well-to-do suburbs became the electoral base, and, despite their small size, now enjoyed an outsized influence in American politics. These self-described "suburban liberals" could not stand the culturally reactionary bent of Ronald Reagan's GOP, yet they still considered the KWNS a largely discredited enterprise, and assumed neoliberalism was its necessary alternative.[19]

By the 1980s, Arkansas Governor Bill Clinton spearheaded a broader effort to make suburban liberals the centerpiece of the Democratic Party. Under the aegis of the Democratic Leadership Council (DLC), Clinton articulated an expressly neoliberal political language to fully realign the party. The reform of capitalism remained a priority, but this project needed to take place through market-friendly initiatives such as public-private partnerships. Meritocratic individualism displaced collective or solidarity appeals. Economic and social policy would continue down the path blazed by Carter (and continued on by Reagan) by focusing on the most dynamic sectors of the economy: finance, insurance, and real estate (the FIRE economy). The political lessons of the crisis of the KWNS set a clear ideological course for the party leaders, apparatchiks, and intellectuals organized around the DLC. Their third-way vision overlapped neatly with the same conclusions reached by European social democrats such as Tony Blair. The redistributive demands of a diverse, largely proletarian base needed to be firmly subordinated to those of the well-to-do suburban liberals.

When the Democrats reclaimed the White House in 1992 after 12 years of Reaganism, the party remained very much in thrall to the prevailing regime. In one policy arena after another, the Clinton administration reaffirmed its fealty to neoliberalism. This meant a drastic retrenchment of the postwar welfare state, all while further building the carceral state. The 1996 Personal Responsibility and Work Opportunity Act "ended welfare as we know it," in Clinton's own words, and in turn provided business with a new reserve army of labor unable to lay claim to federal entitlement payments to help bargain up wages. Proponents of the North American Free Trade Agreement claimed that limitless possibilities for growth existed through global free trade, but these came at the cost of dramatic deindustrialization of the country's unionized manufacturing belt.

Furthermore, Clinton completed the transition from the tax state to the debt state by adhering to an almost single-minded focus on reducing the federal deficit. This all rested on a vast program of deregulation capped off by the repeal of the Depression-era Glass-Steagall Act separating investment and commercial banking with the Gramm-Leach-Bliley Act of 1999. Banks brought up many investment and insurance companies (e.g. Citicorp merged with Traveler Group and Smith Barney), and Gramm-Leach-Bliley explicitly exempted security-based swap agreements and derivative financial products. When Clinton himself declared the "era of big government is over," he was conceding to what presidential scholar Stephen Skowronek called the entrenched governing regime of limited government established by President Reagan.[20]

In the 1980 and 1990s, neoliberalism emerged as a durable and hegemonic regime, one created and nurtured by both major political parties in the United States. Under both Reagan and Clinton, the Republican and Democratic parties seized on neoliberalism to create governing majorities precisely by dramatically narrowing the electoral base of politics. This process of demobilizing the Democrats' cornerstone constituencies proceeded apace with the destruction of the already limited redistributive ambit of the federal government. Privatized Keynesianism provided a workable material base to replace the KWNS for at least several decades. As the dominant regime of the late 1900s and early 2000s, neoliberalism took shape as a formation borne of these historically specific ideological and material forces. The Clinton years in particular represented its apogee as the Democrats and Republicans successfully restructured the institutions and discourses of government to encourage the neoliberal mode of accumulation. Indeed, the 1990s witnessed a dramatic, if unevenly distributed, explosion of economic growth and prosperity. The governing ensemble of neoliberalism, however, would soon be severely tested by the grinding contradictions built into neoliberalism itself.

MELTDOWN

In the glow of the immediate post-Cold War moment, the incredible economic growth of the 1990s made neoliberalism appear triumphant. Aside from the bursting of the "dot-com bubble" in the early 2000s, the American economy grew at an impressive clip with few hiccups. But its benefits remained unevenly allocated, and this fact highlighted a growing set of tensions. In effect, the neoliberal regime only exchanged the specific contradictions of Fordist manufacturing and its attendant KWNS for a novel set of contradictions unique to a financialized economy under neoliberalism. The disappearance of inflation as a chronic problem required the wholesale destruction of an organized working class able to keep wages in line with corporate price increases.

The budget surpluses racked up by the Clinton administration did herald an end to the gnawing fiscal crises of the 1970s. Surpluses, of course, required a concerted project of public austerity and retrenchment that shifted authority over the distribution of wealth to market forces. This shift created a tremulous source of new wealth for financial institutions at the heart of privatized Keynesianism. Shoring up the material foundation of neoliberalism also required new ways to legitimize itself. Privatized Keynesianism filled gaps left by austerity. The ready extension of consumer credit helped keep aggregate demand high, especially through the planned recessions used to discipline labor and depress wage rates. But this whole regime revolved around the hyper-commodification of personal debt on a massive scale through credit cards, student loans, and especially home mortgages.

The growing bubble in the housing market exposed the fatal flaw of privatized Keynesianism, and with it the entire neoliberal organization of the economy and politics. The steady increase in housing prices, matched by a return to low interest rates, convinced lenders to issue mortgages more easily throughout the late twentieth century. These conditions encouraged unprecedented rates of homeownership, and with it a spectacular surge in housing prices. As Crouch makes clear, this all depended on lending practices that extended mortgages well beyond the rather narrow base of consumers who held sufficient collateral or secure employment to issue loans against. Dramatically extending these unsecured loans became the only way for privatized Keynesianism to exert the same countercyclical force on the market as its state-managed variant.[21]

Such risky debt in turn became the very basis of the subprime mortgages that powered the exorbitant profits in the derivatives and futures markets. When the housing bubble burst in 2006, the riskiness of these loans became all too clear as foreclosures and defaults skyrocketed. The major banks across the world that funded rampant speculation behind the subprime mortgages quickly felt the hit. Bank runs not seen since the 1920s devastated the investment banks, and felling giants such as Bear Stearns. The ensuing financial meltdown came from not only relaxed government oversight, but also from a larger neoliberal logic that made financial markets the regulatory mechanism that would ensure the reproduction of mass consumption, mass production capitalism.

The crash that began in 2007 and spilled over into 2009 only amplified a much vaster crisis of capitalism that unfolded amid George W. Bush's second term in office. The collapse of the housing market, and, subsequently, key financial institutions only compounded the near-bankruptcy of the auto industry. Through the Federal Reserve, the government sought to restore liquidity to major banks and investment firms. Likewise, the Treasury issued 50 billion dollars to guarantee investments in money market mutual funds. As Treasury Secretary Henry Paulson urged Congress to pass the Emergency Economic Stabilization Act in the fall of 2008 that created the TARP for extending equity to banks as well as loans to General Motors and Chrysler.

In each case, the Bush administration set in the motion all the key elements of the recovery program that continued well after he left office. According to political scientist Philip Wallach these elements comprised a frantic "adhocracy" of policymaking carried out in the "hurried decisions of unelected officials deriving their authority from obscure sources" rather than duly elected lawmakers.[22] For Wallach, this adhocracy proceeded with quite limited government oversight, and often with dubious legal legitimacy. But the very political economic structure of neoliberalism assumed that any significant democratic input posed a serious risk to investment and prosperity. Just as bureaucratic imperatives transferred essential governing authority to the market, so too would they attempt to restore that system to working order. Thus, the very federal bureaucracies that neoliberalism disempowered in the 1980s and 1990s would now be called upon to rescue neoliberalism. Only now with severely limited resources. The adhocracy of 2007–2008 fit perfectly within the tenets of the neoliberal regime it sought to save. Bush and Obama—like Reagan and Clinton before them—operated firmly within the ambit of neoliberalism. Unlike their predecessors, Bush and Obama needed to rebuild relations, economic structures, and ideologies of policy knowledge driving capitalist governance in the early twenty-first century. Thus, the new Obama administration would implement its recovery program as a fully neoliberal project.

THE OBAMA ADMINISTRATION RESPONDS

When Obama won office in 2008, his signature campaign slogan of "hope and change" offered voters the promise of a decisive break with the Bush years. His campaign came with blistering rhetoric excoriating the greed and ineptitude of bankers and financiers. His language also implicitly suggested an end to the "triangulation" of the late Clinton era and its penchant for deregulation that paved the way for the meltdown. Once in the White House, though, President Obama clearly signaled that his office remained bound to the neoliberal consensus. Obama opted to continue the Bush administration's approach to recovery, and in many cases with the same personnel. The president kept Ben Bernanke at the Federal Reserve and appointed New York Fed president Timothy Geithner, who worked closely with the Bush administration, as Secretary of the Treasury. As a result, the Obama administration's recovery program focused almost exclusively on the commanding heights of financialized, neoliberal capitalism. Together, their plan for economic recovery focused exclusively on shoring up a regime in crisis.

In sum, Obama's administration confronted the near-total destruction of the key bulwarks of America's privatized Keynesianism. At the same time, Obama remained constrained by the contradictions bound up within the neoliberal regime. Parsing out the contending "varieties of Obamaism" requires framing the Obama presidency as a protracted effort to reconcile the competing institutional and coalitional demands of a neoliberal Democratic Party.[23] While his larger objective always focused on preserving the neoliberal project, albeit with a modest liberal entitlement twist, Obama at key moments still needed to accommodate what remained of the Democratic New Deal coalition and make a record on which to run for reelection. To understand the political dynamics of the Obama administration's initial economic recovery, the program must be broken down into three district applications of policy: housing, stimulus spending, and industrial policy.

RECOVERING HOUSING MARKETS

The collapse of the housing market and the subsequent wave of foreclosures formed a critical political venue for Obama to restore confidence in privatized Keynesianism. Dealing with the wave of foreclosures generated by the predatory lending behind the subprime mortgages forced the federal government to address the clear failure of privatized Keynesianism, and more generally the inability of neoliberal governance to prevent total systemic failure. Obama, however, sought to convince the body politic that the government ought to contribute significant resources to right the housing market on terms wholly consistent with privatized Keynesianism. This project came with serious political obstacles. Only a year earlier, the Bush administration's Treasury Secretary Henry Paulson received sharp criticism for refusing to divert TARP resources to assist individuals facing foreclosure. Nor would his successor Timothy Geithner consider such a move until the Fed completed its "stress tests" to determine whether the country's biggest banks held enough capital to withstand the worsening recession.

Writing in his memoir of the crisis, Geithner defended his statements by arguing that there could be no political or economic benefits in helping those who indulged in opulent homes they could not afford or bankrolling failed individual real estate speculators. Nor would he consider "spending billions of taxpayer dollars to restructure mortgages for families who would lose their homes even with government help."[24] Geithner's comments reveal a supreme faith in not only the functional efficacy of privatized Keynesianism, but also its ideological suppositions. Only financial markets could and would efficiently and equitably allocate resources. Nor could it even be considered that the government ought to shoulder any responsibility for providing housing as any kind of de-commodified public good.

This logic became clear in the Public-Private Investments Program (PPIP), the centerpiece of the Obama administration's initial efforts to restore confidence to housing markets. Through partnerships with the Treasury, the PPIP encouraged private investors to purchase equity stakes in pools of mortgages from banks. Backed by debt financing from the Treasury, as well as the Fed and Federal Deposit Insurance Corporation, the PPIP was structured to offer considerable private profit should the mortgages improve even slightly.[25] With this renewed confidence, the private sector could begin issuing loans again at a sufficient clip to stimulate the essential countercyclical function of privatized Keynesianism. In effect, the PPIP leveraged considerable government resources and institutional clout to regenerate profitability by spurring the acquisition of new consumer debt.

Geithner's attempt to outline this program in early February of 2009 still met with popular outcry because it did little to address the rash of foreclosures left in the wake of the meltdown. Geithner's plan focused exclusively on reviving market functions, and did not deal with the social calamity of subprime lending. When Obama went to the hard-hit suburb of Mesa, Arizona, a week later, he attempted to repair the damage done by his Treasury Sectary's remarks. In his Mesa address Obama, promised relief for nearly ten million homeowners (but not profligate "speculators") to refinance or restructure their mortgages. Obama infused two hundred billion dollars into cash-strapped Fannie Mae and Freddie Mac, the two government-sponsored enterprises responsible for ensuring adequate liquidity for housing lenders. Relatedly, the president also unveiled the Home Affordable Modification Program to subsidize any adjustment to the subprime loans held by private mortgage firms. The president touted the package of housing initiatives as an "unraveling of homeownership, the middle class, and the American Dream itself."[26]

The structure of these policy provisions belied such lofty and egalitarian rhetoric. Even Obama admitted that the $270 billion package (only $75 million of which would be directed as relief to homeowners) could hardly be enough to save every home threatened with foreclosure.[27] Nor was that the point. Instead, Obama's housing recovery program was firmly subordinated to the needs of a neoliberal mode of accumulation. Indeed, when Congress finally passed the ambitiously titled Helping Families Save Their Homes Act, the law pointedly avoided amending the personal bankruptcy code to adjust mortgage terms without approval from the lender.[28] This cemented the full-fledged "financialization of urban policy" under the Obama administration.[29] The result reinforced the already deeply unequal distribution of wealth accelerated by privatized Keynesianism. Over a million homeowners received help under the Obama administration's housing programs. But of that number over half fell out of mortgage relief programs because they still could not meet their payments on renegotiated mortgages.[30] Thus, the terms of the housing recovery program starkly foreshadowed just how much the Obama administration continued to operate within the ideological and programmatic framework of neoliberalism. This proved especially true as the administration advanced legislation in the one area that bore even a remote remembrance to the policies of the New Deal regime—stimulus spending.

NEOLIBERAL STIMULUS SPENDING

At first glance, the ARRA passed by Congress in the first days of the Obama administration looked like a classic Keynesian program. The law provided a major fiscal package, totaling some $787 billion. This included infrastructure development, expanded federal unemployment compensation, and money to increase state spending on Medicaid and education. Journalist Michael Grunwald gushed in 2012 that the ARRA stood out as the most ambitious and far-reaching series of economic reforms passed since the New Deal.[31] Ultimately, though, the ARRA did measure up to the nascent social democratic interventions of the 1930s. Fed Chair Ben Bernanke—whose own institution came with a formal mandate to ensure a full employment economy—admitted that "the program was probably too small."[32] He admitted that rebuilding a $15 trillion economy with a recovery package of less than $800 billion would alone be a Herculean effort. Bernanke also noted that certain spending increases were already on the table, so the administration felt no need to go further in actually rebuilding the devastated American welfare state.

More problematically, the ARRA did not come with a clearly defined mass constituency, and instead conjured only popular images of boondoggles and pork barrel expenditures. "Perhaps," Bernanke concluded, "if the package had been more clearly focused and sold as a way of strengthening America's infrastructure and the improving the economy's long-run productive potential, it would have been more broadly supported."[33] Of course reconstructing a financialized, neoliberal regime in crisis could do no such thing. Neoliberal stimulus spending could never consider returning to classic Keynesianism. The turn to neoliberalism in the 1970s came from organized business and its political allies overthrowing the range of economic interventions designed to ensure long-term capitalist functioning through increasing wages and public goods. Such policies only empowered labor as an economic force and an organized political subject able to make demands against capitalist profitability. Neoliberalism, through the mechanism of privatized Keynesianism, depended on markets assuming government authority over the distribution of wealth. This, too, served the interests of the neoliberal Democratic coalition, one led and funded largely by finance capital.

This became all the clearer as the ARRA's identified tax cuts (including a temporary decrease in Social Security payroll taxes) as key tool for economic recovery. In this sense, Obama's ARRA looked quite similar to John F. Kennedy's ostensibly Keynesian 1963 tax cuts. As with Obama's stimulus program, Kennedy defended this proto-supply-side economics policy as a way to encourage renewed business investment rather than increasing mass purchasing or bargaining power.[34] This logic provided a direct through line to the neoliberalism of the 2000s. The federal government used stimulus spending to ensure high aggregate demand for finance capital by reigniting the issuance of loans and easy access to credit. Its most immediate material beneficiaries, therefore, would not be individual consumers, but rather the investment banks. Still, the ARRA did reform the use of TARP funding in a number of ways more broadly acceptable to the Democrats' laboring base. Specifically, the ARRA restricted bonuses paid out to executives at AIG. But the question of TARP funding became much trickier for the Obama administration as it struggled to revive a largely bygone industrial economy.

"Government Motors"

By the 2000s, the once mighty American auto industry had been laid low by decades of mismanagement, growing foreign competition, and failed diversification schemes. The neoliberal shift that traded "factories for finance" also shifted the priorities of policymakers less and less committed to the Fordist economy at the heart of the KWNS.[35] At the same time, the Big Three firms consistently maintained the bottom line by helping to pioneer the widespread financialization of the late twentieth-century economy. General Motors, for instance, pioneered the creation of financing units to drum up sales of cars with payment plans that ended up dwarfing the profits generated by the firm's manufacturing business.[36] Thus, the collapse of the housing market directly impacted automakers reliant on the same streams of easy access to credit that kept car sales going through the neoliberal era. The Bush administration responded by offering TARP loans to keep General Motors and Chrysler—the two automakers closest to bankruptcy—operating, but only for the time being. The Obama administration inherited the much thornier question of what do about the deeply troubled industry.

Perhaps more so than in housing, the question of whether to "bail out" the auto industry tested Obama's ability to act as a coalition manager for a neoliberal Democratic Party. Just as Obama prepared to announce the administration's response to the foreclosure crisis, the troubled automakers submitted the corporate restructuring proposals stipulated by the Bush TARP loan agreements. It soon became clear to the Presidential Task Force on the Auto Industry that the government would need to manage the bankruptcy of both Chrysler and General Motors. The deals hashed out over the spring and summer of 2009 looked quite similar for both firms. Each company would sell off most of its assets to "new" corporate entities (which in Chrysler's case also included a partnership with the Italian automaker Fiat). Furthermore, the deals wrote off much off both firms' debt to its secured creditors, but did much more to protect United Automobile Workers members' pensions from creditors. This move infuriated the neoliberal Democratic Party's cadre in financial circles who feared "Government Motors" as the first step in the nationalization of the corporate industry, not to mention squeezing out creditors.[37]

For President Obama, though, the decision only protected an aging, and thus quite literally disappearing, element of the old Democratic coalition: the unionized manufacturing worker. In the long run, the bankruptcy deals gave far more to corporate managers through dramatically restructuring the day-to-day business of the auto industry, especially through the institution of two-tier collective bargaining that brought new workers into the plants with far lower wages and less generous benefits than their senior coworkers. The terms of the auto bailout placated the dwindling ranks of the organized industrial workers while still offering concrete material incentives for finance capital. Indeed, the bailout likely helped the president win the critical industrial state of Ohio in 2012. The case of the auto industry suggested a way for the Obama administration to reconcile a chief contradiction of neoliberalism for the Democratic Party. But such moves may not legitimate neoliberalism in the long term.

THE FAILURE TO LEGITIMATE NEOLIBERALISM

The administration's economic recovery program begun in 2009 highlighted the ideological coordinates of a Democratic Party committed, above all else, to salvaging the neoliberal regime. This was capped by the expansive 2010 Dodd-Frank Wall Street Reform and Consumer Protection Act. Its constitutive elements promised a sweeping new regulatory apparatus able, according to Bernanke, to "look at the whole system and not just individual components of it."[38] One of the law's most important creations was the Financial Stability Oversight Council to coordinate regulatory oversight to assess capital reserves, conduct stress tests, and so on. These expanded regulatory powers came with restrictions on government regulatory independence as well. Dodd-Frank sought to end the autonomous regulatory power of the Fed, for instance, to determine how to deal with the failure of "systematically critical institutions." Unlike in 2008, the federal government would not be forced to either bail out firms deemed "too big to fail" such as Bear Stearns, Lehman Brothers, or AIG on the taxpayers' dime, or accede to a messy and possibly catastrophic bankruptcy. Title II of the law created the Orderly Liquidation Authority (OLA) to determine the appropriate course of action in concert with the financial apparatuses of the government. The precise power afforded to the OLA, though, remains murky. Without clear guidelines on when or where the OLA could be deployed, its very usefulness in a time of crisis could be severely limited.[39] Even worse, according to Bernanke, the OLA could effectively make it "safe for a big firm to fail."[40] While Dodd-Frank sought to legitimate the mode of accumulation at the heart of the neoliberal order, key pieces of the law failed to fully address the kind of crisis it seeks to prevent.

Nevertheless, Dodd-Frank and the Obama administration's recovery program worked in the immediate term. Obama's management of the crisis achieved a rather remarkable feat by restoring the legitimacy of the neoliberal regime and its mode of accumulation. "For a while, at least," political theorist Nancy Fraser observes, "the 2008 financial crisis put a crimp in privatized Keynesianism. But far from loosening the grip of finance, its effect was to solidify the hold of debt over capital's background conditions, especially public power and social reproduction."[41] Thus, the market-based reforms of the 2009–2010 era consciously, and rather conspicuously, failed to rectify the basic problems of the neoliberal regime. The Obama administration and its network of party leaders, politicians, and allied intellectuals did not seize on this profound moment of crisis to begin sketching out an alternative. The crisis of the postwar KWNS generated—however inadvertently—the material and ideological grist for a new regime. But such a rethinking was well beyond the reaches of the administration's political imagination.

Though the neoliberal regime that staggered out of the crash maintained its grip on power, it did not possess nearly the same legitimacy as before. Over the next four years the terms of the agreement came politically undone. The 2016 Democratic primary reopened debates over the role of government in addressing inequality that the party's neoliberal mainstream considered settled beyond question since the early 1980s. Faced with a slow recovery that only seemed to normalize ever greater precarity, the shibboleths about the natural efficacy of the market to manage the redistribution of wealth could no longer hold. This contradiction also tore apart the uneasy political logic holding the neoliberal Republican Party together. The white supremacist populism of the Donald J. Trump presidential campaign mobilized a rightwing groundswell against neoliberalism that "establishment" politicians from either party could not withstand.

Yet, the globalized and financialized capitalist economy centered in the United States remains hegemonic. But the 2016 election signals that serious cracks in that regime have clearly developed. In this context, it is clear that the Obama presidency reactions to 2008 recession were only a quick fix for neoliberalism as a means of organizing the economy and politics under twenty-first-century capitalism. We only have the books written by Tim Geithner, Ben Bernanke, and others that explained who did what, why, and how. Until the archives are opened, our ability to fully reconstruct the Obama administration's internal decision-making processes remains quite limited. But we can begin laying the foundation for how to evaluate the administration's political response to the crisis by placing it in a longer history. That history seems to reflect a historical arc that follows the rise and fall of neoliberalism.

NOTES

1. Peter Beinart, "The New Liberal Order," *Time* (November 13, 2008).
2. Eric Rauchway, "Neither a Depression nor a New Deal: Bailout, Stimulus, and the Economy," *The Presidency of Barack Obama: A First Historical Assessment*, ed. Julian E. Zelizer (Princeton, NJ: Princeton University Press, 2018), 30–44.
3. "57% of Public Favors Wall Street Bailout," *Pew Research Center*, September 23, 2008; "Support for Stimulus Plan Slips, Poll Finds," *CNN Politics*, March 17, 2009; "Polling Shows Americans Wary of Bailouts," *CBS News*, September 14, 2009.
4. David Harvey, *A Brief History of Neoliberalism* (New York: Oxford University Press, 2010), 2.
5. Stephanie L. Mudge, "What is Neo-liberalism?" *Socio-Economic Review*, 6 (October 2008), 703–31.
6. Daniel Stedman Jones, *Masters of the Universe: Hayek, Friedman, and the Birth of Neoliberal Politics* (Princeton, NJ: Princeton University Press, 2012).
7. Bob Jessop, *The Future of the Capitalist State* (Cambridge, UK: Polity, 2002), 55–93.
8. David Plotke, *Building a Democratic Political Order: Reshaping American Liberalism in the 1930s and 1940s* (Cambridge: Cambridge University Press, 1996).
9. John Maynard Keynes, *General Theory of Employment, Interest and Money* (New Delhi: Atlantic Publishers: 2008 [1936]), 347.
10. Michael Kalecki, "Political Aspects of Full Employment," *Political Quarterly*, 14 (October 1943), 322–30.
11. Ira Katznelson, Kim Geiger, and Daniel Kryder, "Limiting Liberalism: The Southern Veto in Congress, 1933–1950," *Political Science Quarterly*, 108 (Summer 1993), 283–306.
12. Greta Krippner, *Capitalizing on Crisis: The Political Origins of the Rise of Finance* (Cambridge, MA: Harvard University Press, 2011).
13. Wolfgang Streeck, *Buying Time: The Delayed Crisis of Democratic Capitalism* (London: Verso, 2014).

14. Colin Crouch, "Privatised Keynesianism: An Unacknowledged Policy Regime," *British Journal of Politics & International Relations*, 11 (July 2009), 390.
15. Bob Jessop, *The State: Past, Present, Future* (London: Wiley, 2015), 82–83.
16. Stephanie L. Mudge, "What's Left of Leftism?: Neoliberal Politics in Western Party Systems, 1945–2004," *Social Science History*, 35 (Fall 2011), 337–80.
17. Adam Hilton, "Searching for a New Politics: The New Politics Movement and the Struggle to Democratize the Democratic Party, 1968–1978," *New Political Science* 38 (June 2016), 141–159.
18. For the economic politics of the Carter administration, see Judith Stein, *Pivotal Decade: How the United States Traded Factories for Finance in the Seventies* (New Haven, CT: Yale University Press, 2010).
19. For an excellent case study of the politics of the suburban liberals as social bloc, see Lily Geismer, *Don't Blame Us: Suburban Liberals and the Transformation of the Democratic Party* (Princeton, NJ: Princeton University Press, 2015).
20. Stephen Skowronek, *The Politics Presidents Makes: Leadership from John Adam to Bill Clinton* (Cambridge, MA: Harvard Belknap, 1997), 409–446.
21. Crouch, "Privatised Keynesianism," 392.
22. Philip A. Wallach, *To the Edge: Legality, Legitimacy, and the Responses to the 2008 Financial Crisis* (Washington, DC: Brookings Institute, 2015), 17.
23. Lawrence R. Jacobs and Desmond S. King, "Varieties of Obamaism: Structure, Agency, and the Obama Presidency," *Perspectives on Politics*, 8 (September 2010), 793–802.
24. Timothy F. Geithner *Stress Test* (New York: Crown Publishing 2014), 301.
25. Wallach, *To the Edge*, 153.
26. Quoted in Sheryl Gay Stolberg and Edmund L. Andrews, "$275 Billion Plan Seeks to Address Crisis in Housing," *New York Times*, February 19, 2009, p. A1.
27. Ibid.
28. Wallach, *To the Edge*, 150.
29. Robert W. Lake, "The Financialization of Urban Policy in the Age of Obama," *Journal of Urban Affairs*, 37 (February 2015), 75–78.
30. Cedric Herring, Loren Henderson, and Hayward Derrick Horton, "Race, the Great Recession, and the Foreclosure Crisis," in *Repositioning Race: Prophetic Research in a Postracial Obama Age*, ed. Sandra L. Barnes, Zandria F. Robinson, and Earl Wright II (Albany: State University of New York Press, 2014), 101.
31. Michael Grunwald, *The New New Deal: The Hidden Story of Change in the Obama Era* (New York: Simon and Schuster, 2012).

32. Ben S. Bernanke, *The Courage to Act: A Memoir of a Crisis and its Aftermath* (New York: Norton, 2015), 388.
33. Ibid., 389.
34. Kim Phillips-Fein, *Invisible Hands: The Businessmen's Crusade Against the New Deal* (New York: Norton, 2009), 190.
35. Stein, *Pivotal Decade.*
36. Krippner, *Capitalizing on Crisis,* 28–29.
37. Wallach, *To the Edge,* 125–28.
38. Ben S. Bernanke, *The Federal Reserve and the Financial Crisis: Lectures by Ben S. Bernanke* (Princeton, NJ: Princeton University Press, 2013), 118.
39. Wallach, *To the Edge,* 199.
40. Bernanke, *Federal Reserve and the Financial Crisis,* 120.
41. Nancy Fraser, "Legitimation Crisis? On the Political Contradictions of Financialized Capitalism," *Critical Historical Studies,* 2 (Fall 2015), 179.

The Obama Health Care Legacy: The Origins, Implementation, and Effort to Repeal the Affordable Care Act of 2010

Jill Quadagno and Daniel Lanford

For nearly a century, presidents of both parties, powerful elected officials, and social reformers tried and failed to enact some measure that would guarantee that all Americans had access to health insurance. That failure resulted in a health care system that was among the most costly of all developed nations in terms of the portion of GDP spent on health services, with much of the cost borne directly by consumers.[1] It also left the United States behind other nations in terms of health outcomes, ranking at the bottom among wealthy nations in infant mortality and deaths due to preventable disease.[2] In the months leading up to the 2008 election, it is not surprising then that many skeptics did not believe that Barack Obama would be able to keep his

J. Quadagno (✉)
Department of Sociology, Florida State University, Tallahassee, FL, USA
e-mail: jquadagno@fsu.edu

D. Lanford
Scholars Strategy Network, Georgia State University, Emory University, Atlanta, GA, USA
e-mail: daniel@scholars.org

© The Author(s) 2019   69
W. C. Rich (ed.), *Looking Back on President Barack Obama's Legacy*,
https://doi.org/10.1007/978-3-030-01545-9_4

campaign promise to "sign a universal health care bill into law by the end of my first term as president."[3] Yet contrary to expectations, when he was elected president, Obama somehow succeeded in transcending the obstacles that had stymied other leaders, signing into law the Patient Protection and Affordable Care Act (ACA) of 2010. Although the ACA was an imperfect measure that did not achieve universal coverage, it reduced the uninsurance rate and set in motion many important changes to the U.S. health care system. It was Obama's signature achievement and perhaps his greatest legacy.

The main features of the ACA included state insurance exchanges, fines on employers not offering coverage, an individual mandate, a subsidy for low-income people, and an expansion of Medicaid. Further, the ACA specified that the benefit package for the newly eligible Medicaid population had to include ten categories of essential health benefits. The ACA also issued new regulations on insurance companies: a mandate that children be allowed to stay on their parents' policies until age 26, a ban on lifetime benefit limits, and protection for people with pre-existing conditions. In this chapter we discuss the origins of the ACA, the factors that influenced its implementation, and Republican efforts to repeal and replace it. We do so considering the institutional, interest group, and ideological factors that facilitated some provisions of the legislation and undermined others.

The Origins of the ACA

The ACA was arguably the most significant social welfare legislation since the enactment of Medicare and Medicaid in 1965. After nearly a century of failed efforts to promote universal coverage, the ACA signified a promise that the federal government would seek to ensure that all Americans had health insurance. Acting pragmatically, President Obama chose not to replace the health care system in all its complexity, which had been constructed piecemeal after the New Deal. Rather he chose to build upon but improve the structures that were already in place. Although this decision was the only feasible option at that time, it meant that the battle over the health care system would likely continue to rage. The ACA angered liberals, especially Physicians for a National Health Plan who favored a single-payer system, because it retained and even enhanced the private insurance industry. Equally problematic, the ACA infuriated conservatives who decried "Obamacare" as a first step on the road to socialism.[4]

The ACA represented a victory for the Democratic Party in the narrow sense of votes in Congress. It passed, even without a single Republican vote in either the House or the Senate. Yet the ACA was not derived from a model created solely by Democrats. Rather its core provisions were a legacy inherited from other health insurance plans that both Republicans and Democrats had proposed from the 1970s to the 2000s.[5]

The Individual Mandate

Medicare's enactment in 1965 emboldened supporters of national health insurance regarding the prospects for universal coverage, and during the 1970s numerous health insurance bills were introduced. When it appeared that Congress would enact one such program in 1974, President Richard Nixon unveiled his own proposal. One part, the Comprehensive Health Insurance Plan, included an employer mandate specifying that all employers had to provide coverage for their employees. The second part, the Assisted Health Insurance Plan, would have states contract with private insurers to cover low-income and high-risk individuals.[6] Republican support for health insurance legislation ended with Nixon's impeachment, but President Jimmy Carter revived the issues with his own his health insurance plan that included an employer mandate. Carter's plan gained no traction in Congress due to a stalled economy and his general unpopularity.[7] The point, however, is that the employer mandate originated with Republicans.

In the 1980s, rising costs and increasing numbers of uninsured brought health care reform back on the table, and several proposals were raised in congressional committees. While an employer mandate was included in most plans, some conservatives expressed reservations that an employer mandate could create job lock and inflation. Seeking an alternative, conservatives warmed to an alternative proposal from the Heritage Foundation for an individual mandate. An individual mandate would not only avoid job lock but also discourage free riders.[8] In 1991 President George H.W. Bush asked a group of conservative economists to develop a health insurance plan.[9] Their plan laid out the concept of an individual mandate and argued that it could be a counterpoint to either the employer mandate or the single-payer system favored by Democrats:

> All citizens should be required to obtain a basic level of health insurance... Permitting individuals to remain uninsured results in inefficient use of medical care, inequity in the incidence of costs of uncompensated care, and tax-related distortions...(The individual mandate) avoids interfering with labor

markets and employment contracts; it facilitates portability of coverage, employment mobility and a competitive market.[10]

Thus, in its original formulation the individual mandate was being sold as consistent with conservative values that favored a free market and limited state authority.[11] It was incorporated into President Bush's plan, the Comprehensive Health Reform Act of 1992, which would have mandated that each individual purchase a basic benefit coupled with tax credits and deductions to help cover the costs.

American Health Security Act

During the 1992 presidential election, Bill Clinton campaigned on a promise to provide universal coverage, and, when he was elected, he created an outside task force to draft a plan, ignoring ongoing work in congressional committees. The Clinton proposal, the American Health Security Act of 1993 (H.R. 1200), was released seven months later. At the forefront of Health Security were purchasing cooperatives, standard benefit packages, and insurance company regulation as well as a little-noticed provision mandating that individuals purchase health coverage. Section 1002 of the Health Security Act specified that "each eligible individual (1) must enroll in an applicable health plan for the individual and (2) must pay any premium consistent with the Act, with respect to such enrollment." Eligible individuals according to Section 1001 included not only citizens but also nationals, permanent alien residents, and long-term non-immigrants. Thus, under the Clinton plan virtually everyone would be required to enroll in a health insurance plan.[12]

The story of how a coalition of insurers, corporations, and small business groups mobilized against Health Security is well known.[13,14] What is less well known is that following the defeat of the Clinton plan, Republicans devised their own plan that included both an employer mandate and an individual mandate.

The Health Equity and Access Reform Today Act (HEART)

The Republican alternative, the Health Equity and Access Reform Today Act (HEART), was introduced in November 1993 by Senator John Chafee (R-RI). HEART would "guarantee every individual access to affordable and secure health coverage through substantial health insurance market reforms." Insurance plans would have to meet strict requirements including guaranteed eligibility, no pre-existing condition exclusions, guaranteed renewal, and a standard benefit package. Further, large employers would be required to offer coverage to all employees, and small employers (100 or fewer employees) had to offer (but not pay for) a benefit package. Individuals would be required to purchase coverage or pay a substantial penalty "equal to the average yearly premium of the local area plus 20 percent."[15] However, vouchers would be provided to make insurance affordable for low-income individuals.

HEART had the support of half of Republicans in the Senate as well as key House Republicans. When Chafee attempted to move his bill forward, however, conservatives within his own party ruled out mandates. As Senator Trent Lott (R-MI) proclaimed: "Republicans have to make clear we are not signed on to any of this government control and mandate stuff."[16] HEART was never debated in the Senate, and it disappeared from the national policy agenda for the remainder of the 1990s. Nevertheless, it again demonstrates that features later found in the ACA had Republican origins.

Insurance Company Regulation

It is accepted wisdom that Health Security was a failed policy initiative that led to a Republican takeover of the House and Senate in 1994 and undermined support for the Democratic Party for more than a decade.[17] Lost in this interpretation are the Clinton administration's later policy legacies that paved the way for the ACA. One significant legacy was federal regulation of insurance companies. Since 1945 health insurance plans had been regulated by the states. In most states, legislatures enacted the laws under which insurance companies operated, and state insurance departments enforced those laws. In many states, however, insurance companies had considerable influence over the agencies that were supposed to be regulating them and states were unable to halt many of the more egregious insurance company practices.

The failure of the states to rein in the insurers set the stage for greater federal control, and under the Clinton administration some of the regulatory power eventually shifted to the federal government.[18] In 1995 Senators Ted Kennedy (D-MA) and Nancy Kassebaum (R-KS) drafted rigorous federal regulations including guaranteed renewal, guaranteed issue, prohibitions on experience rating, and tightening of pre-existing condition exclusions. Following a barrage of opposition from the insurance industry, however, the proposal was watered down considerably. The bill that

President Clinton signed into law, the Health Insurance Portability and Accountability Act of 1996 (HIPAA), limited the ability of private health plans to impose pre-existing condition coverage exclusions on plan participants, allowed employees who lost group coverage because of a change in personal circumstances to convert to individual coverage, prohibited insurers from charging different premiums for individuals within groups, and required insurers to guarantee renewal to any group.[19] HIPAA did not include any price restrictions, however, making continuing coverage unaffordable for many individuals. Nor did HIPAA guarantee that people shopping for coverage would not be rejected because of health. Further, HIPAA had many loopholes and only applied to small groups.[20] Despite these limitations, HIPAA set an important precedent for federal regulation of the insurance industry.

Medicaid Expansion

A less publicized achievement of the Clinton administration was the expansion of Medicaid beyond the very poor, to near-poor and working-class families. When Medicaid was created as a joint federal–state program under Title XIX of the 1965 amendments to the Social Security Act, states were given considerable leeway in deciding how generous a program to create or even whether to create a program at all. As a result, there was wide variation in terms of protected population groups, eligibility levels, and access to services.

Medicaid expansion was made possible by Section 1115, which allows states to apply for waivers to conduct research and demonstration projects within their Medicaid programs, thus bypassing strict federal rules and regulations. In 1993 the Clinton administration began actively promoting states' use of Section 1115 waivers to expand coverage beyond the very poor and issued new guidelines that streamlined the process. States responded rapidly, raising income and asset limits and incorporating groups not categorically eligible.[21]

Medicaid was further expanded under the State Children's Health Insurance Program (SCHIP) of 1997. SCHIP increased the federal match to the states from 50 percent to 65 percent for eligible beneficiaries and covered children in families with income up to 200 percent of the federal poverty level (FPL). In response, some states created quite generous SCHIP programs.[22] SCHIP rules were subsequently amended to allow states to cover uninsured parents as well as their children.[23]

The Massachusetts Health Care Plan

The most prominent of the state experiments under Section 1115 was the Massachusetts Health Care Reform Plan signed into law by Republican Governor Mitt Romney in 2006. Designed in large part with the assistance of the Heritage Foundation, the plan was "a hybrid approach that incorporated ideas from across the political spectrum."[24] It included a state insurance exchange, insurance company regulations, an employer mandate, and an individual mandate. Health insurance was fully subsidized for adults earning up to 150 percent of FPL and for children of parents earning up to 300 percent of that level. Thus, the Massachusetts plan borrowed many features from HEART but also incorporated the Medicaid expansions that the Clinton administration had made possible. By 2010 more than 98 percent were insured, including 99.8 percent of all children, making Massachusetts' rate of uninsured the lowest in the United States.[25] More significantly, Massachusetts provided the blueprint and evidence that the individual mandate was a workable way to achieve universal coverage with bi-partisan support.

Healthy Americans Act

The success of the Massachusetts plan encouraged members of Congress to consider moving toward universal coverage through an individual mandate, an option that was gathering support among both Democrats and Republicans. In December, 2006, Senator Ron Wyden (D-OR) unveiled the Healthy Americans Act (S. 334), and in May, 2007, Robert Bennett (R-UT), signed on.[26] The Healthy Americans Act was designed to transition away from employer-provided health insurance that the unions had first negotiated in the 1940s. Rather it would shift toward a system of employer-subsidized health insurance by eliminating entirely the tax break that employers received for providing insurance to their employees. It would also require those who did not have insurance to enroll in a state-approved Healthy American Private Insurance Plan, that is, an individual mandate. The bill won more bi-partisan support than any universal health care proposal in the history of the Senate but died in the Senate Finance Committee.

Despite the failure of the Healthy Americans Act, a bi-partisan consensus on the individual mandate seemed to be emerging. Not only did congressional members of both parties support the concept, in the 2008 election campaign, two Democratic candidates—Senators John Edwards (D-NC) and Hillary Clinton (D-NY)—highlighted the individual mandate in their health care plans. The hold-out was Senator Barack Obama.[27] Thus, what began as a conservative, free market approach to health care reform was beginning to morph into a liberal blueprint for change.

The Patient Protection and Affordable Care Act of 2010

When Obama was elected president, Wyden and Bennett wrote a letter recommending legislative goals reflected in the Health Americans Act. They reintroduced their bill on February 5, 2009 with 14 co-sponsors, nine Democrats and five Republicans (S. 391). A companion bill (H.R. 1321) was introduced in the House with ten co-sponsors. Yet in an interview in July 2009 President Obama said that although he agreed with many of the principles in Wyden-Bennett, he felt that the plan was "too radical" and would meet "significant political resistance" because it would virtually eliminate employer-provided coverage.[28]

On July 14, 2009 three House committees reported out the House Tri-Committee America's Affordable Health Care Act (H.B. 3200). The following day the Senate Health, Education, Labor and Pension Committee, of which Obama had been a member when he was a senator, passed its own version, the Affordable Health Choices Act (S. 1679). The legislation that emerged was much more comprehensive than the Healthy Americans Act and less committed to eliminating employer-based coverage. A key provision was the individual mandate, which President Obama now supported: "I was opposed to this idea because my general attitude was the reason people don't have health insurance is not because they don't want it. It's because they can't afford it. I am now in favor of some sort of individual mandate."[29]

Obama's change of heart was pragmatic. Given the extensive bi-partisan support won by previous health care reform plans based on an individual mandate, the president had reason to believe that he might receive a favorable response from Republicans. The ACA's main provisions were nearly identical to the Republican-supported HEART plan. Both HEART and the ACA included an individual mandate, an employer mandate, a standard benefit package, state-based purchasing exchanges, subsidies for low-income people, efforts to improve efficiency, controls on Medicare spending growth, and controls on high-cost plans. Both measures also included stringent regulations on insurance companies including a ban on denying coverage due to pre-existing conditions and a prohibition on insurers from canceling coverage because of health.

HEART and the ACA also differed on a few provisions that, to a large degree, reflected changes that had occurred in the health insurance system during the Clinton administration. One difference was that the ACA but not HEART prohibited insurers from setting lifetime limits on health benefits. Another difference was that the ACA but not HEART extended coverage on private plans to dependents up to age 26. This age group stood out because young adults had the lowest rate of insurance coverage and, unlike children under age 18, were ineligible for SCHIP benefits.[30] Allowing young adults to remain on their parents' plans would immediately reduce the number of uninsured. Both HEART and the ACA included an employer mandate, but whereas it was stringent under HEART, it was more modest under the ACA, as was the individual mandate.

One of the most crucial and original provisions of the ACA was the extension of Medicaid to all children, parents, and childless adults with family incomes up to 133 percent of FPL. As an incentive for states to participate, the ACA made the share of Medicaid costs covered by the federal government significantly larger for expansion populations. Under the ACA, the federal government would cover 100 percent of the states' expansion costs from 2014 through 2016, gradually decreasing to 90 percent in 2020 and thereafter. Further, the federal government would assume some of the costs for segments of the uninsured population that previously came out of state budgets.[31]

The differences between HEART and the ACA were insufficient to trigger the vehement opposition that arose. Rather the Republicans made the political decision to use the ACA to undermine the Obama administration and the Democratic Party. This process began with the implementation of the ACA and continued when the Republicans captured the House, the Senate, and the presidency in the 2016 election.

THE IMPLEMENTATION OF THE ACA

Although the ACA was based on a plan that had received substantial bipartisan support, as noted above, the final vote included no Republicans in either the House or Senate, and Republicans launched an assault against it. The assault did not take place over a single provision but rather varied across provisions, states, and regulatory agencies assigned with implementing the law.

The implementation process was inherently complex, because the ACA was not a coherent program, like Medicare, but rather consisted of a series of policy changes, each with its own institutional structure and political logic.[32] As a result, each provision of the ACA interacted with the federal government in a different way, establishing different sites of contention. The three provisions that generated the most controversy, at least initially, were the health insurance exchanges, the Medicaid expansion, and the regulatory reforms.

The Health Insurance Exchanges

A critical component of the ACA is the health insurance exchange, a state-run marketplace where uninsured people can shop for an affordable policy. Each exchange is supposed to create an accessible website that gives people with little knowledge or training access to information that could guide their choice of a suitable policy. Confounding the issue, the exchanges were also tasked with identifying individuals who would be eligible for federal subsidies, that is, those with income less than 400 percent of FPL. In theory, the exchanges should be attractive to Republican governors, because they are market-based mechanisms that allow consumers to choose among competing private health insurance plans. And indeed, in the months leading up to the ACA, the health insurance exchanges generated little controversy. Once the ACA was enacted, however, they quickly became one of the most contested aspects of the program. As they became entangled in the partisan war over implementation, many Republican governors refused to set up insurance exchanges and some launched a political battle against them.[33]

Several factors contributed to the war between the federal government and the states over the exchanges. First, the exchanges generated controversy because they were associated indirectly with the individual mandate, the least popular provision of the ACA.[34] Although most people would not be insured through the exchange, there was some institutional overlap between people applying for subsidies and the enforcement of the individual mandate through the Internal Revenue Service.[35]

Another factor that made the exchanges contentious was that unlike other provisions of the ACA, such as Medicaid expansion or insurance regulation, the exchanges lacked an institutional precedent. With the exception of Massachusetts, no exchanges existed at the state level. This meant that, under the ACA, states had to establish new institutions that would eventually be self-financing. However, few governors had the authority to authorize the exchanges on their own, nor could administrative agencies simply create exchanges. Rather this process required action by governors and, more importantly, state legislatures, which made the exchanges a prime target for ACA opponents. Exacerbating the problem was that the federal government had no way to punish states that refused to set up exchanges on their own.

The Department of Health and Human Services (HHS) was the federal agency in charge of implementing the law and interacting with the states. To encourage the states to set up the exchanges, HHS agreed to negotiate over key issues regarding implementation.[36] These included allowing joint federal–state exchanges and extending deadlines for compliance. Ironically, when recalcitrant states continued to refuse to set up their own exchanges, the HHS set up federal exchanges for them. Thus, "the conservative crusade against state-run exchanges increased the role of the federal government and the Obama administration in ACA implementation."[37] By 2018, only 12 states had independent exchanges while the others had some combination of a state–federal exchange.[38]

Medicaid Expansion

The day that President Obama signed the ACA, the states made it clear that they would use the courts to challenge the law. Attorney Generals in Republican-controlled states, led by Virginia and Florida and joined by 25 others, filed lawsuits challenging the constitutionality of the individual mandate and the Medicaid expansion. On June 28, 2012, the Supreme Court held that the individual mandate was a constitutional exercise of Congress' power to levy taxes but that the Medicaid expansion was unconstitutionally coercive on the states.[39] The majority decision meant that the federal government could not withhold existing federal Medicaid funds if a state did not comply with the Medicaid expansion, which in practice made the Medicaid expansion optional.[40]

This decision was a major setback for proponents of the law because the Medicaid expansion was a critical component of the ACA. It was one of the most important mechanisms for increasing coverage. It was especially important for lower-income adults with health problems[41] and for racial and ethnic minorities who were more likely than whites to be Medicaid-eligible. Overall, it was estimated that states' decisions to opt out of Medicaid would result in 3.6 million fewer insured and $8 billion less in federal payments to states.[42]

When the expansion went into effect in 2014, 24 states chose not to participate. All Democrat-controlled states expanded Medicaid while most states with unified Republican leadership did not. To say that partisanship was the sole factor determining participation would be misleading, however, for some Republican governors did expand their Medicaid programs. A prime example was Arizona, historically a welfare laggard, which did not even participate in Medicaid at all until 1982. Yet in January of 2013, Governor Jan Brewer, an outspoken critic of Obamacare, nonetheless announced that Arizona would expand Medicaid. Pressures from Latino voters and the potential loss of billions in federal matching funds and health care jobs led to Arizona's decision. Other states that had not publicly committed to expansion still took steps to prepare for future expansion.[43]

An important difference between the recalcitrant response to the state exchanges and the Medicaid expansion was that states already had Medicaid programs in operation, and several, as noted above, had experimented with various ways to increase coverage. These policy legacies continued to influence state Medicaid expansion decisions; in many cases, they were sufficiently influential to break through the partisan gridlock.[44] Thus, despite partisan politics, states that had already instituted more generous coverage were more likely to take advantage of the Medicaid expansion opportunity.

Another factor that influenced Medicaid expansion was a state population's degree of conservatism. Key elements of modern conservatism include opposition to government activism in general and to government spending to redress social ills in particular. Conservatives regularly described the ACA as a huge expansion of federal authority that would be a financial drain on the economy.[45] As expected, states with higher average levels of conservatism were less likely to expand Medicaid, regardless of partisanship among elected officials.[46]

Historically, race has been a fundamental influence on American politics, and racial resentment has proven to be a robust predictor of public attitudes toward race-targeted policies such as affirmative action[47] as well as seemingly non-racial policies such as welfare, crime, and Social Security.[48,49] In the debate over the ACA, racial resentment played a substantial role in shaping public opinion toward various policy proposals because the proposals were often associated with Barack Obama and minority program beneficiaries in public discourse[50,51]; Not surprisingly, states with greater levels of racial resentment were laggards in Medicaid expansion, net of partisan control of government.[52]

Medicaid expansion remains a contested terrain. As of 2018 only 36 states had expanded their Medicaid programs, while others, including Texas and Florida with high numbers of uninsured, had not (Kaiser Family Foundation 2018).[53]

Regulatory Reform

The third arena of ACA implementation involved requiring insurance companies to abide by the new regulations. Compared to the task of creating the exchanges or expanding Medicaid, the roll-out of these regulations was less contentious, despite opposition to some provisions from America's Health Insurance Plans (AHIP), the industry's largest lobbying organization.[54]

One reason why the expansion of regulations proceeded smoothly was because insurance regulation coupled with federal oversight was already a state function. All states had insurance commissioners, and ACA implantation required no new organizations or legislation. Rather in most states insurance commissioners had the authority to simply require insurance companies to comply.[55] Further, opponents of the regulations had little opportunity to mobilize, because HHS quickly set minimum standards that states could adopt, requiring little or no legislative action. Thus, while Medicaid battles played out in state legislatures, regulatory change bypassed this site of contention.

Another factor that minimized conflict was that insurance companies had early-on struck a bargain with the Obama administration. Insurers were willing to accept stricter regulations, including price controls and guaranteed issue without pre-existing condition exclusions, as long as these regulations were accompanied by an individual mandate.[56] An individual mandate would bring young, healthy people into the system to help pay the costs of older, sicker people. Regulation was the price to pay for the mandate.

Finally, insurance regulation proceeded with little controversy because the provisions, especially those instituted first, were designed to expand access to care and were highly popular. Among these early provisions were a prohibition on denying coverage due to pre-existing conditions, allowing children to stay on their parents' policies up to age 26, and an expansion of the scope of coverage. Insurance companies were already widely viewed as public enemy number one, and no insurer wanted to visibly lobby against such unquestionably moral measures.[57]

The Failed (But Ongoing) Effort to Repeal the ACA

As we have seen, the ACA was enacted without a single Republican vote, and between 2010 and 2016 House Republicans voted more than 50 times to repeal, delay, or cripple it. With Democrats in control of the House, however, their votes were merely symbolic. It seemed that the successes of the ACA in reeling in the insurance companies, limiting health insurance premium increases, and expanding coverage would solidify the ACA and also probably result in the eventual full uptake of the Medicaid expansion in all states over time. The end of the battle over the ACA seemed close at hand.

The presidential election of 2016 changed this situation dramatically. During the 2016 election campaign, candidate Donald Trump promised he would repeal and replace Obamacare on day 1, and after Trump won the electoral vote and Republicans took control of Congress, they asserted that they would make good on their promise. The ACA no longer seemed as stable as it had only months before. Yet by the end of summer 2017, efforts to repeal Obamacare had failed. Under the most threatening political conditions, the ACA had proved surprisingly resilient. What factors contributed to the failure of repeal and replace?

Institutional Impediments

One factor was disagreements within the Republican Party between national and state leaders. On May 4, 2017, after months of delay, the House of Representatives passed the American Health Care Act (AHCA) by a slim majority. The AHCA would have allowed states to opt out of some of the ACA's essential health benefits and substantially cut Medicaid. Trump praised the bill, "Yes, premiums will be coming down; yes, deductibles will be coming down, but very importantly, it's a great plan." The non-partisan Congressional Budget Office (CBO) then scored the bill, estimating that by 2026 the number of uninsured would increase by 23 million. Trump then turned on House Republicans, calling the AHCA "mean" and asking the Senate to "spend more on the bill to make it 'generous, kind (and) with heart'."[58]

The Senate's Better Care Reconciliation Act of 2017, which would have repealed some ACA mandates and retained the large Medicaid cuts, fared no better. When the CBO scored the Senate bill, it predicted that 49 million more people would be uninsured by 2026. Then when the nation's governors gathered for their annual summer meeting, governors from both parties came out strongly against the Senate bill. Twenty Republican Senators came from the Medicaid expansion states, and even those that had favored repealing the ACA were now hesitant to support their own Better Care bill. Republican Governor Brian Sandoval of Nevada, an expansion state, summed up the views of many of his colleagues, declaring that he had "great concerns" and that he would not support any bill that cut Nevada's Medicaid program.[59] The Senate became mired in intra-party bickering and finally voted to allow a debate on a non-existent health care bill to proceed. That effort failed on July 28 in the wee hours of the morning when three Republican Senators defected to vote against a so-called "skinny" bill, which would have rescinded some provisions of the ACA but left most of the program in place. A final effort in late September met a similar demise.

Interest Group Opposition

Another major influence was opposition from interest groups. The health care system consists of organizations that form an institutional web governing both the care and the delivery of medical services (hospitals, physician practices, clinics) and that arrange for the financing of care (government agencies, states, local communities, and private insurance companies).[60] All these organizations have a stake in any proposed change to the ACA and thus make up a cadre of potential resistance when their interests are threatened.

The first to speak out were the provider groups. On March 8, 2017 the American Hospital Association, which represents nearly 5000 hospitals, 270,000 physicians, and two million nurses, wrote a letter to the House of Representatives opposing the proposed Medicaid cuts: these cuts would "have the effect of making significant reductions in a program that provides services to our most vulnerable populations ... (and) repeals much of the funding currently dedicated to provide coverage in the future."[61] The following month, on April 17, the American Medical Association released a similar letter urging members of the House to vote against their own bill. They charged that millions of Americans would lose their insurance and they opposed the elimination of insurance regulations regarding pre-existing conditions, guaranteed issue, and parental coverage of young adults. They insisted that Medicaid and safety net programs had to be adequately funded.[62]

When the Senate released the Better Care Act, AARP, the largest voluntary organization in the United States, drew on its extensive lobbying power to rally its members against it. In an open letter, the AARP slammed the Senate bill, labeling it "Wealthcare" and condemning "the Age Tax, which would allow insurance companies to charge older Americans five times more for coverage than everyone else, while reducing tax credits that help make insurance more affordable." AARP also opposed the deep cuts to Medicaid, which would "strip health care from millions of low income and vulnerable Americans" and the cuts to Medicare "which weakens the program."[63]

In July organizations representing the insurance industry, which had largely remained on the sidelines, weighed in. The CEOs of AHIP and the Blue Cross/Blue Shield Association blasted a new provision, the Freedom Option, which would allow insurance companies to sell cheaper policies in the exchanges without the ACA mandates. That option would undermine coverage for people with pre-existing conditions, increase premiums, and cost many people their coverage.[64] The combined opposition of these groups shifted Congress against repeal.

Ideology

A third factor leading to the failure of repeal and replace was the absence of an ideological message that resonated with the public. According to one widely cited argument, the United States has an anti-statist political culture that honors private property, holds individual rights sacred, and distrusts state authority.[65] Anti-statism has been described as an underlying force in various failed attempts to guarantee universal coverage across the entire twentieth century.[66]

During most of its history, anti-statism has been the defining ideology of the Republican Party and it was this theme that became the Republican mantra against the ACA. It was first adopted in early 2009, when a Republican strategist, Frank Luntz, urged Republicans to call the ACA a "government takeover." "Takeovers are like coups," Luntz wrote. "They both lead to dictators and a loss of freedom."[67] That phrase stuck and each time House Republicans voted to repeal Obamacare, they reiterated that message.

The problem was that by 2017 people who had initially believed claims that the ACA represented a government takeover or, worse, socialized medicine had now witnessed the benefits for themselves and their families. Indeed, a June 23 CNN poll reported that 51 percent of the public had a favorable view of Obamacare and the majority opposed cuts to Medicaid.[68] Further, only 17 percent of Americans approved of the Senate Better Care Act, while 55 percent disapproved.[69]

That shift in public opinion left Republicans without a coherent message for rallying support to repeal the ACA and, especially, for drastically cutting Medicaid. Although Medicaid began as a program of welfare medicine, as it expanded to new beneficiary groups, public perceptions of the program were transformed. Medicaid had become the equivalent of an entitlement, nearly as popular as Social Security and Medicare.[70] Robbed of their anti-statist message, Republicans were reduced to simply reiterating criticisms of the ACA that the public no longer believed. Thus, Senator Pat Roberts (R-KS) could only offer as a rationale, "Kansans are losing choices in care, and their costs and premiums are still rising. If we are going to finally reverse the damage of Obamacare, we must act."[71]

Further, much of the initial public hostility toward the ACA was a consequence of racial hostility toward Barack Obama.[72] Since people viewed Obama as closely connected to health care policy, racially resentful whites were more likely to view the ACA unfavorably. With Obama out of the Oval Office, a key mechanism by which racial resentments came to bear on attitudes toward the ACA was removed.

These factors allowed an alternative theme in American culture to emerge, that of a nation constructed upon values of community and solidarity.[73] As a moral concept, solidarity is based on an understanding that individuals and groups share common risks and that citizens of a community are obligated to care for each other in times of hardship. It was this theme that Democrats used to define Republicans' health care plans as divisive and un-American, favoring the rich while taking from the poor. When House Speaker Paul Ryan praised the House bill as "an act of mercy," Rep. Joe Kennedy (D-MA) fired back:

> With all due respect to our speaker, he and I must have read different Scripture. The one that I read calls on us to feed the hungry, to clothe the naked, to shelter the homeless, and to comfort the sick. It reminds us that we are judged not by how we treat the powerful, but by how we care for the least among us.[74]

Other Democrats reiterated that message: that "Trumpcare" would strip insurance from tens of millions of Americans to fund a tax cut for the wealthy. The Republican Senate bill was not a health care measure but actually a transfer of wealth. As former President Obama declared: "It hands enormous tax cuts to the rich and to the drug and insurance industries, paid for by cutting health care for everybody else."[75]

Democrats also presented a dire message of what the Senate bill would mean, focusing on controversial provisions that would harm specific constituencies. According to Senator Chris Murphy (D-CT): "Sick and older people will see costs skyrocket. Protections for people with pre-existing conditions will be gutted with insurance companies put back in charge."[76] Finally, President Obama repeated the theme of social solidarity: "this debate has always been about something bigger than politics. It's about the character of our country – who we are and who we aspire to be."[77]

The Strategy of Incrementalism

In the wake of the failed effort to repeal and replace Obamacare, Republicans have taken a different approach, seeking to undermine the program piece by piece so that it eventually collapses on its own weight. In October of 2017 President Trump issued an Executive Order allowing insurance companies to sell cheaper policies in the exchanges with fewer benefits, thus undermining the principle of the mandated basic benefit package. He also promised that he would end the subsidies to low-income people, creating additional uncertainty in insurance markets. Then Republicans inserted a provision in their 2017 tax overhaul eliminating the enforcement mechanism of the individual mandate—the tax penalty for not purchasing health insurance. The result is likely to be fewer insured people. Further, those choosing not to purchase insurance are likely to be younger and healthier people, leaving sicker and older people in the pool. This outcome would not only increase the cost of coverage but also encourage more insurance companies to withdraw from the exchanges.

DISCUSSION

The ACA led to historic gains in health insurance coverage in the United States. It did so by expanding Medicaid, providing subsidies to low-income people, and creating health insurance marketplaces. In 2010, 16 percent of adults were uninsured; by 2016 only 10.9 percent.[78,79] Still 28 million Americans remain uninsured, and health care spending in the United States continues to outpace ordinary inflation.[80] These numbers illustrate both the achievement of the ACA and its weakness. Clearly, there is work to be done.

In evaluating the ACA, it is important to recognize that legislation, once enacted, must evolve as the initial provisions reveal weaknesses. That is what happened with both Social Security and Medicare, the main social welfare programs of the twentieth century. Initially, Social Security was a modest benefit that paid retirement benefits only to workers. Over decades it expanded to include new categories of beneficiaries (widows, the disabled) and new benefits (early retirement). In the process, program advocates had to fend off efforts by conservatives to roll back the program or even destroy it. Medicare faced less opposition from the start but has been continually embroiled in controversies with physician and hospital groups over payment levels. What has protected both programs is what is termed "path dependency," a process by which institutions create their own constituencies and power points. This process narrows the menu of future options and forms a self-reinforcing path that becomes increasingly difficult to alter. For example, as Social Security expanded, it gave rise to widespread public expectations and a vast network of vested interests ready to lobby against any proposed benefit cuts. Thus, as Skocpol explains, "tracing these feedback processes is crucial for explaining the further development of social provision after initial measures are instituted."[81]

The ACA faces the same challenges as Social Security and Medicare did in their early years. At first glance, it appears that the institutional legacy of Medicaid, the opposition of interest groups, and the lack of an ideological message from opponents may protect the ACA from repeal. The ACA differs from those other programs, however, in that its complexity increases the number of target points opponents can use to undermine it. A seemingly simple setback such as the elimination of the tax penalty behind the individual mandate can have numerous consequences, not only by reducing the number of people who purchase insurance but also by pushing some insurance companies out of the exchanges.

Clearly, the status quo will not be maintained in the future. Republicans and Democrats may work in a bi-partisan way to repair problems in the private insurance market but leave the main tenets of Obamacare in place. Yet progressives are still working to create a single-payer plan, while those on the right hope to destroy the ACA through neglect if they are unable to repeal it outright. The only thing that is certain is that, like all other welfare programs that have experienced change in response to new demographic, economic, and social needs, the ACA will be altered in significant ways for decades to come.

NOTES

1. David Himmelstein, and Steffie Woolhandler, "The current and projected taxpayer shares of US health costs," *American Journal of Public Health* 106, No. 3 (2016): 450.

2. Daniel Lanford, and Jill Quadagno, "Healthcare: Universal" in *The Blackwell Encyclopedia of Sociology*, 2nd Edition, ed. George Ritzer, (New York: Wiley-Blackwell, 2016): Entry 844.

3. Steve Contorno, and Angie Holan, "Five years later, Medicaid opt-outs create holes in universal bill." Politifact, March 25, 2015. http://www.politifact.com/truth-o-meter/promises/obameter/promise/433/sign-a-universal-health-care-bill/

4. Jill Quadagno, "Right Wing Conspiracy? Socialist Plot?: The Origins of the Affordable Care Act," *Journal of Health Politics, Policy and Law* 39, No. 1 (2014): 35.

5. Quadagno, "Right Wing Conspiracy?," 38.

6. Jill Quadagno, *One Nation, Uninsured: Why the US Has No National Health Insurance* (Oxford University Press, 2005), 115.

7. Quadagno, *One Nation, Uninsured*, 125.

8. Quadagno, "Right Wing Conspiracy," 36.

9. Avit Roy, "The Tortuous History of Conservatives and the Individual Mandate." *Forbes*, February 7, 2012. http://www.forbes.com/sites/aroy/2012/02/07/the-tortuous-conservative-history-of-the-individual-mandate/

10. Mark Pauly, Patricia Damon, Paul Feldstein, and John Hoff, "A Plan for Responsible National Health Insurance," *Health Affairs* 10, No. 1(1991): 9–11.

11. Seymour M Lipset, *American Exceptionalism: A Double-Edged Sword* (New York: Norton, 1997), 3.

12. Jill Quadagno, "Interest Group Influence on the Patient Protection and Affordability Act of 2010: Winners and Losers in the Health Care Reform Debate," *Journal of Health Politics, Policy and Law* 36, No. 3 (2011): 444.

13. Quadagno, "Interest Group Influence, 450.

14. Lawrence Jacobs, and Theda Skocpol, *Health Care Reform and American Politics: What Everyone Needs to Know* (New York: Oxford University Press, 2010), 160–163.

15. Congressional Record, Introduction of the Health Equity and Access Reform Today. Hon. William M. Thomas, November 24, 1993, p. E 3078. 103rd Congress. (Washington, D.C.: Library of Congress, 1993).

16. Haynes Johnson, and David Broder, *The System: The American Way of Politics to the Breaking Point* (Boston: Little Brown, 1996), 364.

17. Theda Skocpol, *Boomerang: Health Care Reform and the Turn Against Government.* (New York: W.W. Norton, 1997), 176.
18. Ben Kail, Jill Quadagno, and Marc Dixon, "Can States Lead the Way to Universal Coverage? The Effect of Health Care Reform on the Uninsured," *Social Science Quarterly* 90, No. 5 (2009): 16.
19. Colleen Medill, "HIPAA and Its Related Legislation: A New Role for ERISA in the Regulation of Private Health Plans?," *Tennessee Law Review* 65, No. 2 (1998): 492.
20. M.A Hall, "The Impact of Health Insurance Market Reforms on Market Competition," *American Journal of Managed Care* 6 (2000): 59–61.
21. S.K Schneider, "Medicaid Section 1115 Waivers: Shifting Health Care Reform to the States," *Publius* 27, No. 2 (1997): 104.
22. Lynn Blewett, Michale Davern and Holly Rodin, "Covering Kids: Variation in Health Insurance Coverage Trends by State, 1996–2002," *Health Affairs* 23, No. 6 (2004): 176.
23. P.J Cunningham, "SCHIP Making Progress: Increased Take-Up Contributes to Coverage Gains," *Health Affairs* 22, No. 4 (2003): 168.
24. David Hyman, "Massachusetts Health Plan: The Good, the Bad and the Ugly," *University of Kansas Law Review* 55 (2006): 1106.
25. Huma Kahn, "Has Mitt Romney's Massachusetts Health Care Law Worked?" *The Note* (May 12, 2011). http://abcnews.go.com/blogs/politics/2011/05/has-mitt-romneys-massachusetts-health-care-law-worked
26. U.S. Congress, *Healthy Americans Act.* Bill Summary and Status, 110th Congress. S. 334. (Washington, D.C.: Library of Congress, 2007).
27. Saba Hamedy, "Obama on Senate bill: It's not a health care bill," (July 26, 2017). http://www.cnn.com/2017/06/22/politics/barack-obama-health-care-bill-reaction/index.html
28. "Obama Calls Wyden Plan Radical." *The Oregonion*, (July 2, 2009). http://oregoncatalyst.com/2484-Obama-calls-Wyden-health-plan-radical.html
29. Ezra Klein, "Unpopular Mandate: Why Do Politicians Reverse their Positions," *New Yorker* (June 25, 2012). http://www.newyorker.com/reporting/2012/06/25/120625fa_fact_klein#ixzz2KK6q96lt
30. Benjamin Sommers, Genevieve Kenney and Arnold Epstein, "New Evidence on the Affordable Care Act: Coverage Impacts of Early Medicaid Expansions," *Health Affairs* 33, No. 1 (2014): 83–84.
31. Sommers, Kenney and Epstein, "New Evidence on the Affordable Care Act," 84.
32. Daniel Beland, Philip Rocco, and Alex Waddan, *Obamacare Wars: Federalism, State Politics and the Affordable Care Act.* (Lawrence KS: University of Kansas Press, 2016), 61–63.

33. Tom Cohen, "House Republicans Vote, Again, to Repeal Health Care Law," (July 11, 2012). www.cnn.com/2012/07/11/politics
34. Klein, "Unpopular Mandate."
35. Beland, Rocco and Waddan, *Obamacare Wars,* 65.
36. Simon Haeder, and David Weimer, "You can't make me do it: state implementation of insurance exchanges under the Affordable Care Act," *Public Administration Review* 73, No. S1 (2013): 37.
37. Beland, Rocco and Waddan, *Obamacare Wars,* 66.
38. Kaiser Family Foundation, "Summary of a 1993 Republican Health Reform Plan." *Kaiser Health News* (Feb. 23, 2010). http://kaiserhealthnews.org/Storeis/February/23/GOP-1993-health-reform-bill
39. Jonathan Oberlander, "Under Siege: The Individual Mandate for Health Insurance and Its Alternatives," *New England Journal of Medicine* 364, No. 12 (2011): 1085–87.
40. Kaiser Family Foundation, *A Guide to the Supreme Court's Affordable Care Act Decision,* (July 2, 2012). http://kaiserfamilyfoundation.files.wordpress.com/2013/01/8332.pdf
41. Sommers, Kenney and Epstein. "New Evidence on the Affordable Care Act," 83.
42. Carter Price and Christine Eibner, "For States that Opt Out of Medicaid Expansion: 3.6 Million Fewer Insured and 8.4 Billion Less in Federal Payments," *Health Affairs* 32, No. 6 (2013): 1033–1036.
43. Lawrence R Jacobs and Timothy Callaghan, "Why States Expand Medicaid: Party, Resources, and History," *Journal of Health Politics, Policy and Law* 38, No. 5 (2013): 1031.
44. Jacobs and Callaghan, "Why States Expand Medicaid," 1031.
45. Michael Cannon, *50 Vetoes: How States Can Stop the Obama Health Care Law.* (Washington, D.C.: Cato Institute, 2013).
46. Lanford, Daniel and Jill Quadagno, "Implementing Obamacare: The Politics of Medicaid Expansion under the Patient Protection and Affordable Care Act of 2010," *Sociological Perspectives* 59, No. 3(2016): 628.
47. David Sears, Jim Sidanius, and Lawrence Bobo, eds. *Racialized Politics: The Debate About Racism in America,* (Chicago: University of Chicago Press, 2000).
48. Nicholas Winter, "Beyond Welfare: Framing and the Racialization of White Opinion on Social Security," *American Journal of Political Science* 50, No. 2 (2006): 415.
49. Nicholas Valentino, and David Sears, "Old Times There Are Not Forgotten: Race and Partisan Realignment in the Contemporary South," *American Journal of Political Science* 49, No. 3 (2005): 678.
50. Eric Knowles, Brian Lowery, and Rebecca Schaumberg, "Racial prejudice predicts opposition to Obama and his health care reform," *Journal of Experimental Social Psychology,* 46 (2010): 420–423.

51. Michael Tesler, "The Spillover of Racialization into Health Care: How President Obama Polarized Public Opinion by Racial Attitudes and Race," *American Journal of Political Science* 56, No. 3 (2012): 697–698.
52. Lanford and Quadagno, "The Politics of Medicaid Expansion," 630.
53. Kaiser Family Foundation, *State Health Insurance Marketplace Types,* (December 3, 2018). https://www.kff.org/health-reform/state-indicator/state-health-insurance-marketplacetypes/?currentTimeframe=0&sortModel=%7B%22colId%22:%22Location%22,%22sort%22:%22asc%22%7D
54. Beland, Rocco and Waddan, *Obamacare Wars,* 124–125.
55. Kail, Quadagno and Dixon, "Can States Lead the Way," 17.
56. Jacob Hacker, "Why Reform Happened," *Journal of Health Politics, Policy and Law* 36, No. 3 (2011): 439.
57. Donald Light, "The practice and ethics of risk-related health insurance," *Journal of the American Medical Association* 267, p. 18 (1992): 2503–04.
58. Dan Merica, Jim Acosta, Lauren Fox and Phil Mattingly, "Trump calls House health care bill 'mean,'" (June 14, 2017). http://www.cnn.com/2017/06/13/politics/trump-senators-health-care-white-house-meeting/index.html
59. Jonathan Martin, and Alexander Burns, "Governors shun new health bill from both sides," *New York Times,* July 15, 2017: A1, 13. http://www.nytimes.com/images/2017/07/15/nytfrontpage/scannat.pdf?mcubz=1
60. Jill Quadagno, "Institutions, Interests and Ideology: An Agenda for the Sociology of Health Care Reform," *Journal of Health and Social Behavior* 51 (June 2010): 129.
61. American Hospital Association, "Letter to the U.S. House of Representatives regarding the American Health Care Act." (March 9, 2017). http://www.aha.org/advocacy-issues/letter/2017/170307-let-aha-house-ahca.pdf
62. American Medical Association, "AMA Vision on Health Reform." (Sept. 19, 2017). https://www.ama-assn.org/ama-health-reform-vision/
63. "AARP calls on lawmakers to reject harmful Senate healthcare bill." (June 22, 2017). http://thehill.com/homenews/senate/339098-aarp-calls-on-senate-lawmakers-to-reject-harmful-senate-healthcare-bill
64. Tami Luhby, "Insurers blast Senate health care provision as unworkable." (July 15, 2017). http://money.cnn.com/2017/07/15/news/economy/health-care-insurers-cruz-amendment/index.html
65. Lipset, *American Exceptionalism,* 3–6.
66. Quadagno, *One Nation, Uninsured,* 12.
67. Bill Adair, and Angie Holan, PolitiFact's Lie of the Year: 'A government takeover of health care.' (Dec. 16, 2010). http://www.politifact.com/truth-o-meter/article/2010/dec/16/lie-year-government-takeover-health-care/

68. Dan Mangan, "Obamacare tops 50 percent popularity among Americans for first time in new poll, after Senate unveils bill to gut health-care law." (June 23, 2017). http://www.cnbc.com/2017/06/23/obamacare-tops-50-percent-support-for-first-time-new-poll-shows.html
69. Pramuk, Jacob, "Rough series of polls show Americans broadly disapprove of GOP health-care plan." (June 28, 2017). http://www.cnbc.com/2017/06/28/senate-gop-health-care-bill-has-dismal-approval-rating-poll.html
70. Grogan, Colleen and Eric Patashnik. 2003. "Universalism within targeting: nursing home care, the middle class and the politics of the Medicaid program." *Social Service Review* 7 (1):58.
71. Pat Roberts,"Senator Roberts supports improved health care bill," (July 13, 2017). https://www.murphy.senate.gov/newsroom/press-releases/murphy-trumpcare-40-is-a-disaster-for-connecticut-just-like-every-previous-version
72. Michael Tesler, "The Spillover of Racialization into Health Care: How President Obama Polarized Public Opinion by Racial Attitudes and Race," *American Journal of Political Science* 56, No. 3 (2012): 698–99.
73. James Morone, *The Democratic Wish*, (New Haven, CT: Yale University Press, 1998), 8.
74. Joe Kennedy Jr. Rep. Joe Kennedy Calls Out Paul Ryan for Calling ACA Repeal 'Act of Mercy, (March 9, 2017). https://sojo.net/articles/rep-joe-kennedy-calls-out-paul-ryan-calling-aca-repeal-act-mercy
75. Hamedy, "Obama on Senate bill."
76. Chavez, "ObamaCare repeal without replacement."
77. Hamedy, "Obama on Senate Bill."
78. Steve Contorno and Angie Holan, "Five years later, Medicaid opt-outs create holes in universal bill." *Politifact*, March 25, 2015. http://www.politifact.com/truth-o-meter/promises/obameter/promise/433/sign-a-universal-health-care-bill/
79. Kaiser Family Foundation, *Key Facts about the Uninsured Population*, (Sept. 19, 2017). https://www.kff.org/uninsured/fact-sheet/key-facts-about-the-uninsured-population/
80. Bureau of Labor Statistics, Fact Sheet USDL-16-2302. Consumer Price Index. (December 15, 2016). https://www.bls.gov/news.release/archives/cpi_12152016.pdf
81. Theda Skocpol, *Protecting Soldiers and Mothers*, (Belknap Press 1992), 59.

Appraising the Foreign Policy Legacy of the Obama Presidency

Meena Bose

When President Barack Obama left the White House on 20 January 2017, his foreign policy legacy was largely a work in progress. In his first term in office, he kept a 2008 campaign promise to withdraw US military forces from Iraq (where the United States had maintained an active military presence since the 2003 war), but then had to send back troops in his second term to combat terrorists in the Islamic State of Iraq and Syria (ISIS) network. In Afghanistan, Obama approved a major troop increase at the end of 2009 to establish stability in a country where the United States had waged war against terrorists since 2001. He subsequently pledged to withdraw US forces in his second term, but more than 8000 troops remained at the conclusion of his presidency. Obama won the Nobel Peace Prize in 2009 primarily for the promise his presidency brought for diplomacy and multilateral action on key global issues, from combating terrorism to addressing climate change. Eight years later, that promise appeared to be evident more in public communication than in policy making.

In some respects, Obama's limited record in foreign affairs was unsurprising. Apart from his campaign pledge to end the Iraq War, Obama had

M. Bose (✉)
Hofstra University, Hempstead, NY, USA
e-mail: meena.bose@hofstra.edu

run for president on a platform focusing on domestic and economic policies, specifically enacting universal health care and ending the US financial crisis stemming from the late 2007–early 2008 recession. With limited political experience—eight years in the Illinois Senate and four years in the US Senate—Obama pledged a new approach to policy making in Washington, as his campaign slogan "Change We Can Believe In" indicated.[1] In foreign affairs, he made a similar pledge to work with other nations on pressing global matters, in contrast to the unilateralism of the George W. Bush presidency. Once in office, however, Obama demonstrated both continuity with and change from his predecessor's foreign policies, particularly for combating terrorism.[2] The continuity reflected both constraints from external events and the challenges—both domestic and international—of casting a new direction for the United States in global affairs.

This chapter evaluates the accomplishments and challenges of the Obama administration in foreign policy. It begins by examining Obama's pre-presidential views on the Iraq War, treatment of suspected terrorists, and other key foreign policy debates in the 2008 campaign for the White House. It then discusses the Obama White House's foreign policy goals, as presented in both official documents and presidential speeches. The chapter next evaluates the Obama administration's actions in a few key policy areas: wars, combating terrorism, and international diplomacy. While a comprehensive assessment of Obama's foreign policy legacy requires more extended study, this chapter examines the issues that will largely define the historical record for the administration. The chapter concludes with a discussion of how Obama's legacy will influence, through constraints and opportunities, both his successor's foreign policy agenda and those of future presidents in the coming years.

OBAMA'S PRE-PRESIDENTIAL VIEWS ON US FOREIGN POLICY

Although he did not have professional expertise in foreign affairs before becoming president, Barack Obama's family background and childhood experiences informed his views on the US role in the world. The son of a father from Kenya and a mother from Kansas, who met at the University of Hawaii, Obama lived with his mother and maternal grandparents in Hawaii until he was six, when he and his mother moved to Indonesia, her second husband's home. Obama lived in Jakarta until he was ten, when he returned to Hawaii and completed his secondary schooling there, staying with both his grandparents and his mother, who returned briefly for graduate study. Obama came to the continental United States for college, studying first at Occidental College in Los Angeles and then completing his undergraduate degree at Columbia University in New York. After college, he worked in Chicago as a community organizer for a few years before going to Harvard Law School.[3]

In a memoir that he published after law school (for which he received a book contract after becoming the first black president of the *Harvard Law Review*), Obama reflected on how his family and home transitions shaped his views on politics and world affairs. As he wrote in 2004, after winning the Democratic nomination in the US Senate race in Illinois, domestic and global conflict in the twenty-first century over poverty, diversity, religion, and more "is the struggle set forth, on a miniature scale, in this book."[4] While he did not present policy prescriptions, Obama did say, "The hardening of lines, the embrace of fundamentalism and tribe, dooms us all."[5]

With just four years in the US Senate, the last two of which focused primarily on his presidential run, Obama had little time to develop foreign policy expertise in Washington. He had entered the Senate with a clear (albeit not publicly acknowledged at the time) goal of entering the 2008 race for the White House, and thus needed to plan strategically in his legislative work. He opposed the 2006 Military Commissions Act, which permitted the military to employ special interrogation procedures for certain suspected terrorists. Obama also worked with US Senator Richard Lugar (R-IN) to pass legislation to stem the global proliferation of both conventional weapons and weapons of mass destruction.[6] (Lugar chaired the Senate Foreign Relations Committee, which Obama had joined upon taking office, having expressed keen interest following the election in that appointment.[7]) Citing concerns about government electronic surveillance, Obama joined with other Democrats to oppose renewal of the Patriot Act. In addition to the Senate Foreign Relations Committee, Obama also served on the Environment and Public Works Committee as well as the Committee on Veterans' Affairs. After Democrats won control of the chamber in 2006, he switched from the Environment Committee to Health, Education, Labor and Pensions, and Homeland Security and Governmental Affairs, again bolstering his professional experience in national security and foreign affairs with the latter.[8]

When Obama announced his candidacy for president on 10 February 2007, he referred to the need for change in Washington, in both politics and policy making. In foreign affairs, Obama discussed the importance of battling terrorism on multiple fronts, using military, economic, and intelligence resources. He also declared that "ultimate victory against our enemies will come only by rebuilding our alliances and exporting those ideals that bring hope and opportunity to millions around the globe."[9] Obama was critical of the Iraq War, which he had opposed from the outset as a state senator, declaring in an October 2002 speech that "I don't oppose all wars … What I am opposed to is a dumb war."[10] In 2002, Obama called for continued United Nations arms inspections in Iraq, as part of a broader strategy of reducing nuclear proliferation and promoting economic development and civil liberties around the globe. He continued these themes in the 2008 presidential campaign, declaring in his Democratic nomination acceptance speech that he would "build new partnerships to defeat the threats of the 21st century: terrorism and nuclear proliferation, poverty and genocide, climate change and disease."[11] Upon winning the presidential election, Obama spoke directly to people abroad, saying, "Our stories are singular, but our destiny is shared, and a new dawn of American leadership is at hand."[12] As president, he moved swiftly to explain what the new US role in the world would entail.

DEFINING FOREIGN AND NATIONAL SECURITY POLICY IN THE OBAMA ADMINISTRATION

The Obama administration's guiding principles for foreign and national security policy were presented consistently in presidential speeches and strategy reports as well as through executive appointments. In each area, the president focused on multilateral engagement and cooperation to advance US interests abroad. This approach contrasted sharply with the perceived unilateralism of the previous administration, particularly in how the George W. Bush administration pursued the war on terror through interrogations and surveillance, and waged the Iraq War. The Obama administration recognized the importance of an active US presence in global affairs, but it maintained that working with other nations was essential to achieving international security and stability, and to promoting democratic values around the globe.

In his inaugural address, Obama obliquely criticized the previous administration's policies by stating, "We reject as false the choice between our safety and our ideals," alluding to such controversies as treatment of detainees and surveillance of suspected terrorists, but he did not delve into specifics.[13] The president spoke directly to the Muslim world, calling for "a new way forward, based on mutual interest and mutual respect," and he emphasized the importance of diplomacy, promising corrupt or illegitimate leaders that "we will extend a hand if you are willing to unclench your fist." He reiterated this point in his first speech before Congress, declaring that "In words and deeds, we are showing the world that a new era of engagement has begun."[14]

Perhaps the best evidence of early "engagement" by the Obama administration was the president's travel abroad. In his first six months in office, President Obama made trips to both large and small countries, including Russia and Ghana, as well as four Middle Eastern states: Egypt, Iraq, Saudi Arabia, and Turkey. In Egypt, Obama gave a widely publicized speech at Cairo University in which he called for a "new beginning between the United States and Muslims around the world."[15] He also participated in three European summit meetings and signed agreements to regulate the global financial system more effectively, address climate change, and promote security in Afghanistan. According to Brendan J. Doherty, who has examined early presidential travel across administrations, Obama spent 25 days or 14 percent of his first six months in office (calculated from 20 January to 30 June 2009) on international trips.[16]

When President Obama won the Nobel Peace Prize in 2009, the award committee explicitly recognized his "extraordinary efforts to strengthen international diplomacy and cooperation between peoples."[17] In his acceptance speech, Obama addressed the importance of collective action, stating that "in a world in which threats are more diffuse, and missions more complex, America cannot act alone. America alone cannot secure the peace."[18] When military force is necessary, Obama emphasized the need for nations to follow accepted international rules of behavior: "I am convinced that adhering to standards, international standards, strengthens those who do, and isolates and weakens those who don't."[19] Obama reaffirmed these points in his 2014 commencement speech at the United States Military Academy at West Point, declaring that "in the 21st century American isolationism is not an option," and noting that post–World War II international institutions such as the United Nations and the World Bank "are not perfect, but they have been a force multiplier."[20]

The Obama administration's national security doctrine explicitly discussed the importance of multilateral cooperation. The 2010 National Security Strategy report called for "engagement with other countries," starting with allies who have "shared interests and shared values."[21] The report also declared the need to "pursue engagement with hostile nations to test their intentions, give their governments the opportunity to change course, reach out to their people, and mobilize international coalitions."[22] Such interactions would "underpin our commitment to an international order based upon rights and responsibilities."[23] Five years later, the Obama administration's second National Security Strategy document declared the need for US leadership in the world to "mobiliz[e] collective action to address global risks and seize strategic opportunities."[24]

The national security team in the Obama White House further demonstrated the president's commitment to global cooperation. Obama selected several senators to serve in his administration, from Vice President Joe Biden for both terms to Secretary of State Hillary Rodham Clinton in his first term and then Secretary of State John Kerry in his second. Their legislative expertise varied greatly, but all three shared a commitment to diplomacy and continued engagement with other countries. For Defense Secretary, Obama initially asked Bush appointee Robert Gates, a career intelligence official who had served as Deputy National Security Advisor and Director of Central Intelligence in the first Bush presidency, to stay in office. He subsequently appointed Leon Panetta, Chuck Hagel, and Ashton Carter, bringing a combination of legislative and executive-branch experience to the position. For National Security Advisor, Obama first appointed former Marine Corps Commandant and North Atlantic Treaty Organization (NATO) Supreme Allied Commander James L. Jones, and then appointed two advisors with State Department expertise, first Thomas E. Donilon and then Susan Rice. The collective legislative and diplomatic expertise of Obama's national security team was consistent with the president's goal of continued, sustained engagement with other nations.

WAR AND DIPLOMACY IN THE OBAMA ADMINISTRATION

The Obama administration's foremost challenge in foreign affairs was determining when to use military force. With US troops stationed in both Afghanistan and Iraq at the start of his presidency, Obama faced immediate expectations of fulfilling campaign pledges to establish stability in both countries. During his presidency, he additionally had to decide whether to send troops to Libya and Syria for security and humanitarian purposes, as civil wars raged in both countries. The rise of the ISIS terrorist network in the Middle East raised further questions about the need for US military force in the region. And the Obama White House also had to contend with ongoing global efforts to halt the development of nuclear weapons in Iran and North Korea, successfully reaching an agreement (albeit a highly controversial one) with the former, but experiencing numerous setbacks with the latter. In each case, Obama maintained his commitment to multilateralism, but faced criticism for perceived indecisiveness and lack of timely action on key issues affecting US security interests.

Afghanistan and Iraq

Soon after taking office in 2009, Obama announced a policy review on the US war in Afghanistan. After an initial increase of about 17,000 US troops (bringing the total number of American forces in the country to nearly 70,000), the Obama White House decided in the fall that a broader counter-insurgency operation, popularly known as COIN, was required to develop solidly functioning roads, schools, and political institutions.[25] In December, Obama announced that the United States would send an additional 30,000 troops to Afghanistan for 18 months to establish security and stability in the war-torn country.[26] The "surge" in Afghanistan achieved some success in defeating the fundamentalist, anti-democratic, Taliban forces, and that progress was further bolstered in 2011, when US Special Forces killed Osama bin Laden, the al Qaeda leader who had directed the 9/11 terrorist attacks, in a raid in Pakistan.[27] In the spring of 2012, Obama traveled to Afghanistan to sign a strategic partnership agreement that stated the United States would withdraw combat forces and turn over security to Afghan forces by the end of 2014.[28]

By the end of Obama's second term, security in Afghanistan had become much more elusive. Taliban forces had regrouped, instigated terrorist attacks in the Afghan capital of Kabul, and initiated military offensives in parts of the country, while the ISIS terrorist network in Iraq had begun recruiting Afghan supporters. In 2015, Obama announced that he would halt the drawdown of US forces, who would remain in the country well after he left office.[29] While US allies—including the UK, Australia, Georgia, Germany, and Turkey—also had sent troops to fight the Taliban in Afghanistan, the war had been a US-led mission from the outset. Even after NATO formally assumed control of peacekeeping forces in 2003, US participation was critical to the operation.[30] When NATO ended the combat mission in December 2014, three-quarters of the 13,000 troops that stayed in the country to assist with military training and counter-terrorism operations were American.[31] And when Obama left office in 2017, about 8400 US troops remained in Afghanistan.[32]

The US-led invasion of Iraq in 2003 was more controversial, both domestically and internationally, than the war in Afghanistan.[33] Even before Obama took office, his predecessor, President George W. Bush, had signed a Status of Forces Agreement with Iraq that required all US troops to depart the country by the end of 2011, unless Iraq agreed to extend their mandate. In February 2009, Obama announced that most of the approximately 142,000 US combat forces in Iraq would depart by the summer of 2010; the remaining 35–50,000 troops that remained to train Iraqi forces and complete other tasks would leave in 2011, as negotiated by the outgoing Bush administration.[34] Obama followed through with this plan, but continuing conflict and the rise of the brutal ISIS terrorist network prompted him to send US troops back to Iraq in 2014, with some 5000 military personnel there when he left office.[35]

Libya and Syria

In addition to ongoing military engagements, Obama also had to contend with sudden crises in foreign affairs that raised the question of whether the United States would use military force. Civil war in both Libya and Syria raised this issue, and in the first case, the Obama administration decided to engage for a short time, while in the second case, it demurred, ultimately not following through on a promise to get involved if the Syrian government used chemical weapons. In both countries, Obama declared the United States would act in concert with other nations; but action or the lack thereof ultimately was dependent on US interests and support from political leaders and the public.

In response to a United Nations Security Council Resolution led by the Obama administration, in the spring of 2011 the United States decided to act in concert with other NATO countries to prevent a humanitarian disaster in Libya. Democracy protests, popularly known as the "Arab Spring," had toppled authoritarian governments in Egypt and Tunisia, and rebels in Libya sought to do the same by overthrowing Libyan dictator Muammar al-Qaddafi. Fears of a civilian massacre prompted the United States and allies to assist democracy protesters in Libya by establishing a no-fly zone over the region and bombing al-Qaddafi's forces.[36] Obama did not seek congressional support for military action, saying it was unnecessary because NATO soon took responsibility for the fly zones, and that the UN Resolution limited air action to protecting civilians. Although the Republican-led House of Representatives, with some Democratic support, rejected a bill in June 2011 that would have authorized the intervention, Western support continued through the fall, when rebels succeeded in taking control of the government and killing al-Qaddafi.[37]

The United States declared the intervention a success, but the fledgling democratic government in Libya did not endure. The ensuing civil chaos raised questions about the military action, particularly following the tragic death of four Americans in an attack on the US consulate in Benghazi in September 2012.[38] Members of Congress criticized the Obama administration for not seeking legislative authorization for the 2011 intervention, and Republicans were highly critical of Secretary of State Hillary Clinton and US Permanent Representative to the United Nations Susan Rice for their statements and actions following the 2012 attack.[39]

By 2014, civil war had returned to the country, making it fertile territory for terrorist groups. In 2016, Obama said failing to plan for what to do after intervening in Libya was probably his worst mistake as president, though he continued to defend the intervention itself.[40] He described the country as chaotic (using far more colorful language), and acknowledged that the mission "didn't work."[41] In some respects, then, the intervention demonstrated parallels to US military action in Afghanistan and Iraq; as one analyst wrote, "The American way of war encourages officials to fixate on removing the bad guys and neglect the post-war stabilization phase."[42] A strong critique of the Bush administration now seemed applicable to the Obama White House as well.

Perhaps at least partly in reaction to the ongoing turmoil in Libya, the Obama administration demonstrated far greater reluctance to intervene in the civil war in Syria. In March 2011, pro-democracy protestors in Syria demanded the resignation of President Bashar al-Assad, and, as his security forces tried to stifle dissent, civil war erupted across the country, with hundreds of thousands of people opposing Assad's brutal rule. By the summer of 2013, 90,000 people had died in the conflict, and the number had nearly tripled to 250,000 two years later.[43]

A few months after the civil war began, Obama said Assad should resign so the Syrian people could determine their own political system—a view shared by US allies Great Britain, France, and Germany, which joined the

US call for Assad's ouster—and the United States imposed sanctions on Syria.[44] In 2012, Obama pledged to take military action if the government crossed a "red line" of using chemical weapons against its people. When that happened the following year, however, the White House backed down, saying it would act only with congressional authorization, which was not forthcoming.[45]

While Russia ultimately negotiated an agreement to have Syria destroy its chemical weapons stockpile, the civil war continued—with no international punishment for the Assad regime's horrific actions—and the ISIS terrorist network established a base of operations in the war-torn country. By the time Obama left office, his administration faced widespread criticism for its failure to follow through on the "red line" warning and take military action in Syria. As one scholar writes, "In correcting for Bush's overly aggressive foreign policy, Obama went too far in avoiding confrontations … he wound up neither strengthening his country's influence and status nor its power to bring about its ultimate goal of a safer and more peaceful world."[46]

International Diplomacy

The ambivalence that Obama demonstrated about US military action abroad was not evident in his international diplomacy, which illustrated the commitment to multilateral action presented in the president's speeches and strategy documents. During the 2008 presidential campaign, Obama had expressed willingness to have discussions with US adversaries "without preconditions," stating, "Under certain conditions, I always believe in talking. Sometimes it's more important to talk to your enemies than your friends."[47] Perhaps Obama's most significant effort in this area was the multilateral agreement to halt Iran's nuclear program in his second term.

In 2015, the Obama administration successfully concluded a two-year effort to create an historic seven-nation accord that imposed restrictions on Iran's development of nuclear weapons in return for the lifting of some economic sanctions. The five United Nations Security Council Permanent members (China, France, Great Britain, Russia, and the United States), Germany, and Iran reached an agreement, known as the Joint Comprehensive Plan of Action, that Iran would remove fissile material that could develop a nuclear weapon, and would permit international inspections to ensure compliance. (Without the agreement, negotiators had estimated that Iran would be able to develop a nuclear weapon within a few months.) In return, the European Union, the United Nations, and the United States pledged to suspend some sanctions on Iran. The restrictions were set to expire after 10 years for centrifuges and 15 years for low-enriched uranium, and the inspections had an expiration date as well.[48]

While the agreement had strong international support, it was widely disputed in the United States, with fierce opposition in Congress from Republicans and concerns raised by some Democrats as well. In particular, critics questioned whether inspections would ensure verification of the agreement, and whether strengthening Iran through lifting sanctions might present a threat to Israel. Although the agreement was not a treaty (which would have required a two-thirds vote in the Senate), the Obama administration had previously agreed that Congress could vote on a resolution to disapprove the agreement.[49] But the president could veto the resolution, and given that the White House had the votes to sustain a veto (i.e., Congress did not have the two-thirds support required in both chambers to override), the resolution of disapproval did not pass in 2015. However, because the deal was not a treaty, it was subject to change by subsequent administrations, and in May 2018, President Donald J. Trump withdrew the United States from the agreement.[50]

The Obama White House also sought to ease tensions with Cuba and North Korea. During the early Cold War, the United States had supported the dictatorial Batista regime due to its anti-communist position. But after communist rebel leader Fidel Castro took power in 1959, the United States cut off diplomatic ties with Cuba and then imposed a trade embargo. More than 50 years later, the Obama White House restarted diplomatic relations, permitted some travel and trade, and no longer identified Cuba as a state sponsor of terrorism.[51] Negotiations with North Korea were more problematic, as it conducted several nuclear tests during the Obama presidency, blocking any possibility of a non-proliferation agreement.[52] Nevertheless, Obama did follow through on his campaign promise to pursue diplomacy with US adversaries, and he achieved some notable successes, though the early presidency of Donald Trump raised questions about their continuation.

COMBATING TERRORISM IN THE OBAMA ADMINISTRATION

Since the 9/11 terrorist attacks, the looming threat of harm to the United States has informed American foreign policy. To protect US interests, the George W. Bush administration waged war on Afghanistan and Iraq, detained suspected terrorists at Guantanamo Bay, conducted domestic surveillance without warrants on communications with suspected terrorists, and created the Department of Homeland Security, among other actions. As discussed earlier, Obama's 2008 presidential campaign criticized some of Bush's foreign policy choices, but also made clear that the United States would continue to take necessary measures to combat terrorism. In some areas—particularly treatment of detainees, use of drones to destroy terrorist cells, and surveillance of suspected terrorists—the Obama administration's actual policies showed more continuity than change with the actions of the Bush administration.

In the post-9/11 world, the Bush White House suspended the writ of habeas corpus for what it termed "enemy combatants," declared that those combatants could be tried in military tribunals, and issued memoranda granting broad latitude in interrogation of detainees.[53] Congress and the Supreme Court attempted to restore a balance of power with the executive branch in combating terrorism, but still gave the president wide latitude to protect US national security.[54] Within days of taking office, President Obama issued executive orders to close the Guantanamo Bay detention facility for suspected terrorists within one year, and to ban torture, or "enhanced interrogation," of detainees. Doing so, Obama said, would "restore the standards of due process and the core constitutional values that have made this country great even in the midst of war, even in dealing with terrorism."[55] But the Obama White House faced congressional resistance to bringing the Guantanamo detainees to the United States, and in eight years, the administration was unable to negotiate an agreement with Congress to resolve the situation.[56] When Obama left office in 2017, the prison remained open, albeit with a small number of detainees—from just over 240 prisoners when Obama took office (from a high of nearly 700 in 2003) to 41 at the end of his term.[57]

Obama's campaign pledge to combat terrorism without infringing upon civil liberties also was tested during his presidency. Six weeks after the 9/11 attacks, Congress passed the USA Patriot Act, which gave law enforcement agencies broad power to examine business, electronic, and other records of suspected terrorists.[58] During his 2004 Senate campaign, Obama criticized the law's infringement on individual privacy, stating in his keynote address at the Democratic National Convention that "we don't like federal agents poking around in our libraries."[59] (Federal searches of library records had sparked controversy.) But as senator, Obama voted to reauthorize the Patriot Act in 2006, and as president, he voted to renew the Patriot Act in 2011. In each case, Obama endorsed additional civil liberties protections, but critics said those efforts were insufficient. The issue became even more contentious when former National Security Agency (NSA) contractor Edward Snowden leaked thousands of classified documents to journalists in 2013 that revealed the NSA had instituted mass data collection programs for Americans' telephone calls. (Obama's predecessor, President George W. Bush, had faced similar criticism for authorizing the NSA to conduct electronic surveillance without warrants.) In 2015, Obama signed the USA Freedom Act, which ended bulk collection of metadata and imposed other restrictions as well as transparency provisions for federal information gathering.[60]

The Obama administration additionally faced criticism for its extensive use of remotely piloted aircraft, or "drones," to attack terrorists. The George W. Bush administration had conducted drone strikes in Pakistan, Somalia, and Yemen on a limited basis until mid-2008, when the CIA expanded the program, demolishing more terrorist targets, but with increased civilian casualties, including deaths of children. Bush authorized approximately 50 air strikes as president, and Obama increased the number by more than tenfold, killing ten times as many terrorists (an increase from almost 300 to more than 3000 people), but also doubling civilian deaths. The so-called "surgical" strikes sparked much controversy around the world (and in the United States as well, though they commanded strong congressional and general public support), because of the many casualties, as well as limited information about how they were conducted.[61] As one commentator noted, "More consequential than the growth in drone strikes, is the Obama administration's efforts to institutionalize and normalize the practice... A central component of Obama's drone warfare legacy will be the unfilled gap between how his administration has justified drone strikes and how they are conducted."[62]

INTERNATIONAL AGREEMENTS IN THE OBAMA ADMINISTRATION

In keeping with his commitment to multilateralism, Obama pursued opportunities for the United States to pursue common interests with other countries in such areas as the environment and trade. The Obama administration enacted several environmental policy changes through executive action, and also signed a major international agreement in 2015 to reduce carbon emissions to combat climate change. As with the Iran nuclear deal, though, this agreement was not subject to Senate ratification, as the administration said it was not a treaty, and the Trump White House withdrew from the agreement in 2017. The Obama White House also pursued a free trade partnership in the Pacific, but halted efforts after the 2016 presidential election, given strong domestic opposition from the public as well as both major-party presidential candidates.

In a 2007 campaign speech in Iowa, Obama had identified environmental issues as a critical challenge for the country: "We are in a defining moment in our history. Our nation is at war. The planet is in peril."[63] As president, Obama approved federal funding for renewable energy and energy efficiency programs, worked with the automobile industry to increase fuel-economy standards, endorsed reduction of carbon pollution from coal, and protected land and water through national monument designations.[64] And in the highly contentious debate over the proposed Keystone XL pipeline that would bring crude oil from Canada to Texas, Obama exercised his veto power for just the third time to reject legislation authorizing its completion while the project was still under review in early 2015. By the end of the year, he announced that he would not approve a permit for the pipeline, due to environmental concerns.[65]

The Obama administration's most significant action in environmental policy was signing the historic 2015 Paris Agreement on climate change, which set goals for countries to reduce their emissions in the next 15 years. The 195 signatories to the agreement—almost every country in the world—included the three that produce the most greenhouse gases, namely, the United States, China, and India.[66] While the agreement was voluntary (it did not require congressional approval, which almost certainly would not have been possible in 2015, given high polarization between Democrats and Republicans, and divided party control of the White House and Congress), it set a clear direction for international cooperation on reduction of greenhouse gases. One year after Obama left office, the United States was the only country opposed to the agreement, indicating the strong and widespread global support for the initiative.[67]

Trade policy also was contentious for the Obama White House, particularly during the 2016 presidential race, when domestic concerns stymied the administration's efforts to win legislative approval for an international agreement to expand US global commerce. In 2016, the United States and 11 other countries signed the Trans-Pacific Partnership to bolster trade among participants by cutting tariffs, setting labor and environmental rules, developing common regulations, and more. Obama had secured "fast track" authority from Congress the previous year to have a yes or no vote on the legislation (without amendments), but election politics intervened. Both Democratic nominee Hillary Clinton and challenger Bernie Sanders opposed the legislation, as did Republican nominee Donald Trump. The Obama administration mounted a major campaign to win bipartisan support for the trade deal, but with strong opposition from politicians, business groups, and labor and environmental organizations, the White House decided after the election to halt its efforts.[68]

CONCLUSION

As this brief overview of major foreign policy choices and debates in the Obama administration illustrates, the 2008 campaign theme of unilateralism versus multilateralism belied the complicated issues at stake in defining US interests in world affairs. As promised, the Obama administration made some major changes in American foreign policy, most significantly in withdrawing US troops from Iraq. But the return of troops toward the end of Obama's presidency, along with the postponement of a full troop withdrawal from Afghanistan, indicated the difficulties with shifting the US role in the world. While other countries participated in both military interventions, the United States was the primary force behind both. Obama did pursue multilateral policy making in other areas, such as environment and trade, but progress was stymied by domestic politics, particularly during the contentious 2016 presidential race. Furthermore, Obama's reluctance to engage American forces in such conflicts as the Syrian civil war, or to remain engaged in chaotic states such as Libya, may have left open opportunities for terrorist networks such as ISIS to expand. While Obama's foreign policy legacy will not be established definitively for some time, this initial appraisal finds mixed success with both the president's goals and reactions to unexpected events in the world.

NOTES

1. Barack Obama, *Change We Can Believe In: Barack Obama's Plan to Renew America's Promise* (New York: Crown, 2008).
2. For a comparison of the two presidencies, see, for example, Meena Bose, ed., *Change in the White House? Comparing the Presidencies of George W. Bush and Barack Obama* (New York: Nova Science Publishers, 2014.
3. For a meticulously researched biography of Obama, including extensive detail on both his maternal and paternal ancestry, see David Remnick, *The Bridge: The Life and Rise of Barack Obama* (New York: Knopf, 2010).
4. Barack Obama, *Dreams From My Father: A Story of Race and Inheritance* (New York: Crown Publishers, 1995; reprint ed., 2004), Preface to 2004 edition.
5. Ibid.
6. David Mendell, *Obama: From Promise to Power* (New York: HarperCollins, 2007; rev. ed. 2017), ch. 22, "The Senator."
7. David J. Garrow, *Rising Star: The Making of Barack Obama* (New York: HarperCollins,), ch. 10, "Disappointment and Destiny: The U.S. Senate, November 2004–February 2007).
8. Ibid.
9. "Senator Obama's Announcement," *New York Times*, 10 February 2007.
10. "Transcript: Obama's Speech Against the Iraq War" (Chicago, 2 October 2002), *National Public Radio*, 20 January 2009.
11. "Barack Obama's Acceptance Speech" (2008 Democratic National Convention, Denver), *New York Times*, 28 August 2008.
12. "Full Transcript: Sen. Barack Obama's Victory Speech," *ABC News*, 4 November 2008.
13. Barack Obama, "Inaugural Address," 20 January 2009. Available at www.obamawhitehouse.archives.gov. These two paragraphs on Obama's early speeches and travel originally appeared in Meena Bose, "The President and Foreign Policy," in *New Directions in the American Presidency*, ed. Lori Cox Han (New York: Routledge, 2010). Some examples here of Obama's foreign policy decisions also draw upon that chapter, as well as an updated version in a forthcoming second edition of the volume (Routledge, 2018).
14. Barack Obama, "Address to Joint Session of Congress," 24 February 2009. Available at www.obamawhitehouse.archives.gov
15. Barack Obama, "Remarks by the President on a New Beginning," Cairo University, Cairo, Egypt, 4 June 2009. Available at www.obamawhitehouse.archives.gov
16. For comparisons to other recent presidents' early travel, see Brendan J. Doherty, "POTUS on the Road: International and Domestic Presidential Travel," *Presidential Studies Quarterly* 39, no. 2 (June 2009): 322–46.

17. Statement by Norwegian Nobel Committee, "The Nobel Peace Prize for 2009," 9 October 2009, at http://nobelprize.org/nobel_prizes/peace/laureates/2009/press.html
18. President Barack Obama, "Nobel Lecture: A Just and Lasting Peace," 10 December 2009. Available at https://www.nobelprize.org/
19. Ibid.
20. President Barack Obama, "Remarks by the President at the United States Military Academy Commencement Ceremony," 28 May 2014. Available at https://obamawhitehouse.archives.gov/
21. President Barack Obama, "National Security Strategy," May 2010, p. 3. Available at http://nssarchive.us/
22. Ibid.
23. Ibid.
24. President Barack Obama, "National Security Strategy," February 2015, p. 3. Available at http://nssarchive.us/
25. Mark Landler, "The Afghan War and the Evolution of Obama," *New York Times*, 1 January 2017. Also see Bob Woodward, *Obama's Wars* (New York: Simon & Schuster, 2010). Not all White House and military officials supported the "surge" in Afghanistan; both Vice President Joe Biden and US Ambassador to Afghanistan/retired Lieutenant General Karl W. Eikenberry, for example, expressed concerns at the time about the reliability of Afghan President Hamid Karzai and the difficulty of achieving security and political stability in the country. See Elisabeth Bumiller and Mark Landler, "U.S. Envoy Urges Caution on Forces in Afghanistan," *New York Times*, 11 November 2009; and Eric Schmitt, "U.S. Envoy's Cables Show Worries on Afghan Plans," *New York Times*, 25 January 2010.
26. President Barack Obama, "The New Way Forward," United States Military Academy at West Point, New York, 1 December 2009.
27. CNN Library, "Death of Osama bin Laden Fast Facts," 23 April 2017.
28. Mark Landler, "Obama Signs Pact in Kabul, Turning Page in Afghan War," *New York Times*, 1 May 2012.
29. Landler, "The Afghan War and the Evolution of Obama."
30. Amy Waldman, "NATO Takes Control of Peace Forces in Kabul," *New York Times*, 13 August 2003.
31. "How Many Foreign Troops Are in Afghanistan?" *BBC News*, 15 October 2015.
32. Christi Parsons and W.J. Hennigan, "President Obama, Who Hoped to Sow Peace, Instead Led the Nation in War," *Los Angeles Times*, 13 January 2017.
33. See, for example, Richard N. Haass, *War of Necessity, War of Choice: A Memoir of Two Iraq Wars* (New York: Simon & Schuster, 2009); and David

E. Sanger, *The Inheritance: The World Obama Confronts and the Challenges to American Power* (New York: Crown Publishers, 2009).

34. Peter Baker, "With Pledges to Troops and Iraqis, Obama Details Pullout," *New York Times*, 27 February 2009.

35. Tony Karon, "Iraq's Government, Not Obama, Called Time on the U.S. Troop Presence," Time, 21 October 2011; Scott Wilson and Karen DeYoung, "All U.S. Troops to Leave Iraq by the End of 2011," *Washington Post*, 21 October 2011; Ben Hubbard, Robert F. Worth, and Michael R. Gordon, "Power Vacuum in Middle East Lifts Militants," *New York Times,* 4 January 2014; Mark Thompson, "Number of U.S. Troops in Iraq Keeps Creeping Upward," *Time*, 18 April 2016.

36. Alan J. Kuperman, "Obama's Libya Debacle: How a Well-Meaning Intervention Ended in Failure," *Foreign Affairs* 94, no. 2 (March/April 2015).

37. Charlie Savage and Mark Landler, "White House Defends Continued U.S. Role in Libyan Operation," *New York Times*, 15 June 2011; Jennifer Steinhauer, "House Spurns Obama on Libya, But Does Not Cut Funds," *New York Times*, 24 June 2011.

38. Paul Richter and Christi Parsons, "U.S. Intervention in Libya Now Seen as Cautionary Tale," *Los Angeles Times*, 27 June 2014; Sarah Aarthun, "4 Hours of Fire and Chaos: How the Benghazi Attack Unfolded," *CNN World,* 13 September 2012.

39. Charlie Savage, "Attack Renews Debate Over Congressional Consent," *New York Times*, 21 March 2011; Charlie Savage and Thom Shanker, "Scores of U.S. Strikes in Libya Followed Handoff to NATO," *New York Times*, 20 June 2011; David M. Herszenhorn, "House Benghazi Report Finds No New Evidence of Wrongdoing by Hillary Clinton," *New York Times*, 28 June 2016.

40. Dominic Tierney, "The Legacy of Obama's 'Worst Mistake'," *The Atlantic*, 15 April 2016; Shadi Hamid, "Everyone Says the Libya Intervention Was a Failure. They're Wrong," Brookings Institution, 12 April 2016.

41. Tierney, "The Legacy of Obama's 'Worst Mistake'."

42. Ibid.

43. "Syria: The Story of the Conflict," *BBC News*, 11 March 2016.

44. Scott Wilson and Joby Warrick, "Assad Must Go, Obama Says," *Washington Post*, 18 August 2011.

45. Peter Baker and Jonathan Weisman, "Obama Seeks Approval By Congress for Strike in Syria," *New York Times*, 31 August 2013; Haley Bissegger, "Timeline: How President Obama Handled Syria," *The Hill*, 15 September 2013.

46. David Greenberg, "Syria Will Stain Obama's Legacy Forever," *Foreign Policy*, 29 December 2016.

47. Associated Press, "Clinton: Obama is 'Naïve' on Foreign Policy," *The Debates on NBCNews.com*, 24 July 2007; Marc Ambinder, "On Iran, Parsing Obama, Without Preconditions or Preconceptions," *The Atlantic*, 21 May 2008.
48. Michael R. Gordon and David E. Sanger, "Deal Reached on Iran Nuclear Program; Limits on Fuel Would Lessen With Time," *New York Times*, 14 July 2015; Obama White House, "The Historic Deal That Will Prevent Iran from Acquiring a Nuclear Weapon," https://obamawhitehouse. archives.gov/node/328996; Zachary Laub, "The Impact of the Iran Nuclear Agreement," *Council on Foreign Relations Backgrounder*, 18 May 2018.
49. David M. Herszenhorn, "The Iran Nuclear Deal: Congress Has Its Say," *New York Times*, 7 September 2015; Jonathan Weisman and Peter Baker, "Obama Yields, Allowing Congress Say on Iran Nuclear Deal," *New York Times*, 14 April 2015.
50. Jennifer Steinhauer, "Democrats Hand Victory to Obama on Iran Nuclear Deal," *New York Times*, 10 September 2015; Manu Raju, "How the White House Kept Democrats From Killing the Iran Deal," www.cnn.com, 11 September 2015; Jim Zarroli, "As Sanctions on Iran Are Lifted, Many U.S. Business Restrictions Remain," *National Public Radio*, 26 January 2016; Stephen Collinson, "Iran Deal: A Treaty or Not a Treaty, That is the Question," www.cnn.com, 12 May 2015; Mark Landler, "Trump Abandons Nuclear Deal He Long Scorned," *New York Times*, 8 May 2018.
51. Jeremy Diamond, "U.S.-Cuba Relations: 10 Questions on the Embargo, Embassies and Cigars," www.CNNPolitics.com, 1 July 2015; Ted Piccone, "On Cuba, Obama Looks Beyond 2016," Brookings Institution, 14 October 2016; Council on Foreign Relations, "U.S.-Cuba Relations, 1959–2018." Available at www.cfr.org
52. Victor Cha, "The Unfinished Legacy of Obama's Pivot to Asia," *Foreign Policy*, 6 September 2016; Amanda Erickson, "A Timeline of North Korea's Five Nuclear Tests and How the U.S. Has Responded," *Washington Post*, 14 April 2017.
53. James P. Pfiffner evaluates the George W. Bush presidency's actions in these areas, arguing that they "undermined the constitutional balance among the branches" (p. 4), in *Power Play: The Bush Presidency and the Constitution* (Washington, D.C.: Brookings Institution Press, 2008).
54. Full assessments of Bush's foreign policy include Peter Baker, *Days of Fire: Bush and Cheney in the White House* (New York: Doubleday, 2013); James Mann, *George W. Bush: The 43rd President, 2001–2009* (New York: Times Books, 2015); Jean Edward Smith, *Bush* (New York: Simon & Schuster, 2016).

55. "Obama Signs Order to Close Guantanamo Bay Facility," www. CNNPolitics.com, 22 January 2009.

56. Connie Bruck, "Why Obama Has Failed to Close Guantanamo," *New Yorker*, 1 August 2016.

57. Ryan Browne, "Obama's Last Transfer of Gitmo Detainees, Trump Inherits 41," www.CNNPolitics.com, 19 January 2017.

58. USA PATRIOT is an acronym for Uniting and Strengthening America by Providing Appropriate Tools Required to Intercept and Obstruct Terrorism Act of 2001, but all capital letters typically are not used in referring to the law. See Public Law 107–56, 26 October 2001.

59. "Barack Obama's Keynote Address at the 2004 Democratic National Convention," *PBS Newshour*, 27 July 2004; Jason M. Breslow, "Obama on Mass Government Surveillance, Then and Now," *PBS Frontline*, 13 May 2014.

60. The George W. Bush administration's secret NSA program of surveillance without warrants was first revealed in James Risen and Eric Lichtblau, "Bush Lets U.S. Spy on Callers Without Courts," *New York Times*, 16 December 2005. Analyses of Obama's surveillance policies include James Bamford, "Every Move You Make," *Foreign Policy*, 7 September 2016; and Lauren C. Williams, "Obama Leaves Behind a Mixed Record on Technology and Surveillance," www.thinkprogress.org, 22 December 2016.

61. Steve Coll, "The Unblinking Stare: The Drone War in Pakistan," *New Yorker*, 24 November 2014; Jack Moore, Drone Strikes Under Obama Killed Up to 117 Civilians Worldwide, Intelligence Report Claims," *Newsweek*, 20 January 2017.

62. Micah Zenko, "Obama's Embrace of Drone Strikes Will Be A Lasting Legacy," *New York Times*, 12 January 2016.

63. Barack Obama: "Remarks at the Iowa Jefferson-Jackson Dinner in Des Moines," November 10, 2007. Online by Gerhard Peters and John T. Woolley, *The American Presidency Project*. http://www.presidency.ucsb. edu/ws/?pid=77021

64. Michael Brune, "Let's Celebrate the Environmental Progress Made During the Last Eight Years," *Sierra Magazine*, 3 November 2016.

65. Jeff Brady and Scott Horsley, "What You Need to Know About the Keystone XL Oil Pipeline," *National Public Radio: All Things Considered*, 17 November 2014; Juliet Eilperin and Katie Zezima, "Obama Vetoes Keystone XL Bill," *Washington Post*, 24 February 2015; Laura Barron-Lopez, "Obama Vetoes Keystone XL Bill," *The Hill*, 24 February 2015; Elana Schor, "Obama Rejects Keystone XL Pipeline," *Politico*, 6 November 2015.

66. White House, "President Obama: The United States Formally Enters the Paris Agreement," 3 September 2016; "Paris Climate Deal: Nearly 200 Nations Sign in End of Fossil Fuel Era," *The Guardian,* 12 December 2015; Lee H. Hamilton, "Obama Foreign Policy: Significant Success and Notable Missteps," *Huffington Post,* undated.
67. Brian Resnick, "4 Things to Know About the Paris Climate Agreement," *Vox,* 1 June 2017; Jonathan Ellis, "The Paris Climate Deal: What You Need to Know," *New York Times,* 1 June 2017; Lisa Friedman, "Syria Joins Paris Climate Accord, Leaving Only U.S. Opposed," *New York Times,* 7 November 2017.
68. Timothy B. Lee, ed., "The Trans-Pacific Partnership, Explained," *Vox,* 25 July 2016; Barack Obama, "Statement by the President on the Signing of the Trans-Pacific Partnership," 3 February 2016, www.obamawhitehouse-archives.gov; Jackie Calmes, "Obama Readies One Last Push for Trans-Pacific Partnership," *New York Times,* 21 August 2016; William Mauldin, "Obama Administration Gives Up On Pacific Trade Deal," *Wall Street Journal,* 11 November 2016; David Lawder, "Obama Administration Suspends Pacific Deal Vote Effort," *Reuters,* 11 November 2016.

The World We Have Lost: US Labor in the Obama Years

Ruth Milkman

Barack Obama was the most labor-friendly US president in at least a generation. As he recalled in his 2006 best-seller, *The Audacity of Hope*, he had been a strong union ally as an Illinois State senator, "sponsoring many of their [labor's] bills and making their case on the floor." He went on to play a similar role as a US senator. Later in the book, he endorsed the key provisions of organized labor's top legislative priority at the time, the Employee Free Choice Act (EFCA):

> ... to help workers gain higher wages and better benefits, we need once again to level the playing field between organized labor and employers ... We should have tougher penalties to prevent employers from firing or discriminating against workers involved in organizing drives. Employers should have to recognize a union if a majority of employees sign authorization cards choosing the union to represent them. And federal mediation should be available to help an employer and a new union reach agreement on a contract within a reasonable amount of time.[1]

R. Milkman (✉)
Department of Sociology, City University of New York Graduate Center,
New York, NY, USA
e-mail: rmilkman@gc.cuny.edu

© The Author(s) 2019   115
W. C. Rich (ed.), *Looking Back on President Barack Obama's Legacy*,
https://doi.org/10.1007/978-3-030-01545-9_6

Yet another reflection of his union sympathies was Obama's mantra "Yes We Can!"—an English rendition of "Si Se Puede!," the United Farm Workers' iconic labor organizing slogan. AFL-CIO General Counsel Craig Becker, a member of the National Labor Relations Board under Obama, declared that no "president since Roosevelt has been rhetorically as open about his support for the labor movement."[2]

When Obama was elected president, organized labor was in a period of deep soul-searching, after decades of decline in union membership and clout. The Service Employees International Union (SEIU), along with UNITE HERE! (the name of the hotel and garment workers' unions after their 2004 merger) and a few other unions had left the AFL-CIO just three years earlier to form Change to Win, a rival labor federation.[3] The SEIU and UNITE HERE's Chicago affiliates had endorsed Obama's 2004 Senate run; these two unions were also early supporters of his candidacy in the 2007 presidential primaries.[4] Obama was also friendly to the AFL-CIO unions.

The 2008 financial meltdown, the deepest economic crisis since the Great Depression and a key factor in Obama's election victory, led many progressives and labor leaders to urge him to replicate some of the New Deal initiatives of the 1930s that had established key legal protections for workers and sparked the nation's last great union upsurge. Unions had invested millions of dollars in Obama's 2008 election campaign, and his professed commitment to the labor cause led many to hope that he would follow up on his pledge to support EFCA and take a leadership role in helping win its passage.

Shortly after the November 2008 election (but before Obama's inauguration), rank-and-file workers occupied the Republic Windows factory in Obama's adopted hometown of Chicago. The strike came in protest of a planned plant shutdown that would have violated a federal law requiring employers to provide advance notice to affected workers. In part because it broke out during the holiday season and amid the chaos of the financial crisis, the Republic Windows workers captured broad public sympathy. Obama (along with many other elected officials) spoke out in support of their action, further adding to the expectations that the inauguration of the nation's first African-American president, a self-proclaimed union supporter, would be a new day for the U.S. labor movement.

At first, these hopes seemed amply justified. SEIU President Andy Stern was the single most frequent visitor to the White House in the first half of 2009. AFL-CIO President John Sweeney, who had been invited to the

White House only once during the entire eight years of the previous administration, was there at least once a week in the early months of Obama's presidency; later Sweeney's successor, Richard Trumka, was also a regular guest. Obama also made a series of pro-labor appointments immediately upon taking office, including Hilda Solis, a California congresswoman with strong union ties, who became his Secretary of Labor in 2009, and Wilma Liebman, a labor attorney previously employed by the Bricklayers union, to head the National Labor Relations Board (NLRB).[5] And the very first bill Obama signed into law was the Lilly Ledbetter Fair Pay Restoration Act, which was designed to make it easier for workers to sue for pay discrimination.[6]

However, the economic team Obama assembled to address the financial crisis was dominated by Wall Street loyalists and was far less union-friendly than many progressives had hoped. It famously prioritized financial and business interests over those of labor and working people in addressing the financial crisis. And although organized labor strongly supported Obama's health care reform effort, his decision to prioritize the Affordable Care Act over all other legislative goals during the administration's first year was among the factors leading to failure of the EFCA campaign. As many commentators have noted, EFCA might well have been defeated in any case, but at the time its collapse was a huge disappointment for labor, which had poured vast resources into the effort to win its passage.[7]

Obama did deploy his executive powers in support of labor interests throughout his eight years in office. He made a series of progressive appointments to the U.S. Department of Labor (DOL) and the NLRB—despite considerable Congressional resistance in regard to the. latter. Obama's DOL ramped-up enforcement of wage and hour laws, occupational health and safety rules, and other worker protections. He also issued various Executive Orders and administrative regulations extending minimum-wage and overtime protections to home care workers, restricting unpaid internships, increasing the wage threshold for overtime eligibility, requiring federal contractors to provide paid sick leave, and raising the minimum wage for workers employed by federal contractors. In addition, the Obama NLRB issued a steady stream of union-friendly rulings, making it easier for sports players, taxi drivers, graduate student employees and faculty to unionize, and issued rules designed to streamline the union representation election process.

These actions significantly improved the situation of workers and their unions for the duration of Obama's two terms in office, but most of them proved short-lived. Some were successfully challenged in the courts, and nearly all the others would be reversed soon after the 2016 election of Donald Trump. Meanwhile, at the state level, even during Obama's first term, immediately after the 2010 midterms, newly elected Republican governors and legislators launched coordinated efforts to restrict public-sector unions (which unlike their private-sector counterparts are governed by state-level laws), with considerable success. Wisconsin's 2011 law restricting public-sector union rights under Governor Scott Walker is the best-known case, but there were similar developments in many other states.

Unionization rates continued their long decline in the Obama years. In 2008, 12.4 percent of the nation's wage and salary workers and 7.6 percent of those in the private sector were union members; by 2016, the figures were 10.7 percent and 6.4 percent, respectively.[8] However, even as union membership waned, the number of non-union organizations like worker centers and community-based organizations grew steadily during the Obama years. Such "alt-labor" groups, along with traditional unions, helped secure passage of pro-labor legislation in several states and cities where Democrats retained political power, providing new protections for vulnerable occupational groups (e.g., domestic workers), increasing penalties for violations of labor and employment laws, increasing state and local minimum wages, and establishing paid sick leave and paid family leave programs in various jurisdictions.

The Failure of the Employee Free Choice Act

The aspect of this eight-year period of labor history that has been most studied is the failure to win EFCA. After the 2008 elections, with a union-friendly president and a filibuster-proof majority in the Senate, labor leaders believed they finally had a chance to secure this reform, which consisted of a set of amendments to the 1935 National Labor Relations Act (NLRA). EFCA had first been introduced in Congress in 2003 and had been labor's top legislative priority ever since. The measure was designed to address the tactics that employers had developed since the late 1970s to delay and undermine the NLRB election process, typically with the help of "labor consultants" (known as "union busters" in the vernacular).

EFCA had three key provisions. First, it would have required the NLRB to certify unions if a majority of workers signed valid union authorization cards, rather than requiring a secret-ballot election. Secondly, in newly unionized workplaces, EFCA would have mandated binding arbitration after 90 days of collective bargaining if agreement had not yet been reached on a first contract. Third, it would have stiffened penalties for employer "Unfair Labor Practice" violations, like firing workers involved in organizing or threatening to close a business if workers voted to unionize—actions that have long been illegal under the NLRA but are widely practiced, in part because the penalties are minimal.

The business lobby shared organized labor's perception that EFCA (or a compromise measure including many of its provisions) had a serious chance of passage under Obama, who had pledged to sign it into law if it got through Congress. Employer organizations mobilized intensively to defeat the proposed measure, with the US Chamber of Commerce alone devoting $20 million for this purpose in 2009 and 2010.[9] Bernie Marcus, the CEO of Home Depot, went so far as to declare that EFCA would mean "the demise of civilization."[10] The business counter-campaign, along with the unexpected victory of Republican Scott Brown in the special election to replace Senator Edward Kennedy after his death in 2009, which cost the Democrats their filibuster-proof Senate majority, effectively killed the bill.[11]

EFCA's failure was deeply demoralizing to organized labor and its supporters. "We had put all of our eggs in that legislative basket and we didn't win," labor attorney and former Kennedy staffer Sharon Block later recalled.[12] "For American labor, year one of Barack Obama's presidency has been close to an unmitigated disaster," veteran labor journalist Harold Meyerson wrote in early 2010, adding that EFCA's defeat was "devastating and galling."[13] Instead of the breakthrough for labor law reform that so many had dreamed of after Obama's election, EFCA's defeat became another chapter in the decades-long history of union decline.

Obama's Economic Recovery Program: No New Deal

Another source of disappointment for labor was the administration's response to the economic crisis. Obama's progressive campaign rhetoric and the massive popularity he enjoyed in the immediate aftermath of his election in 2008 inspired widespread hopes that he might replicate the kinds of public policies that had followed the 1929 stock market crash: efforts to stem or reverse the growth of inequality, a massive job creation program, and other measures to help working people recover from the massive employment and housing losses they suffered after the 2008 financial meltdown. Initially, there were some promising signs along these lines, most notably the American Recovery and Reinvestment Act (ARRA), which provided a major economic stimulus of $787 billion and included significant tax cuts benefitting working people. But the ARRA was more modest in scale and scope than many progressives had hoped and conspicuously lacked a New Deal-style jobs program. More important, the economic team Obama appointed to address the crisis was dominated by economists drawn from Wall Street, and it soon became clear that their priority was rescuing financial institutions with bailouts and tax cuts, rather than addressing the pressing economic concerns of ordinary Americans.[14]

Thus like EFCA, labor's hopes for a new New Deal were left unfulfilled. In the 1930s, President Franklin D. Roosevelt had taken a bold stand in support of unions and collective bargaining and launched large-scale job creation programs and other measures to assist workers, while confronting business opposition head on. This was the period of landmark legislation creating Social Security, the first federal minimum-wage law, and other bedrock labor protections. Crucially, Roosevelt had the political leverage to carry out this agenda, most of which was passed with bipartisan support. In contrast, Obama faced a sharply divided Congress from the outset, a situation that would deteriorate dramatically after the 2010 midterm elections. That many on the political Right demonized the president on an openly racial basis further limited his room for maneuver.

Perhaps Obama could have been bolder during the "honeymoon period" at the start of his first term, but the political reality he faced in 2009 and 2010 bore little resemblance to that of the New Deal era. He did make numerous labor-friendly appointments to the DOL and NLRB; otherwise his actions in support of working people and the labor movement were largely confined to administrative measures and Executive Orders.

LABOR-FRIENDLY EXECUTIVE ORDERS, POLITICAL APPOINTMENTS, AND ADMINISTRATIVE ACTIONS

Presidents have the power to issue Executive Orders, and to reverse those issued by their predecessors, without Congressional approval. Obama used this power to deliver on some of his campaign promises immediately upon taking office. For example, he issued an Executive Order that prohibited federal contractors from using government funds for anti-union expenditures, another that required contractors to post notices informing workers of their rights to unionize, and a third encouraging them to adopt Project Labor Agreements (short-term agreements that resemble union contracts) for construction projects. Another Obama Executive Order re-established a labor-management council within the federal government.[15]

In addition to choosing Hilda Solis as his Secretary of Labor, Obama made several other labor-friendly appointments in 2009 that reinvigorated the department. In the first two years of the Obama administration, the DOL also hired hundreds of new wage-and-hour investigators, along with new staffers in various other agencies assigned to enhance enforcement of workplace protections.[16] This enabled DOL to ramp-up enforcement of minimum-wage, overtime, and occupational health and safety laws. The Department's Wage and Hour Division began to shift resources toward more proactive enforcement efforts, rather than simply responding to complaints, and greatly increased its outreach efforts to educate workers about their rights and to communicate their renewed determination to more effectively address violations.[17]

The Obama DOL also extended minimum-wage and overtime protections to nearly two million previously exempted home care workers, and required businesses to disclose any outside legal advice they received in regard to union organizing campaigns (the "persuader rule"). It also issued new regulations limiting worker misclassification as independent contractors, setting stricter limits on unpaid internships, and expanding eligibility for overtime pay to millions of additional workers.[18] However, with the exception of the measures for home care workers, which survived a legal challenge in the federal courts, all of these efforts would be scaled back or reversed after Obama left office.

The NLRB was also far more labor-friendly under Obama than it had been under the Bush administration, but in contrast to the DOL, there was a lengthy delay before it could begin its work. The 2009 appointment of Wilma Liebman to chair the NLRB was warmly welcomed by organized labor.[19] However, in response to vigorous opposition from the business lobby, Republicans successfully filibustered confirmation of Obama's nominees to fill two additional vacancies on the NLRB, Craig Becker and Mark Pearce, for nearly a year. In April 2010, they were finally installed through "recess appointments" that could be made by executive authority when the Senate was not in session. The time limits on recess appointments meant that this drama would be repeated: similar controversy surrounded Obama's subsequent appointments to the NLRB, and in 2012

Republicans went so far as to challenge his right to make recess appointments, although the administration ultimately prevailed.

Despite this protracted process, the Obama NLRB actively deployed its rule-making power to help speed up union elections. Employers were newly required to post notices informing workers of their legal right to unionize under the NLRA, to provide unions with workers' email addresses and phone numbers, and to postpone any legal challenges to NLRB elections until after the workers had voted. However, this approach proved short-lived as nearly all these rules were successfully challenged in the courts.[20] Instead, the Obama NLRB, like its predecessors, used its power of adjudication in regard to the specific cases that came before it.

Historically, NLRB rulings have long followed a partisan pattern, with more labor-friendly rulings under Democratic administrations and more business-friendly rulings under Republican ones.[21] The Obama NLRB was no exception, with decisions in a number of key cases that facilitated union organizing and protected workers' rights to engage in "concerted activity for mutual aid and protection" under Section 7 of the NLRA, that is, the right of workers to collectively address work-related issues on the job, not only by organizing unions but through other types of collaborative activity.

One arena in which the Obama NRLB made path-breaking new rulings involved the use of social media in the workplace. In a 2012 decision, *Costco Wholesale Corp.*, it ruled that policies in employee handbooks prohibiting workers from using electronic postings criticizing their employers were unlawful. Two years later in *Three D, L.L.C.*, it ruled that Facebook communications among employees were protected concerted activity; in 2014, it ruled in *Purple Communications Inc.* that employees could not be prohibited from using employer-provided email for organizing and other concerted activity. The Obama board also weighed in on conventional forms of workplace communication in the 2014 *Plaza Auto Center, Inc.* case, finding that a worker's verbal complaints to other workers on the job were protected speech.[22]

In 2012, the Obama NLRB issued an especially high-profile decision in *D.R. Horton, Inc.*, banning employers from requiring workers to pursue individual arbitration (and thus requiring that they waive their right to class arbitration or other collective legal action), as a violation of the NLRA's provision protecting the right to concerted activity. This was reaffirmed in another case two years later, *Murphy Oil USA, Inc.*[23] However, it has been the subject of court challenges and will soon come before the U.S. Supreme Court for a final resolution.

Another critical issue the Obama NLRB took up was the scope of "bargaining units" under the NLRA. In 2011, it ruled in *Specialty Healthcare Center of Mobile* that units that did not include all employees in a workplace were permitted. For example, a nursing home bargaining unit could include only certified nursing assistants but not cooks, janitors and clerical workers. Although business opponents criticized this decision as allowing "micro-units," in this case the unit was twice the median size of bargaining units the NLRB had certified over the previous decade; the real issue was not size but whether the unit involved a "readily identifiable" group.[24]

A series of additional decisions by the Obama NLRB expanded the coverage of the NLRA to include groups of workers whose status was ambiguous or who had been excluded from coverage in the past. The Board expanded eligibility for union representation to include non-tenure-track faculty members and graduate student assistants at private colleges and universities. Taxi drivers dispatched by a company were also deemed employees (rather than independent contractors), as were FedEx delivery drivers, and thus eligible for unionization under the NLRA.[25] In another key case, *Browning-Ferris Industries*, which the NLRB ruled in 2015 that a company that hires a contractor or franchisee to run one of its outlets may be considered a "joint employer" of the workers employed there, even if it does not actively supervise them. Although the *Browning* case concerned a different industry (recycling), it has implications for the fast-food industry, where the SEIU has been attempting to organize workers at McDonald's franchises (the SEIU campaign is discussed further below).[26]

The impact of these NLRB rulings has been limited, however. Even before the election of Donald Trump, whose NLRB appointees are highly likely to reverse many of them in future cases, many of these decisions faced court challenges and in some cases could be nullified by new legislation. For example, the *Browning-Ferris* case has already been reversed by the new Trump NLRB, but business opponents fearful that the pendulum could swing in the other direction under a future Democratic administration are lobbying for legislation to address the issue.[27]

In summary, while Obama's Executive Orders and his political appointments fulfilled his promises to support organized labor, and on his watch both the DOL and NLRB delivered many labor-friendly rulings between 2009 and 2016, those gains were highly precarious. There was an uptick in union win rates during the Great Recession, which persisted through-out the Obama years.[28] However, as noted above, unionization rates con-tinued their relentless decline during his two terms. Meanwhile, new political struggles over public-sector labor rights emerged at the state and local level after 2010, along with cases that came before the US Supreme Court.

ATTACKS ON PUBLIC-SECTOR UNIONS: WISCONSIN TO THE FRIEDRICHS CASE

Starting in 2010, the absolute number of public-sector union members began to decline, reflecting cutbacks tied to austerity measures precipi-tated by the 2008 financial crisis. In efforts to reduce or eliminate budget shortfalls, more than half the states laid off public employees in fiscal years 2010 or 2011. Moreover, after the 2010 midterm elections brought Republicans into political power in many key states, austerity measures were coupled with a wave of direct political attacks on public-sector col-lective bargaining to produce an unprecedented fall off in public-sector union density. Ironically, Wisconsin, where these political attacks were especially prominent, in 1959 had been the first state to pass legislation creating collective bargaining rights for public-sector workers. The 2011 attack on public-sector bargaining rights led by Wisconsin Governor Scott Walker sparked vigorous resistance and a dramatic political struggle, including a month-long occupation of the state legislature building, but ultimately Walker prevailed.[29]

This was not merely a continuation of previous anti-union efforts, which had been escalating since the late 1970s. Whereas those efforts had been concentrated in private companies, after 2010, for the first time the public sector became a central battleground. And in contrast to earlier years, the attacks did not come directly from employers—which in the public sector were government agencies—but rather from elected officials, under pres-sure from lobbyists and campaign donors. Attempts at undermining pub-lic-sector unions had appeared periodically before, but they accelerated enormously with the Great Recession and the state and local budget defi-cits that it helped to create. The new attacks on public-sector unions that emerged in 2011 were nakedly political in character. The ties between organized labor and the Democratic Party, and unions' long-standing tra-dition of generously supporting Democratic candidates, had long made unions anathema for the political right. Now anti-union organizations such as the American Legislative Exchange Council (ALEC) capitalized on the unique opportunity presented by the wave of state-level Republican victories in the 2010 midterm elections. In 2011 and 2012 alone, 15 states passed laws restricting public employees' collective bargaining rights (although three of these were later overturned in popular referenda). ALEC wrote model legislation and disseminated it to sympathetic elected officials in various states, an approach that proved highly effective.

Although this public-sector anti-union offensive was the most distinctive feature of the post-2008 labor landscape, anti-union efforts continued to escalate in the private sector as well. ALEC and other right-wing groups promoted proposals for "right-to-work" legislation, which prohibits collective bargaining agreements that require that all covered workers pay union dues. Right-to-work laws were introduced in 19 states in 2011 and 2012, and were soon passed in three former union bastions in the Midwest: Indiana in 2012, followed by Michigan in 2013 and Wisconsin in 2015. ALEC also promoted other types of labor legislation at the state level including bills eliminating New Deal-era "prevailing wage" laws that require firms with public contracts to pay the wages and benefits that the majority of workers in a region and occupation receive (in practice, typically those specified in collective bargaining agreements).

The conservative interests that animated ALEC also pursued their anti-union agenda in the federal courts. The most important example, *Friedrichs v. California Teachers Association*, became the focus of a dramatic set of developments during Obama's final year in office. *Friedrichs* challenged the right of public-sector unions to collect "fair share service fees," also known as "agency fees," to cover the cost of union representation for government workers who chose not to become union members. As the U.S. Supreme Court had established in a 1977 case, such fees had long been deemed lawful in light of the fact that unions are required to represent both members and non-members in collective bargaining. *Friedrichs* revisited this question, with the plaintiffs arguing that agency fees violated the First Amendment's guarantee of free speech.

Most observers had expected the Supreme Court to side with the plaintiffs, but the sudden death of Justice Antonin Scalia in 2016 instead led to a tied 4-4 vote, which meant the lower court decision, which favored the union, remained in force.[30] The subsequent success of conservatives in blocking Senate confirmation of any replacement for Scalia on the Court, and Donald Trump's choice of Neil Gorsuch for that position in 2017, set the stage for a replay of this drama. A new case pivoting on the same issue, *Janus v. AFSCME*, was decided by the Court in June 2018. As most observers had anticipated, the Court sided with the plaintiffs and struck down agency fees, which will be a major blow to public-sector union treasuries.

Alt-Labor and Blue State Legislative Initiatives

In the aftermath of EFCA's failure, hopes for labor movement revitalization have increasingly focused on the "alt-labor" (alternative labor) organizations that had begun to proliferate in the 1990s. Also known as "worker centers," these are not traditional unions but community-based groups that organize and advocate for low-wage immigrants and others concentrated at the bottom of the labor market. Alt-labor organizing campaigns typically involve "naming and shaming" employers who exploit such workers, focusing media and public attention on violations of labor and employment law, such as payment below the legal minimum wage (or in some cases outright nonpayment). Many worker centers also engage in litigation to secure back pay and other remedies for the victims. Initially, traditional unionists were skeptical about these efforts, but that had changed by the time Obama took office. By 2009, several labor unions as well as the AFL-CIO had entered into partnership agreements with worker centers, and some unions even began to emulate their tactics.

There were 160 worker centers in the United States in 2007; in the aftermath of the Great Recession, the number grew to over 200 by 2010 and, according to one estimate, to a total of 230 by 2013.[31] In addition, several worker centers that began as local operations expanded during this period into national operations. These include the Restaurant Opportunities Centers United (ROC-United), with 11 local organizations across the nation; the National Domestic Workers Alliance, with 42 affiliates; and the National Day Laborers Organizing Network, with 43 affiliates.[32] Other examples include the Food Chain Workers' Alliance (with which ROC-United is also affiliated) and the National Guestworker Alliance. Although there are no reliable data as to how many workers are affected by these efforts, many of which are modest in size, the Food Chain Workers' Alliance alone claims to represent 300,000 workers.

Another high-profile organizing initiative emerged in the wake of the 2011 Occupy Wall Street movement: the SEIU fast-food workers' campaign, centered on demands for wages of $15 per hour and the right to unionize. Launched in New York in late 2012, the "Fight for $15" soon spread nationwide, propelled by a series of one-day demonstration strikes that garnered extensive publicity. Although funded by a traditional labor union, the SEIU, this campaign was initially spearheaded by a community organization (New York Communities for Change), and it adopted the strategic repertoire of the worker center movement, shining a bright light on low wages and workplace abuses in the fast-food industry and operating entirely outside the NLRA framework. The Fight for $15 expanded to include workers in other low-wage sectors: in December 2014, April 2015, and November 2015, airport workers, domestic workers, convenience store employees, and even college-teaching adjuncts joined in the one-day strike demanding a $15 hourly wage. Another worker center-like union-sponsored campaign was OUR (Organization United for Respect) Walmart, which launched a series of "Black Friday" strikes as well as other efforts to put pressure on the nation's largest employer to improve its employment practices.

The $15 per hour demand first floated by the SEIU fast-food organizing also inspired efforts across the nation to raise the minimum wage in cities and counties where unions still had a strong presence and significant political leverage. Seattle and SeaTac in Washington State, along with San Francisco, Emeryville, and Los Angeles in California, and more recently New York City and State, all passed laws gradually raising the overall minimum hourly wage to $15 or more. Advocates also won more modest increases in minimum wages in more than a dozen other cities and states across the nation.

Like the Fight for $15 itself, these minimum-wage campaigns built directly on the Occupy movement's successes in raising public awareness of skyrocketing inequality. In 2014 alone, 14 states raised their statewide minimum wages.[33] At least two million workers benefitted from these new city-level laws from 2012 to 2016 alone, and about three million from the statewide minimum-wage increases legislated between 2008 and 2014. As of 2010, only a handful of cities had passed their own minimum-wage ordinances, but between 2012 and early 2016, 32 municipalities did so. In September 2015, seven cities in the San Francisco Bay Area announced plans to work together to establish a regional minimum wage, another recent innovation. Organized labor has also promoted a variety of legislative measures at the state and local levels aimed at improving the situation of low-wage workers, mandating benefits like paid family leave and paid sick days, and ramping up enforcement of state and local labor standards.[34]

These legislative initiatives as well as the spurt of alt-labor organizing efforts that emerged in the Obama years harken back to pre–New Deal labor movement strategies, in contrast to the NLRA-based union campaigns that dominated in the mid-twentieth century. In the Progressive Era, when unionization rates were comparable to those of the early twenty-first century, labor reform groups and their middle-class allies publicized sweatshops and employer abuses and provided educational and social services for immigrant workers in much the same way that worker centers do today. These reformers also campaigned for progressive legislation, including the first state minimum-wage laws. With the failure of EFCA and in an institutional environment increasingly hostile to unions, the labor movement has returned to its pre–New Deal strategic repertoire.[35]

ALEC and the other anti-union organizations allied with it have not stood by idly in the face of these new efforts. They argue that worker centers are unions in disguise and should be governed by the NLRA. That particular claim has not gained much traction, but in many states where Republicans have won political control, they have enacted preemption legislation that prohibits cities and counties from increasing minimum-wage laws or other measures benefitting workers. By 2017, 25 states had enacted minimum-wage preemption laws, 12 of which were passed after 2013, in direct response to the post-Occupy Wall Street wave of efforts to win minimum-wage increases at the city and county level. A few states have enacted blanket preemption laws designed to preclude local legislation on a wide variety of matters.[36] And a Republican-sponsored proposed federal law, H.R.4219, the "Workflex in the 21st Century Act," introduced in November 2017, would extend this logic to preempt all state and local paid leave laws.

CONCLUSION

Although Obama was far more supportive of unions than any president in decades, he was unable to deliver lasting gains to organized labor. The EFCA debacle was only the first blow. For six of his eight years in power, Republican control over Congress severely constrained Obama's room for maneuver, which was essentially limited to administrative actions—Executive Orders and DOL regulations and policies, as well as appointing DOL and NLRB officials. With the election of Donald Trump, moreover, most if not all of what Obama achieved in the labor policy arena will be reversed. Union power is increasingly confined to "Blue" states and cities; although some cherish the hope that on the national level, a day will come when the pendulum will swing back to the progressive side. As Obama himself remarked the day after Donald Trump was elected, "The path that this country has taken has never been a straight line. We zig and zag, and .... if we lose, we learn from our mistakes, we do some reflection, we lick our wounds, we brush ourselves off, we get back in the arena. We go at it. We try even harder the next time."[37]

NOTES

1. Obama, Barack. 2006. *The Audacity of Hope*. New York: Three Rivers Press.
2. Minchin, Timothy J. *Labor Under Fire: A History of the AFL-CIO Since 1979*. Chapel Hill: University of North Carolina Press.
3. Milkman, Ruth and Stephanie Luce. 2017. "Labor Unions and the Great Recession," *RSF: The Russell Sage Foundation Journal of the Social Sciences* 3(3): 145–65.
4. Obama, Barack. 2006. *The Audacity of Hope*. New York: Three Rivers Press.
5. Minchin, Timothy J. *Labor Under Fire: A History of the AFL-CIO Since 1979*. Chapel Hill: University of North Carolina Press.
   Warren, Dorian. 2010. "The American Labor Movement in the Age of Obama: The Challenges and Opportunities of a Racialized Political Economy," *Perspectives on Politics* 8(3): 847–60.
6. Lofaso, Anne Marie. 2011. "Promises, Promises: Assessing the Obama Administration's Record on Labor Reform," *New Labor Forum* 20(2): 65–72.
7. Warren, Dorian. 2010. "The American Labor Movement in the Age of Obama: The Challenges and Opportunities of a Racialized Political Economy," *Perspectives on Politics* 8(3): 847–60.
8. Hirsch, Barry T. and David A. MacPherson. 2017. *Union Membership and Earnings Data Book*. Bloomberg—Bureau of National Affairs.
9. Hamburger, Tom. 2009. "Labor Unions Find Themselves Card-Checked," *Los Angeles Times*, May 19.
10. Lofaso, Anne Marie. 2011. "Promises, Promises: Assessing the Obama Administration's Record on Labor Reform," *New Labor Forum* 20(2): 65–72.
11. See Warren, Dorian. 2011. "The Unsurprising Failure of Labor Law Reform and the Turn to Administrative Action," in Reaching for a New Deal, eds. Theda Skocpol and Lawrence R. Jacobs. New York: Russell Sage Foundation.
12. Cohen, Rachel. 2018. "How the Labor Movement Is Thinking Ahead to a Post-Trump World," *The Intercept* (Jan. 21) https://theintercept.com/2018/01/21/labor-movement-us-unions/

13. Meyerson, Harold. 2010. "Under Obama, Labor Should Have Made More Progress," *The Washington Post*, February 10.
14. Skocpol, Theda and Lawrence R. Jacobs, "Reaching for a New Deal: Ambitious Governance, Economic Meltdown and Polarized Politics," in *Reaching for a New Deal*, eds. Theda Skocpol and Lawrence R. Jacobs. New York: Russell Sage Foundation.
15. Warren, Dorian. 2011. "The Unsurprising Failure of Labor Law Reform and the Turn to Administrative Action," in Reaching for a New Deal, eds. Theda Skocpol and Lawrence R. Jacobs. New York: Russell Sage Foundation.
16. Warren, Dorian. 2011. "The Unsurprising Failure of Labor Law Reform and the Turn to Administrative Action," in Reaching for a New Deal, eds. Theda Skocpol and Lawrence R. Jacobs. New York: Russell Sage Foundation.
17. Semuels, Alana. 2017. "The Future of the Department of Labor under Trump," *The Atlantic*, March 6.
18. Scheiber, Noam. 2015. "As His Term Wanes, Obama Champion's Workers' Rights," *New York Times*, August 31.
    Gitis, Ben. 2017. "Obama-Era Labor Regulations: Where Are They Now?" *American Action Forum*, September 21. https://www.americanactionforum.org/insight/obama-era-labor-regulations-now/
19. Lofaso, Anne Marie. 2011. "Promises, Promises: Assessing the Obama Administration's Record on Labor Reform," *New Labor Forum* 20(2): 65–72.
20. Garden, Charlotte. 2015. "Toward Politically Stable NLRB Lawmaking: Rulemaking vs. Adjudication," *Emory Law Journal* 64: 1469–1494.
21. Moe, Terry. M. 1982. "Regulatory Performance and Presidential Administration," *American Journal of Political Science* 26(2): 197–224.
22. Green, Michael Z. 2015. "The NLRB as an Uberagency for the Evolving Workplace," *Emory Law Journal* 64: 1621–1646.
23. Green, Michael Z. 2015. "The NLRB as an Uberagency for the Evolving Workplace," *Emory Law Journal* 64: 1621–1646.
    Becker, Craig. 2012. "The Continuity of Collective Action and the Isolation of Collective Bargaining: Enforcing Federal Labor Law in the Obama Administration" *Berkeley Journal of Employment & Labor Law* 33: 401–17.
24. Becker, Craig. 2012. "The Continuity of Collective Action and the Isolation of Collective Bargaining: Enforcing Federal Labor Law in the Obama Administration" *Berkeley Journal of Employment & Labor Law* 33: 401–17.
25. Lewin, Tamar. 2014, "Labor Ruling Could Allow More Faculty to Unionize," *New York Times*, December 22.

Scheiber, Noam. 2016. "Grad Students Win Right to Unionize in an Ivy League Case," *New York Times*, August 23.

DePillis, Lydia. 2015. "Labor Board's Shift in Legal Interpretation Could Allow Many Taxi Drivers to Unionize," *Washington Post* Wonkblog, October 29. https://www.washingtonpost.com/news/wonk/wp/2015/10/29/labor-boards-shift-in-legal-interpretation-could-allow-thousands-of-taxi-drivers-to-unionize/?utm_term=.679ec54ab7e4

26. Scheiber, Noam. 2015. "As His Term Wanes, Obama Champion's Workers' Rights," *New York Times*, August 31.

27. Scheiber, Noam. 2017. "Labor Board Reverses Ruling That Helped Workers Fight Chains," *New York Times*, December 14.

28. Milkman, Ruth and Stephanie Luce. 2017. "Labor Unions and the Great Recession," *RSF: The Russell Sage Foundation Journal of the Social Sciences* 3(3): 145–65.

29. Milkman, Ruth and Stephanie Luce. 2017. "Labor Unions and the Great Recession," *RSF: The Russell Sage Foundation Journal of the Social Sciences* 3(3): 145–65.

Lafer, Gordon. 2017. *The One Percent Solution: How Corporations are Remaking America One State at a Time.* Cornell University Press.

30. Liptak, Adam. 2016. "Victory for Unions as Supreme Court, Scalia Gone, Ties 4–4," *New York Times*, March 29.

31. Fine, Janice. 2011. "New Forms to Settle Old Scores: Updating the Worker Center Story in the United States," *Relations Industrielles/Industrial Relations* 66: 604–30.

Narro, Victor. 2013. "Perspectives: Worker Centers and the AFL-CIO National Convention," *Law at the Margins* blog, September 3. Available at: http://lawatthemargins.com/perspectives-worker-centers-and-the-afl-cio-national-convention/

32. Fine, Janice. 2015. "Alternative labour protection movements in the United States: Reshaping industrial relations?" *International Labour Review* 154(1): 15–26.

33. Luce, Stephanie. 2015. "$15 per Hour or Bust: An Appraisal of the Higher Wages Movement," *New Labor Forum* 24(2): 73–78.

34. Milkman, Ruth and Stephanie Luce. 2017. "Labor Unions and the Great Recession," *RSF: The Russell Sage Foundation Journal of the Social Sciences* 3(3): 145–65.

35. Milkman, Ruth. "Back to the Future? U.S. Labor in the New Gilded Age," *British Journal of Industrial Relations* 51: 645–66.

36. Riverstone-Newell, Lori. 2017. "The Rise of State Preemption Laws in Response to Local Policy Innovation," *Publius: The Journal of Federalism*, 47(3): 403–425.

37. https://obamawhitehouse.archives.gov/the-press-office/2016/11/09/statement-president

Swimming the Multiple Currents: The Political and Racial Time of Barack Obama's Presidency

Kimberley S. Johnson

The presidency of Barack H. Obama was, in his words, an improbability: a man with the middle name of Hussein who was born in Hawaii, a grandson of white Kansas' Greatest Generation; and the son of a Kenyan student, was the least likely person to have been elected to the American presidency. Yet, he was elected; and now that this two-term administration is over, political scientists and historians can begin to put the Obama presidency into a broader historical and political context. Understanding the Obama presidency means placing his administration not only in what some political scientists call "political time," but also in what I call "racial time" as well.

Obama's presidency cannot be understood by looking at it through an institutional lens; nor should an evaluation of his presidency take place solely through the lens of racial politics. Instead, inasmuch as Obama would have argued, we must do both. The Obama presidency cannot be understood unless we evaluate him within the contours of American polit-

K. S. Johnson (✉)
New York University, New York, NY, USA
e-mail: kj37@nyu.edu

© The Author(s) 2019   133
W. C. Rich (ed.), *Looking Back on President Barack Obama's Legacy*,
https://doi.org/10.1007/978-3-030-01545-9_7

ical institutions. Yet at the same time, we cannot divorce American political institutions—from how they are shaped to how they structure politics and policies—without placing America's racial orders as an important constituent element of the American political system.[1] Obama was a *black president* inhabiting both political as well as racial time.[2] This duality shaped Obama's presidency into a singular presidency whose successes as well as failures will be endlessly debated as those evaluations will be contingent on where a judge stands within both political and racial time.

At its beginning, Barack Obama's presidency seemed to confirm theories of the presidency rooted in "political time." By political time is meant the interplay between what Stephen Skowronek has called institutional orderings of the presidency: constitutional, organizational, and political.[3] By constitutional, it is meant the "political disruption" that ensues as each president "seizes control of the formal powers of his office and attempts to exercise them in his own right." Organizational orderings are the "institutional resources, relationship and responsibilities" that make up the "working modes of governmental operation." The third element is "political ordering" defined as the "government's basic commitments of ideology and interests [which] have tended to congeal institutionally around relatively durable partisan regimes, and those orderings frame the recurrent pattern of founding, fragmenting and disintegrative governing coalition and party systems."[4] All presidents both shape and are shaped by these political orderings. In short, a president doesn't stand out of time or orders/arrangements—they are deeply embedded within these arrangements. Yet, within each presidency is a unique individual who simply by inhabiting the office changes the "range of political possibilities." Obama, then, can be seen as a president who can be fitted within previously identified types of presidencies.

At the same time, Obama's political premise was based on a racial premise—not one in which he was the embodiment of the Civil Rights revolution, but rather a racial premise rooted in an embodiment of a postracial transcendence. Certainly, Obama would make the claim via his white mother and Kenyan father that he was a physical manifestation of his ability and eagerness to transcend the still raw wounds that slavery, Jim Crow, the Civil Rights movement and white backlash had kept barely managed. His Kenyan father, largely absent from his childhood, would play a pivotal role in his origin story of *Dreams of My Father*, marking Obama of African descent, but isolating him from the still publicly verboten aspects of slavery and Jim Crow that American society had deemed not fit for public discussion.[5] At the same time that Obama would make claims to a post-racial and post-"political" transcendence, he would also stake a claim to be carrying forth the mantle of the Civil Rights movement or at least a hoped-for "color-blind" post-racialism.

In his way then, Obama inhabited racial time. By racial time, I mean the particular structuring of ideas, institutions, practices and beliefs rooted around notions of "race" that shape the boundaries of black and white lives at particular moments in time. These kinds of structures can be thought of as racial orders.[6] Thus the antebellum United States was a distinctive racial order, as was the Jim Crow order which followed Reconstruction. The "long civil rights movement" of the twentieth century culminated in what King and Lieberman have called the Civil Rights State. This Civil Rights state—always contested—entered the beginnings of its decline with the Reagan administration and its embrace of "color-blind" policy.[7] Thus, in Barack Obama's presidency, racial time could not but intersect with the political time of his presidency leading to a president who could only both exceed and fall short of the impossible demands imposed by the cross-currents of time within which he was embedded.

PLACING BARACK OBAMA IN POLITICAL TIME

Outside of political scientists and historians, the most common ways the "political time" of presidencies is understood is via the metric of "presidential greatness." Will a president be a success or a failure? How much can a president shape his or her legacy, and how much of a president's actions is constrained by the hand of history? For Obama, the expectations were outsized—and indeed improbably so—because of his race but also because of the economic crisis that was engulfing the United States and global economy. When *Time* magazine pictured him on its cover as an ersatz Franklin Roosevelt wearing a jaunty fedora and cigarette holder in his mouth, the raised expectations were made clear.[8] Not only was Obama to be the first black president, he was also destined to be an FDR, much greater and less tarnished than the last occupants of the White House, Bill Clinton and his wife Hillary Rodham Clinton, who had just lost a bruising Democratic primary to Obama. Indeed, the journalist Andrew Sullivan saw Obama as a needed break from the post-Vietnam War baby-boomer politics that had paralyzed the American political system during the Clinton era.[9]

How then to understand Obama? Skowronek's model of presidential leadership is one way. Skowronek's model posited four broad types of presidencies: (1) politics of reconstruction; (2) politics of disjunction; (3) politics of preemption; and (4) politics of articulation.[10] Given Obama's emergence in a moment of economic and political crisis, as well as his political and rhetorical commitments—a politics of articulation—which exist when "established commitments of ideology and interest are relatively resilient, providing solutions to the governing problems of the day"—was not a possibility.[11] While the failures of the Bush administration precluded a politics of articulation, so too was a politics of disjunction as Obama seemed both able and willing to "break free from weakened political and institutional commitments."[12]

The two paths lay before Obama:—prospectively—and given the out-size expectations—was the path of reconstructive politics. Retrospectively, however, Obama's presidency was not one of reconstruction but rather of preemption. Certainly, a politics of reconstruction seemed possible at the beginning of Obama's presidency since under a reconstructive politics, the reigning political order has proven vulnerable opening the way up for a president who can engage in a "wholesale reconstruction of the standards of legitimate national government."

Yet implacable Republican and hard right opposition, as well as Obama's own political disposition and commitments stayed his ability or desire to embrace a reconstructive politics. Obama ultimately embodied a fourth type of presidency—a "politics of preemption" in which presidents are opposition leaders whose authority is constrained by the "political, institutional, and ideological supports that the old establishments maintains."

The path to Obama's preemptive presidency initially seemed to take a reconstructive aspect. First, the faltering of what had been touted by Karl Rove as a "permanent majority" that opened up the possibility of Obama leading the Democrats into a new moment that would capitalize on the growth of a new liberal coalition that united the college educated, suburban white women, people of color, the LGBTQ community and left/progressives. While union households and the white working class were welcome to join, the media focused on the literally more colorful—and in some ways more culturally resonant—elements of the new Obama coalition in which some of the media saw in themselves.

New coalitional possibilities were just one of the only elements which animated beliefs that the Obama presidency would be reconstructive/

transformative. The other key element was the collapse of the housing and real estate market, which in turn led to a collapse of the American economy as well as the global economy. The rise of the tech industry and social media also portended the emergence of a new economy in which brains not brawn would definitively prevail, and one in which economic relations were "free" and "fluid" based on "gigs" and "personal branding" rather than the stable (and sometimes unionized), long-term jobs of the industrial era. For some, this presaged a new era of worker mobility and freedom, while to others it signaled further economic impoverishment as employer-based social welfare system disappeared as the "gig economy" gained market share. Thus, part of Obama's reconstructive mandate was to figure out how to move American society and its employer-centered social welfare system away from one based on manufacturing and large corporations to a new social contract based on rising numbers of people employed in part-time, temporary or contingent positions, where family, health insurance and retirement benefits were simply unavailable.

Of these mandates to move the two key elements of the American social welfare system into the twenty-first century, Obama proved to be non-transformational. In the education arena, rather than repudiating No Child Left Behind and the broader school reform agenda of charter schools, high stakes testing, and so on, Obama in fact embraced it with the development of his Race to the Top Program. Rhetorically, he would tell audiences that the problem of growing economic inequality was not the economic forces that had triggered the Great Recession but rather a belief that the United States couldn't compete in global markets because Americans lacked "skills." Education and especially higher education would be the path forward.

Left unacknowledged was that global competition in the form of low wages and less stringent regulation—as well as American tax and industrial policy had effectively gutted manufacturing. College for all could not be a panacea for a global race to the bottom or a bulwark in the face of rising automation and AI. The appearance of the Occupy Movement in 2011 and the subsequent public discussion or economic inequality—which had not really happened in the first two years of Obama's presidency—finally got an airing. And with this airing, at least economically speaking, any pretension that Obama was a reconstructive president was laid to rest. Rather than forcefully addressing the growing impact of Wall Street, the financializing of the economy, and the broader forces of neoliberalism, Obama, whether by choice or by the constraints placed on him, chose to embrace a reformist path. While these reforms—ranging from Dodd-Frank to the Consumer Financial Protection Board—were needed, they did not fundamentally change the country's economic path and particularly the yawning gap between the 1% and the rest.

Health care reform, which had notably eluded the Clinton administration, became the other element in making the claim for a reconstructive Obama presidency. By Obama's election, both liberals and conservatives recognized the growing crisis of health affordability and coverage, as well as the rising amount of the nation's GDP that the health care sector consumed. Each side had put forth policy proposals that attempted to address these problems. The Great Recession exacerbated this crisis as unemployment skyrocketed and many of those formerly comfortably ensconced in (or in many cases teetering on the edge of) the middle class saw themselves and their children subject to precariousness of health care and its attendant financial risks. Yet, even in this policy arena, where there was consensus that something had to be done, Obama stepped back from a truly transformative policy change. To be fair, one could argue that he was constrained by political and institutional structures. Though Obama had a majority Democratic Congress, he had a significant number of Democrats on the right who favored minimal reform; while on his left were Democrats who pushed for a more comprehensive approach.

True to his transcendent rhetoric, Obama pushed mightily for a plan that bore strong similarities to plans put together by then moderate groups like the Heritage Foundation and political figures like former Massachusetts governor, Mitt Romney. In the end, while Obama did manage to push through a health care reform bill, the Affordable Health Care Act (ACA) or "Obamacare," it came at a huge political cost. It animated the "Tea Party" movement and others, some of whom argued that the ACA was a form of reparations. Thus, in this moment of triumph, a major political achievement (a "big f*****g deal" in the words of Joe Biden) was reduced to racial reparations payback at best, and the rise of imminent Bolshevism at worse.[13]

At the close of his second edition of *Presidential Leadership in Political Time*, Skowronek noted that while Obama, based on his own rhetoric as well as the political and economic crisis brewing in the 2008 election year, may have had the capacity to be a reconstructive president; by the time of Skowronek's 2011 reappraisal, the possibilities of reconstruction had worn off. Instead of a re-ordering of politics, presidential time had pushed Obama into a politics of preemption.

Indeed, far from being able to create a new set of political commitments and ideologies that would strengthen his political prospects, the Obama presidency had created a relatively cohesive oppositional coalition. This new coalition brought together the faltering elements of the Republican coalition that had begun to splinter as George W. Bush's final term came to its dispiriting end, as well as a growing number of primarily white voters who were either unable to vote for Hillary Clinton and/or embraced the economic anxiety/white identity politics ultimately articulated by Donald Trump.

Obama was a reconstructive-like figure; but not for the Democrats but rather for the Republicans who won a decisive 2010 midterm elections—a "shellacking"—after which any further Obama victories or even normal day-to-day exercises of presidential authority would be continually contested and ultimately blocked. By the end of his presidency, Obama-governed power and authority lay largely constrained by a deeply hostile and recalcitrant Republican-majority Congress. Obama's promise of political transcendence was unfulfilled. Political polarization not bipartisanship had come to define his presidency. In this way, Obama left office not as FDR but rather like Johnson or Carter, an attempt to define a new order was repudiated and the old order that it was focused on was able to reconstitute itself.

In retrospect, Obama's ability to affect a transformative effect on the presidency was in fact highly constrained not only by political and secular time but also racial time. Obama's presidency reshaped and reconfigured by the racial politics that emerged out of his identity as a *black* president and out of the new racial order that had already been under construction since at least the Clinton presidency.

PLACING BARACK OBAMA IN RACIAL TIME

The second claim of this essay is that Obama's presidency cannot be understood separately from his racial identity. Obama not only engaged in presidential political orderings, but he engaged in racial re-ordering as well. This claim may be a puzzle as Obama repeatedly backed away from presenting himself as nothing more than a symbol of racial transcendence. Yet even as he was developing and deploying this symbolism, he also engaged in twenty-first century racial politics. By racial politics, I draw on Hanchard and Chung's definition of racial politics as a mode of politics wherein the "idea of race is invoked and practiced in political rhetoric, electoral competition, and public opinion as well as other modes of political competition and conflict."[14] "Race" and by extension, racial politics is a political phenomenon wherein racial identity is not a given; rather racial identity is constructed by political institutions and processes across time and across changing historical contexts.[15] Obama's repeated invocation of both his Kansas grandparents and the Chicago Southside roots of Michelle Obama—were attempts to create post-Civil Right Era definition of race as not something biologically immutable but rather a choice of community and culture. If race was a choice, it could also be in the Obama worldview, an identity to be affirmatively embraced within a framework of tolerance and inclusion. Race could be transcended by appeals to everyone's "American-ness."

Yet here as well, Obama's framing of race actually embodies a new kind of racial politics: a neoliberal politics of race in which structural inequalities are elided away in favor of neoliberal approach in which the failures of capitalism vis-à-vis black and brown communities are laid at the feet of the individuals most oppressed by the political and economic structures of neoliberalism.[16] Like all workers in a neoliberal economy, it was up to African Americans to develop their own human capital. The racial twist on this was that under the neoliberal rubric, blacks (in-)ability to develop their human capital was not a result of decades of under- and dis-investment in schools, housing and communities; nor was it the result of the spreading tentacles of mass incarceration state whose broad and insidious reach created in many communities a virtual school-to-prison pipeline. Instead, Obama would repeatedly refer to the lack of responsibility and particularly the "absence of black fathers" as both the cause as well as the solution for the devastating economic inequality that afflicted black communities. These policy prescriptions, which culminated with the rolling out of his program, My Brother's Keepers, was a neoliberal racial politics in which the state was not obligated to address inequality, rather it was the legitimation of a particularly neoliberal belief system, that it was up to each individual (or their community) to confront the racial inequity of the market on their own.

The neoliberal politics of race was not only deployed against blacks, it was also deployed against whites. If race was a choice, so too was racism especially if that racism was derived from economic anxiety. Obama's major utterances on white racism are telling. In the first instance, Obama was recorded as saying that some whites "clung to the guns and religion" as a result of their real (or perceived) economic marginalization.[17] Implicit in that judgment was a belief that a lack of success in the "market" leads to atavistic beliefs such as racism. Hence the solution to white racism was not condemnation, but rather understanding; and more importantly, making ever more visible the administration's efforts to make the "market" work for whites. Such an approach rests upon a deeply neoliberal belief that humans are rational actors; and that given the cost-benefit calculus of "clinging to racism" and coal jobs versus jobs in the solar industry, whites would choose the latter. Indeed, in the aftermath of Reverend Jeremiah's Wrights sermons condemning white racism, Obama gave a speech on race that was widely lauded by white liberals.[18] In this speech, while he acknowledged past white racism, Obama hastened to reassure whites that Wright's views on race was a "profoundly distorted view of this country—a view that sees white racism as endemic, and that elevates what is wrong with America above all that we know is right with America."

Obama in this speech while acknowledging the past effects of discrimination and segregation and allowing for lingering ongoing inequality admonishes blacks for not letting go of the past and taking responsibility for deficiencies in education, housing and families. For whites, Obama offers an exculpatory hand,

> Just as black anger often proved counterproductive, so have these white resentments distracted attention from the real culprits of the middle class squeeze—a corporate culture rife with inside dealing, questionable accounting practices, and short-term greed; a Washington dominated by lobbyists and special interests; economic policies that favor the few over the many. And yet, to wish away the resentments of white Americans, to label them as misguided or even racist, without recognizing they are grounded in legitimate concerns—this too widens the racial divide and blocks the path to understanding.[19]

The goal then of neoliberal racial politics is to address racial inequality and animosity not by addressing what he calls the "stalemate" of race, but rather making all citizens better able to compete for jobs, education and housing. While stating that racism comes out of a belief that we live in a zero-sum society, Obama's response was not to fundamentally change that society, but rather to give everyone a chance to compete, and to not especially and visibly hinder the status of whites.

Yet, while Obama can be (and certainly was) criticized for this speech, a more charitable understanding of the speech can be seen. As the embodiment post-Civil Rights racial reconciliation and progress, Obama could not acknowledge black pain—that would be entirely too credulous for mainstream white liberal supporters (and insulting and perhaps a bridge too far for his black supporters as well). At the same time, however, the impact of an even older structuring of racial time—"race relations"—can be seen in his approach. By "race relations," it is meant a mode of racial politics that "emphasize[s] an implementation strategy to obtain peaceful and consensual relations between the two races even if the result is the domination of one and the subordination of the other."[20]

The "race relations" approach places considerations of race and politics as secondary, as something to be examined elsewhere or at some other time. Fundamental to race relations' modes of time is the belief that American political system is basically healthy except for "race relations," which require management to minimize antagonism not between races, but rather antagonism and fear from whites toward blacks. Under racial relations, whites could never be held fully accountable for the past. Instead, the metric is defined as how harmonious or not was their perception of their relationship with those who lay on the darker side of the color line. The logic of neoliberalism in many ways follows the logic of race relations, although with the extension of class as well as race as being outside of the pale of argument.

CONCLUSION

In perhaps one of the most unfortunate subtitles in recent political analysis, Shelby Steele in his book, *A Bound Man: Why We Are Excited About Obama and Why He Can't Win*—wrote that Barack Obama's ability to find his political voice would be fundamentally constrained by the dual position many black leaders found themselves to be in: both bargainer and challenger.[21] In the former, black leaders downplay race as a way for racial politics to not be deployed against them. By the same token, to be taken as credible especially by black voters, black leaders must in some way challenge or obliquely confront the role of white racism in creating black inequality. This delicate dance between acknowledgment and abnegation is central to a deracialization strategy that black leaders have employed in the wake of the Civil Rights State.[22]

Certainly, Obama's embrace of a neoliberal politics of race in which politics of admonishment and/or responsibility toward blacks, as well as a plea for transcendence from whites reflected the deracialization strategy, he embraced as both bargainer as well as challenger.[23] As the *black* president, Obama essentially took structural racial inequality off the table for discussion while proposing "beer summits" and individual responsibility as the solution to the everyday racial aggressions encountered by blacks. With the full logic of neoliberalism racial politics behind him, black members of the Obama coalition found themselves unable to call attention to the particularities of American racial inequality that market solutions not only failed to solve but, in some case, exacerbated.

As a result of these twin embraces, Obama and indeed mainstream black leadership was caught off-guard by the emergence of Black Lives Matter movement (much like mainstream Democrats had been caught off-guard by the Occupy Movement. The feeble response of Obama to these killings (in part because he was politically and racially *bound*), and the widespread publicized display of militarized police repression marked in some ways the end of the Civil Rights State and the beginning of a new racial time. The neoliberal race politics embodied by Obama could not address a new moment in which right-wing white populism sought a new racial order in which whites could be assured of political and social ascendancy after putatively losing it under the Obama administration.

Obama's presidency was thus similarly bound—by political time and by racial time. Obama did not question—at least publicly—the ascendant worldview of neoliberalism. Markets for all were taken to be a given—the best that a liberal could do would be to ensure that all had a fair shot at competing and succeeding in these markets. Thus, critics on the farther left quickly understood that no grand "new" New Deal of infrastructure spending or War on Poverty-like social programs would be forthcoming. Such programs identified groups of winners and losers, rather than the empowered rational actors that neoliberal governance preferred. But more importantly, the political time of party coalitions and commitments also haunted Obama's ability to be truly transformative. Democrats had regained the White House but the grip of neoliberal orthodoxy made the party leadership shy away from policies and programs that would have cemented a new political ordering. While voter outreach and get out the vote efforts brought new voters in who were crucial to Obama's win, this organizational structure was not made permanent. Charisma and a bad economy had helped to bring Obama into office, but the Democratic Party did not seem to be interested in making permanent the grassroots political organization that had brought Obama into office. Tolerance and diversity certainly brought old and new supporters together, but these connections would never be cemented via policy such as labor-friendly policies like card check that could have shored up the desperately needed union vote. Indeed, while extolling the American immigration story, Obama would step up deportations of undocumented America residents. Only toward the end of his term, would Obama move to tentatively unwind America's carceral state, while at the same time he stepped up drone strikes against majority Muslim countries.

Race also came to be bound up in shaping the way his political time and his presidential orderings unfolded. While Republicans since the Clinton presidency had long demonized and attempted to de-legitimate Democratic leadership and the party, Obama's election raised it to a new level. From the beginning of his administration, Republicans pledged to remain implacable in their opposition. This implacable opposition was reflected in small and large ways from the unprecedented death threats issued against him, to having his family (particularly his daughters) slandered, to being publicly insulted in his State of the Union speech by a member of Congress.

While the rise of Tea Party was an early sign of the de-legitimization of Obama's presidency, it was the rise of birtherism (and related claims about Obama's religion, his elitism and his lack of "love for America") which would rejuvenate the ailing Republican coalition into a proto-populist party with white supremacy moving from its fringes to its core. It is the rise of birtherism that makes Obama's presidency *sui generis*. All presidents face criticism, and indeed many face invective and slander—yet no president in recent history had their fundamental right to be president—their citizenship questioned and treated as if it was a perfectly acceptable topic for debate. This slow drip of de-legitimation was accompanied by the final shattering of political norms and understandings (particularly in Congress) that had become undone since at least the Clinton administration. The Obama presidency made the final shattering of these norms justified. Mitch McConnell, the Senate Majority Leader, could state that Obama could not appoint a vacancy on the Supreme Court with more than a year left in his presidency because "the people" need a chance to have a say. By implication, Obama and his coalition were not legitimate representatives for "the people." Far from transformative, the Obama presidency ended in a fog of nostalgia, and with a political legacy that could and would be swiftly dismantled. In the end, far from being a reconstructive president, and rather than being the orthodox-innovator that he intrinsically was, Obama was forced into a preemptive presidency whose contested legitimacy based in part because of his race. This in turn has set the stage for the disjunctive presidency which has followed Obama's.

Will Obama be considered a "great president"? At the time of this chapter's publication it is certainly too early to tell. At least though at first glance, the prospects for greatness lay more in his race than in his office. The durability of his political and institutional changes triggered by his inhabitance of the office has yet to be seen. If they do endure, then perhaps he will be recognized both as a great president, and as a great black president. Yet, Obama's election also triggered a virulent racialized "frontlash" in which new racial orderings are imagined and articulated. The question remains open about whether Obama's time in office will be subjected to what W.E.B. DuBois called the "propaganda of history."[24] Will Obama's legacy be similar to the fate of southern black office holders in the Reconstruction South—held as failures rather than the brave pioneering politicians that they actually were? Time—and the voices of political scientists and historians—will tell.

NOTES

1. See Kimberley S. Johnson, "The Color Line and the State: Race and American Political Development," *The Oxford Handbook of American Political Development,* Robert C. Lieberman, Suzanne Mettler, Rick Valelly, eds. (Oxford University Press, 2016); on racial orders see Desmond King and Rogers Smith, "Racial Orders and American Political Development" *APSR* 99 (2005): 75–92; also see Michael Omi and Howard Winant, eds., *Racial Formation in the United States: From the 1960s to the 1990s* (New York: Routledge, 1994).
2. On Obama as a "black president" see Ta-Nehisi Coates, *We Were Eight Years In Power: An American Tragedy* (One World Books, 2017).
3. The broader discussions of presidential types and times comes from two sources: Stephen Skowronek, *The Politics Presidents Make: Leadership form John Adams to Bill Clinton* (Cambridge. MA: Belknap Press of Harvard University Press, 1997); and, *Presidential Leadership in Political Time: Reprise and Reappraisal* (Lawrence, KA: University Press of Kansas, 2011 (rev)).
4. See also Skowronek and Orren's (2004) definition of "political order" as a "constellation of rules, institutions, practices, and ideas that hang together over time, a bundle of patterns...exhibiting coherence and predictability while other things change around them" (Karen Orren and Stephen Skowronek, *The Search for American Political Development* (Cambridge University Press, 2004), pp.14–15.

5. Barack Obama, *Dreams From My Father: A Story of Race and Inheritance* (Broadway Books, 2004); as well as his *The Audacity of Hope* (Vintage, 2008).

6. For fuller discussion of racial orders, see Johnson, "The Color Line and the State," and King and Smith, "Racial Orders and American Political Development".

7. For discussion of Civil Rights State, see Desmond King and Robert Lieberman, "The Civil Rights State," in K. Morgan & A. Orloff (Eds.), *The Many Hands of the State: Theorizing Political Authority and Social Control* (Cambridge: Cambridge University Press, 2017); and Hanes Walton, Jr., *When the Marching Stopped The Politics of Civil Rights Regulatory Agencies* (SUNY Press, 1988).

8. See Peter Beinart, "The New New Deal: What Barack Obama Can Learn from F.D.R. and What the Democrats need to do," *Time* (November 24, 2008).

9. See Andrew Sullivan, "Goodbye to All That: Why Obama Matters," *The Atlantic*, December 2007.

10. For quotations see Skowronek, *The Politics Presidents Make*, pp. 39–44.

11. According to Skowronek, presidents in this mode are "orthodox-innovators" who "galvanize political action with promises to continue the good work of the past and demonstrate the vitality of the established order in changing times. As the fount of political orthodoxy, their office is a sacred trust full of obligations to uphold the gospel and deliver the expected services in the prescribed manner," p. 41.

12. Indeed according to Skowronek, the disjunctive president "can neither shore up the faltering system nor repudiate it," p. 39.

13. See Christopher S. Parker, and Matt A. Barreto. *Change They Can't Believe In: The Tea Party and Reactionary Politics in America* (Princeton University Press, 2013). For Biden quote see "Joe Biden: This a Big Fucking Deal," *The Guardian*, March 23, 2010.

14. See Michael Hanchard and Erin Aeran Chung, "From Race Relations to Comparative Racial Politics: A Survey of Cross-National Scholarship in Race in the Social Sciences," *DuBois Review* 1: 2(2004): 319–343, 332.

15. We can also think of this as a "racial order," defined as a political order in which "political actors… adopted (and often adapted) racial concepts, commitments, and aims in order to bind together their coalitions and structure governing institutions that express and serve their architects," King and Smith, 2005, p. 75.

16. On neoliberalism and black politics, see Michael C. Dawson and Megan Ming Francis, "Black Politics and the Neoliberal Racial Order," *Public Culture* 1 January 2016; 28 (1 (78)): 23–62.; as well as Lester K. Spence, *Knocking the Hustle: Against the Neoliberal Turn in Black Politics* (Brooklyn, NY: Punctum Books, 2015).

17. Obama quote from Katharine Q. Seelye and Jeff Zeleny, "On the Defensive, Obama Calls His Words Ill-Chosen," *New York Times*, April 13, 2008.
18. Jeremiah Wright speech from Brian Ross, "Obama's Pastor: God Damn America, U.S. to Blame for 9/11," ABC News; "Barack Obama's Speech on Race [transcript], *New York Times*, March 18, 2008.
19. See "Barack Obama's Speech on Race [transcript], *New York Times*, March 18, 2008.
20. See Hanes Walton and Robert C. Smith, "The Race Variable and the American Political Science Association's State of the Discipline Reports and Books, 1907–2002." In *African American Perspectives on Political Science*, edited by Wilbur C. Rich (Philadelphia: Temple University Press, 2007), p. 28.
21. See Shelby Steele, *A Bound Man: Why We Are Excited About Obama and Why He Can't Win* (Free Press, 2007); but also see Ralph J. Bunche, *A Brief and Tentative Analysis of Negro Leadership.* Edited by Jonathan Scott Holloway (NYU Press, 2005).
22. For early discussion of deracialization see Georgia Persons, ed. *Dilemmas of Black Politics* (HarperCollins 1993).
23. See Fredrick Harris's *The Price of the Ticket: Barack Obama and the Rise and Decline of Black Politics* (Oxford University Press, 2012).
24. See the chapter "The Propaganda of History," in W.E.B. DuBois, *Black Reconstruction in America, 1860–1880* (Free Press 1997 [1935]).

The Legacy of President Obama in the U.S. Supreme Court

Isaac Unah and Ryan Williams

The election of Barack Obama in November 2008 was heralded as a new beginning for the United States and for institutional governance. Americans were growing increasingly weary from two long wars far away in Afghanistan and Iraq and from the growing threat of international terrorism. Domestically, the nation was experiencing a devastating economic recession. The housing market bubble popped and the credit market crashed, bringing great losses and pain to American households. Approximately 11.1 million persons were out of work, pushing the national unemployment rate to 7.2 percent and climbing.[1] Private capital retreated, making it extremely difficult for small businesses and ordinary citizens to borrow money to finance economic projects. Amid this devastation, Americans entrusted their future to a 47-year-old African American man "with a funny name!"[2] In that sense, Obama's election was also seen as a hopeful sign for improved race relations and a dialing back of social class and political friction in America (Esposito and Finley-Barry 2009).

I. Unah (✉) • R. Williams
Department of Political Science, University of North Carolina
at Chapel Hill, Chapel Hill, NC, USA
e-mail: unah@unc.edu

© The Author(s) 2019   149
W. C. Rich (ed.), *Looking Back on President Barack Obama's Legacy*,
https://doi.org/10.1007/978-3-030-01545-9_8

For the U.S. Supreme Court, Obama's election presented an opportunity to address important legal conflicts. Issues such as protections for civil rights and liberties, voting rights, same-sex relationships, religious freedom, immigration rights, discrimination, affordable healthcare for Americans, and gun rights would likely compete for space on the Court's crowded plenary agenda. Expectations were extremely high for the new president; after all, he campaigned on the comforting and unifying themes of hope and change and his election marked a significant swing to the left from his predecessor, George W. Bush. However, as a former community organizer, Obama understood that political and legal change takes time and requires diligence and perseverance. But these ideals would be insufficient. To meet his pressing goals and fulfill campaign promises, Obama would also need some luck in the creation of vacancies in the Supreme Court, vacancies that he could fill with individuals whose role orientations as jurists could support his policy agenda while maintaining fidelity to the Constitution and the rule of law.

In this chapter, we examine Obama's legacy in the Supreme Court. We argue that Obama's presidency produced a mixed record. He experienced both successes and challenges in attempting to shape the Court in his own image, but he largely succeeded in using the Supreme Court to secure some of his biggest policy victories as president. Ultimately, Obama's biggest and perhaps insufficiently acknowledged success was in slowing down the aggressive rightward shift of the Court with his appointment of two relatively liberal female justices. These appointees, Elena Kagan and Sonia Sotomayor, became effective counterweights to the Court's conservative majority but have not moved the Court dramatically to the left. Moreover, analysis of Obama's judicial legacy would be incomplete without examining his appointments to lower federal courts. We tackle this aspect of his legacy by documenting both Obama's difficulties in filling these lower federal judgeships and his remarkable success in improving descriptive representation on the federal bench.

Our discussion proceeds in four sections. The first section addresses Obama's overall success in the Supreme Court during his two terms as president compared to the success of other recent presidents, including Reagan, H.W. Bush, Clinton, and W. Bush, and considers Obama's track record of appointments to the lower federal courts. The second section examines how Obama's tenure helped shape the landscape of judicial selection to the Supreme Court. We focus on the politics surrounding the selection of Justices Sotomayor and Kagan. Most importantly, we examine the President's failed nomination of Court of Appeals for the District of Columbia Chief Judge Merrick Garland to fill the vacancy created by the sudden death of conservative icon Justice Antonin Scalia on February 13, 2016. The political machinations and procedural changes in Senate rules prompted by efforts to fill Scalia's seat have the greatest potential to alter the institutional foundations of Senate confirmation of Supreme Court nominees for the foreseeable future. In the third section, we analyze Obama's Supreme Court legacy by comparing the performance of Obama's Justices to the performance of the justices they replaced on the Court. Most observers, as well as ideologically-based theories of judicial behavior, would expect the voting pattern of Obama's Justices to lean heavily in a liberal direction. But does this expectation hold up when subjected to close empirical scrutiny? In the last section of the chapter, we analyze some of the big cases and monumental legal issues of the Obama Era, focusing on the domestic issues of healthcare, marriage equality, and immigration.

BARACK OBAMA AND THE GROWING EXPANSION OF JUDICIAL POWER

Throughout much of American history, the development of constitutional doctrine on the relationship between the executive branch and the Supreme Court has prized judicial restraint and deference to executive authority over judicial activism and policy innovativeness by justices. Because ours is a government of separate institutions sharing power, the defining feature of the relationship between the Supreme Court and the executive branch is a tendency toward deference to the unique constitutional authority and prerogatives inherent in each other.

The Supreme Court's role is to "patrol" the boundaries of the Constitution as a way of checking the actions of the other branches and bringing them into compliance with the Constitution and the rule of law. As such, the Supreme Court does occasionally hold the president accountable by ruling against the executive branch when justices think the president, an agency, or official within the administration has exceeded allowable constitutional or statutory authority (see, e.g., *Youngstown Steel Corp v. Sawyer* (1957)). However, conventional wisdom holds that presidents usually win in the Supreme Court. For instance, in their analysis of federal regulatory commission cases appealed to the Burger Court, Spaeth and Teger (1982) reported that the Court supported federal regulatory agencies 72 percent of the time (p. 278). Other scholars have reported similarly high win rates for executive branch agencies in the 70–85 percent range (Canon and Giles 1972; Crowley 1987; Handberg 1979; Sheehan 1992). In foreign policy, the win rate and hence overall level of deference to presidential administrations is decidedly substantial (Breyer 2016; Entin 2012; *United States v. Curtis-Wright Export Corp.* 1936).

This presidential dominance perspective is based on the Court's historical tendency to allow a wide berth, greater flexibility, and discretion for executive authority when interpreting the meaning of federal statutes and their manner of enforcement. That perspective was solidified in the case of *Chevron v. Natural Resources Defense Council* (1984). Over the last four decades, however, this tendency toward Supreme Court deference to executive authority has decreased as justices have become more assertive in their approach to judicial review of administrative and legislative actions. The Court is increasingly unwilling to acquiesce to the decisions of federal bureaucrats. Instead, the Court is increasingly assuming a more assertive (even activist) posture in its dealings with the executive branch, regardless of partisan affiliation of the administration in power. As Jeffrey Segal noted, "The Court has been striking down cases involving federal agencies, which is unusual given the deference that they are supposed to show under *Chevron*" (quoted in Roeder 2015). Consequently, one would expect the claims and positions of recent presidents, including Obama, to have tepid performance in such a reinvigorated Supreme Court.

The clear implication of this development is that in a wide variety of statutory and constitutional areas of policy, the power of the Supreme Court has expanded and is continuing to expand in ways unimaginable just a few decades ago. Justice Stephen Breyer acknowledged this development in his recent book, *The Court and the World*, which he describes as a report from the judicial "front lines" about how things have changed regarding the "foreign" aspects of the Court's docket in the age of globalization and international terrorism (Breyer 2016).

It is within this context of expanding judicial power and the seemingly long-term retreat of presidential dominance that we must evaluate Obama's legacy in the Supreme Court. How did President Obama fare in the Supreme Court relative to other recent presidents? How successful have his appointees been in shaping legal policy in the Court? These are certainly interesting and important questions that must be addressed in systematic ways, and some scholars have already started the task. In a recent empirical examination of Supreme Court deference to executive authority, Eric Posner and Lee Epstein used a database of 3783 Supreme Court cases that concerned American presidents from 1932 to 2016 (Posner and Epstein 2018). These cases are deemed to be of interest to presidents because they involve either an executive branch official or federal agency as a direct party.

If, as we indicated, the strategy of the Court has changed from deference to a more assertive posture, then one cannot expect any modern president to fare too well in any judicial system where justices enjoy the constitutional protections of judicial independence. Indeed, this is exactly what Posner and Epstein reported in their examination of presidential success rates in the Supreme Court. According to Posner and Epstein (2018), presidential dominance in the Supreme Court ended during the Reagan administration. While the average win rate is 65 percent for all presidents from 1932 to 2016, Ronald Reagan proved to be the most successful of recent presidents, with a win rate of approximately 76 percent. Interestingly, win rates have declined steadily for every subsequent president since Reagan, culminating with Obama, who clocked in with a win rate of just over 50 percent (Posner and Epstein 2018, pp. 845–846). The expectation is that this trend will continue, suggesting that there is turbulence ahead for President Donald Trump.

Several factors potentially account for this development, including ideological incongruence between the Court and the president and the possibility that federal agencies are overreaching. However, we agree with Posner and Epstein that one empirically plausible reason is the growing specialization of the Supreme Court bar rather than executive overreach or ideological differences between the Supreme Court and the president (Posner and Epstein 2018). Scholars often attribute presidential success in the Supreme Court to the influence of the U.S. Solicitor General (SG), the administration's chief representative before the Supreme Court. Many scholars have documented the greater success the SG achieves relative to other litigants as both direct party and as an amicus participant (Black and Owens 2011; Salokar 1992; Segal 1990). Some researchers attribute this success to the SG's status as the ultimate repeat player (McGuire 1995, 1998) and the privileged position the SG occupies before the Court, where the SG provides credible information and arguments to the justices and serves, in effect, as a "tenth justice" (Caplan 1987; Pacelle 2003). However, this repeat player advantage is challenged by the emergence of an elite Supreme Court bar, a select group of highly influential lawyers, many of whom are former SGs, department of justice officials, and Supreme Court law clerks. These elite members of the Supreme Court bar achieve greater success than other private attorneys in getting their clients' certiorari petitions accepted, and rival the SG in winning before the Court (McGuire 1993; Biskupic et al. 2014).

It would be altogether myopic and misguided to view Obama's relatively low win rate as evidence that he lacked success in the Supreme Court, as some commentators have come to believe (see Shapiro 2016). Instead, the relatively low win rate should be considered a byproduct of larger trends in the United States and worldwide, including the global expansion of judicial power (Tate 1995), the acceptance of legal realism by jurists (Gibson and Caldeira 2011), and the global judicialization of politics (Hirschl 2011). Legal realism, for example, dictates that Supreme Court justices vote their sincere preferences in most legal conflicts. Under this principle, judging is not value-free. Rather, it is preference-based (Segal and Spaeth 2002; Unah and Hancock 2006). Private lawyers in boutique law firms that specialize in Supreme Court advocacy understand this reality all too well and construct their arguments to profit from the pull of legal realism.

When it comes to the Supreme Court and the Obama Administration, we can surmise that where justices stand on the cases and controversies involving the administration depends largely on their ideology. Most conservatives in the right wing of American politics detested Obama's progressive policies, especially those Tea Party conservatives who listened to right-wing talk radio and its constant drumbeat of negativity toward Obama and his actions as president (see Bullock and Hood 2012; Maxwell and Parent 2012). Likewise, the Supreme Court, as a reflection of the American polity, was highly polarized along ideological lines during the Obama Era, with some legal news reporters and analysts proclaiming the Roberts Court as "the most conservative in decades" (Liptak 2010) and as the most polarized in recent memory (Whitehouse 2015). Interestingly, the ideological polarization in the Court does mirror polarization in the body politic. As Dahl (1957) reminded us, the Supreme Court is a majoritarian institution whose decisions reflect prevailing governing majorities and hence the psyche of the American people. Therefore, it should surprise no one that Obama would enjoy a relatively low win ratio in a Supreme Court that is highly polarized and significantly more conservative than his administration. Evidence of this ideological incongruence is displayed in Fig. 1. Using data from Bailey (2013), we plot the ideal point estimates of

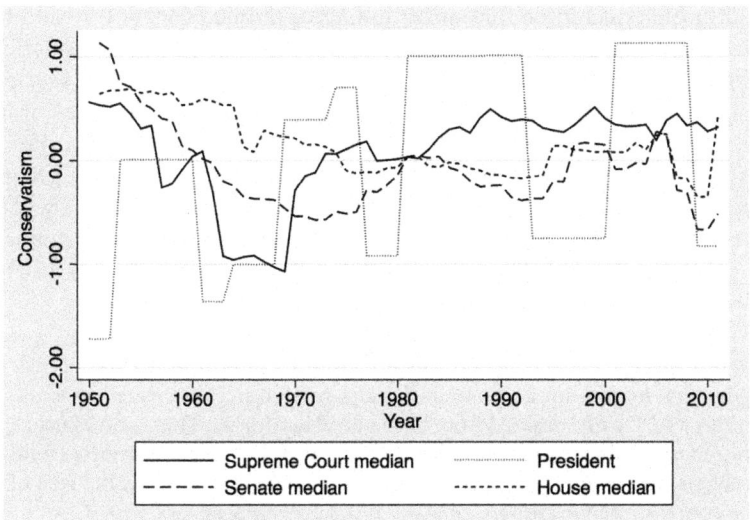

Fig. 1   Ideology of Congress, the Supreme Court, and the President (1950–2011)

ideology for the Supreme Court, president, and congressional medians. During the first three years of the Obama presidency (2009–2011), the Supreme Court was clearly more conservative than the President.

Another possible explanation for the low win rate is that Obama did not prioritize the judiciary as the venue to bring about profound and lasting policy changes. As such, he was less aggressive in pursuing wins in the Supreme Court than he could have been. This comports with Obama's credo that the electoral process, not the halls of justice, is where lasting policy change must be derived. As a senator, Obama explained his disillusionment with using the courts to achieve social change: "I wondered if, in our reliance on the courts to vindicate not only our rights but also our values, progressives had lost too much faith in democracy" (Obama 2006, as quoted in Toobin 2012, p. 27). According to Jeffrey Toobin (2012), Obama's unease with using the courts for social change came early on as a state legislator when he analyzed the implications of the Supreme Court's decision in *San Antonio School District v. Rodriguez* (1973). It was the case that motivated Obama to think seriously about staying in and using politics to achieve social change, especially with respect to redistribution and wealth inequalities, which courts are ill-equipped to address (Toobin 2012, p. 32). In *Rodriguez*, the Court decided 5 to 4 that there is no constitutional guarantee for equal funding of public education within the same state, ignoring the reality of pervasive resource inequality in American primary and secondary schools, which rely heavily on property tax receipts. Respondents in the case were advancing claims that they thought, if left unaddressed, would exacerbate economic and racial inequality. During an interview with a local Chicago public radio station in 2001, Obama described the *Rodriquez* decision by saying the Court "basically slaps those kinds of claims down" because "the institution just isn't structured that way" (quoted in Toobin 2012, p. 32).[3] Jeffrey Toobin (2012) described the "Obama credo" as follows:

> To [Obama], the courts were (or should be) static in their protection of basic rights, but he was not going to push judges and justices to create new ones. In this way, Obama differed from both liberal heroes like Thurgood Marshall and conservative icons like Antonin Scalia; they believed the courts could deliver social change. Obama did not, and this diffidence about the role of the courts shaped his professional life and, later, his presidency. (p. 32)

Today, some scholars continue to attribute pervasive and growing class inequality in the United States partly to the Court's decision in *Rodriguez* and its failure to level the playing field regarding school funding and the availability of educational opportunity for all of America's children (Stone n.d.).

Moreover, Obama has been criticized for being too slow and not sufficiently aggressive in filling federal judgeships (Savage 2012) and for not fighting hard enough to fill the vacancy created by Scalia's death. In his defense, Obama did face, for most of his tenure, a highly unified, uncooperative, and recalcitrant Congress, with a House and Senate[4] controlled by Republicans whose leadership had conspired to mount an unyielding opposition to each of the President's policy moves right from the genesis of his administration. Figure 2 shows the number of federal district and appellate court vacancies in December of each year of the Bush and Obama presidencies.[5] Year 0 refers to the December of the year prior to each president's first year of office, December 2000 and December 2008 for Bush and Obama, respectively. Year 1 refers to December 2001 for Bush and December 2009 for Obama. The figure partially corroborates the criticism that Obama was relatively less successful at filling federal judgeships. Compared to Bush, Obama consistently faced a higher number of federal district court vacancies; this demonstrates a lack of urgency in filling those

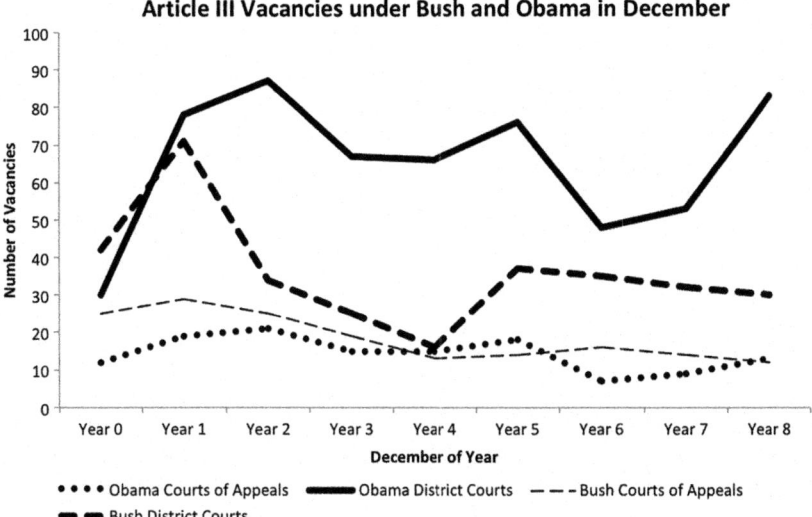

Fig. 2   District and appellate court vacancies under Bush and Obama

judgeships, particularly when Democrats had majority control of the Senate until 2015. Moreover, the sharp uptick in vacancies in Obama's final year speaks to the recalcitrance of Senate Republicans in confirming Obama's nominees, usually by withholding blue slip approval[6] in hopes of keeping the seat vacant (Slotnick et al. 2017; Wheeler 2017; Feinstein 2017). In contrast, the number of appellate court vacancies during the Obama presidency was comparable to those seen during the Bush years.

Perhaps most interestingly, Slotnick et al. (2017) note that at the end of the Obama presidency, almost half of the 99 Article III court vacancies were without a nominee. Moreover, more than 70 percent of the vacancies without a nominee were in states with at least one Republican senator. This suggests that Obama was discouraged by the blue slip approval process, which Republican senators used as a powerful tool to stymie Obama's judicial nominations.

Obama did achieve greater success in seeing his lower court nominees confirmed when Democratic Senate Majority Leader Harry Reid initiated the nuclear option for lower federal judicial nominations in November 2013. This unprecedented action was undertaken in reaction to Republican obstructionism. By invoking the nuclear option, the Senate was able to

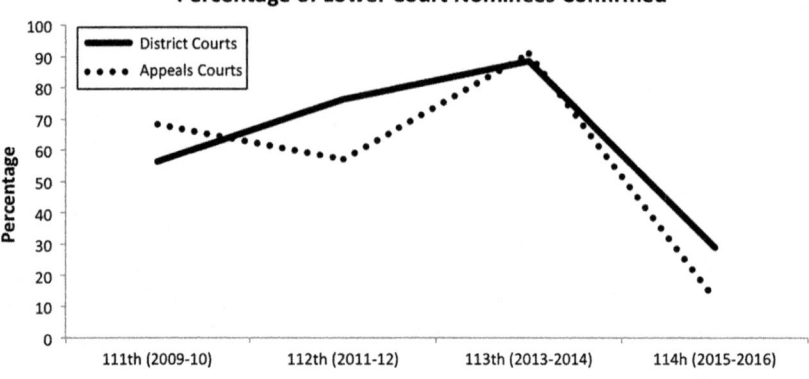

Fig. 3 Percentage of Obama's lower federal judicial nominees confirmed. (Source: Slotnick et al. 2017)

approve judicial nominees with a bare majority vote. However, Obama's success rate plummeted when the Senate reverted to Republican control during Obama's final two years in office. Indeed, the confirmation process for lower court nominees essentially shut down with the nomination of Merrick Garland to fill Antonin Scalia's seat (Slotnick et al. 2017). Figure 3 shows the percentage of Obama's district and appellate court nominees confirmed by the Senate from the 111th–114th Congresses (2009–2016).[7]

Ultimately, Slotnick, Schiavoni, and Goldman find that while Obama was criticized for his inability to see his lower court judges confirmed, he did prioritize the selection of diverse judicial nominees, as more than 60 percent of his confirmed nominees were women, racial minorities, or openly gay. Indeed, Obama outpaced all recent presidents in the percentage of female and minority judges appointed to the federal judiciary. More than 40 percent of Obama's district and appellate court appointees were women, and almost 20 percent were African American. In comparison, women were less than 30 percent of Clinton's appointees and just over 20 percent of George W. Bush's appointees. African Americans constituted about 17 percent and 8 percent of Clinton and Bush's appointees, respectively. Obama's appointments of Hispanic Americans also exceeded those of previous presidents.

In sum, Obama's prioritization of diversity in appointments to the district and appellate courts has important consequences for descriptive representation in the judicial branch. From the time Obama took office in 2009 to the time he left in 2017, the percentage of women judges in U.S. district courts increased by 17.5 percent and by 20 percent in federal appellate courts. Moreover, the percentage of African Americans in the Court of Appeals increased by 50 percent, while the percentage on the district courts increased by 11.8 percent (Slotnick et al. 2017). This is a laudable legacy that is bound to enhance the judicial process and expand the boundaries of legal interpretations of law.

Ultimately, the Republican Party's primary governing objective during the Obama years was, in the words of Senate Majority Leader Mitch McConnell (R-KY), "to make Barack Obama a one-term President" and to just say no to each of his policy proposals (Frontline 2013). While Obama went on to win a second term, the hostility of House and Senate Republicans did significantly stifle Obama's policy pursuits and help explain why he reverted to using his executive powers and "bureaucratic bulldozing rather than legislative transparency" to achieve many of his pressing policy goals (Applebaum and Shear 2016). During his 2014 State of the Union address, Obama responded to Republican obstruction by saying, "Whenever I can take steps without legislation to expand opportunity for more American families, that's what I'm going to do."[8] That is what he did.

OBAMA AND THE LANDSCAPE OF JUDICIAL SELECTION TO THE SUPREME COURT

Every American president relishes an opportunity to place his administration's imprimatur on the Supreme Court through the appointment of justices. The creation of vacancies in the Supreme Court is a rare and random event. Empirical research suggests that a new vacancy is created in the Court every 22 months (Dahl 1957). There is an element of luck involved in accounting for why some presidents are blessed with more vacancies (e.g., Ronald Reagan) than others (e.g., Jimmy Carter). However, when a vacancy does arise, it takes commitment and dedication for the president and the candidate to navigate the political storms that often accompany modern Supreme Court nominations. An appointment to the Supreme Court establishes an opportunity for a long-term legacy for the president. For this reason, presidents take appointment to the Supreme Court more seriously than they do other appointments. President Obama was fortunate to have three vacancies during his two terms.

The retirement of Justice David Souter in 2009 soon after Obama's election presented the new president with a golden opportunity to place his ideological stamp on the Court. Obama quickly nominated Sonia Sotomayor of New York to replace Souter. Sotomayor was confirmed by a vote of 68 to 31, not exactly smooth sailing but quite a respectable level of support across the two political parties. The vote differential betrays the level of ideological conflict surrounding the nomination. Even though most Republicans spoke glowingly about Sotomayor's storied background and her 27 years of experience as a federal judge, including 11 years on the Court of Appeals for the Second Circuit, only 9 Republican senators ultimately voted for her confirmation, providing evidence that sharp disagreements between the political parties remain a fixture of Supreme Court confirmations.

Sotomayor's appointment was historic. She is the first Hispanic to serve on the Supreme Court and the third woman to do so. As such, Sotomayor's appointment is a key Obama legacy. Her background as the daughter of poor Puerto Rican parents and her reputation as a hard worker and a diligent exponent of the law meant broad support, even among many of the Republican senators who ultimately voted against her. Senators often have multiple reasons for not voting to support a judicial nominee. For example, they must consider how a yea vote might be perceived by constituents and by potential electoral opponents. In the case of Sotomayor, some senators had expressed concern that she would be biased as a Supreme Court justice based on a statement she made during a public lecture at the University of California, Berkeley School of Law: "I would hope that a *wise Latina* woman with the richness of her experiences would more often than not reach a better conclusion than a white male who hasn't lived that life" (Sotomayor 2002).

We think that a more important reason why many Republicans failed to support Sotomayor is that the National Rifle Association (NRA), at Senate Majority Leader Mitch McConnell's request, had announced to senators that the organization would "score" the Sotomayor confirmation vote in its rating of senators (Washington Post 2009). It was the first time the NRA used a Supreme Court confirmation vote in its gun-support rating, and it was a direct threat to Republican senators who receive significant support from the organization (Greenhouse 2012).[9] For Republican senators, a vote for Sotomayor would surely lower their NRA rating and conservative credentials and harm their reelection prospects. Strategically, then, if Senate Republicans could vote nay and still see Sotomayor confirmed, it was the way to go.

Of the many questions asked during Senate debate on the Sotomayor nomination, Senator John Kerry (D-MA) asked the most pertinent one for our purposes: "What direction will this nominee take the Supreme Court?" (Goldstein and Kane 2009). Kerry answered his own question: "I have concluded that she is someone with whom our rights and freedoms are safe." In the next section of the chapter, we bring some empirical evidence to bear on this question by comparing the voting behavior of Justice Sotomayor with that of her predecessor, Justice David Souter.

Barack Obama's Supreme Court vacancy fortunes increased when Justice John Paul Stevens (a 1975 Ford appointee) announced in April 2010 that he intended to retire at the end of the term after 35 years on the Court. Justice Stevens was known generally as a leader of the liberal wing of the Court even though he was appointed by a Republican president. He was also a vociferous defender of abortion rights. Moreover, he favored expanding protections for LGBT people, restricting the availability of the death penalty, and ensuring a robust role for judges in interpreting the nation's laws and curbing executive power. As the most senior Associate Justice who, by his seniority, speaks after the Chief Justice and assigns the majority opinion writer when the Chief Justice votes in the minority, Stevens's departure was sure to affect the internal workings of the Court. The President praised Justice Stevens and said he would move quickly to nominate an individual who possesses "an independent mind, a record of excellence and integrity, a fierce dedication to the rule of law and a keen understanding of how the law affects the daily lives of the American people" (Barnes 2010).

As many informed observers expected, Obama nominated his SG, Elena Kagan, a former Harvard Law School Dean, to fill the vacancy. It would be his second consecutive female nominee to the Supreme Court. The nation had never witnessed such a development before. Indeed, the President had already changed the history books when in 2008 he named Kagan to be SG. No woman in American history had ever served in this important federal government role. The SG is the most important government lawyer, representing the federal government before the Supreme Court, screening federal government cases, and preparing them for appeal to the Supreme Court. As such, the tenor of the relationship between the executive branch and the Supreme Court often rests on the SG's shoulders. Kagan's Senate confirmation was relatively smooth as she faced little serious opposition from Republicans, although some Republican senators were concerned about her lack of prior experience as a judge. We address Kagan and Sotomayor's impact on the Court in the next section by considering their liberalism compared to their predecessors' (Justices Souter and Stevens) as a way of assessing what direction they are taking the Supreme Court.

We now turn to the failed nomination of D.C. Circuit Chief Judge Merrick Garland following the death of Justice Scalia. The presidential election campaign was in full swing when Scalia died in February 2016. The Senate was still controlled by Republicans and their concern was the critical nature of this vacancy. If Obama nominated successfully, this would shift the ideological balance of power in the Court from conservative to liberal. The stakes were unusually high. As such, it was going to be an uphill battle for Obama to get any nominee confirmed for Scalia's seat no matter how qualified or how moderate.

Obama nominated the well-qualified and ideologically moderate D.C. Circuit Chief Judge Merrick Garland. Prior to the nomination, Obama had sought the advice of Senate leaders, including conservative leaders, for an "appropriate" candidate. For Republican leaders, an appropriate candidate in a Democratic administration would be a moderate jurist they could tolerate. Several longtime GOP members of the Senate Judiciary Committee had actively and publicly lobbied for Garland's selection in the past (Memoli and Mascaro 2016). Yet Senate Majority Leader Mitch McConnell (R-KY) and other key Republicans registered their opposition right after Garland's nomination by invoking the so-called "Biden Rule"[10] to block his confirmation.

The Biden Rule was never an institutional rule but an opinion of one individual senator. It came from a floor speech that then Senate Judiciary Committee Chairman Joe Biden (D-DE) gave in 1992 urging President George H.W. Bush not to nominate someone *if* a vacancy should open in the summer before the upcoming presidential election. Biden further implored the judiciary committee to not hold hearings should a nomination be made under the circumstance. The speech was not a widespread norm, let alone proposed as a rule, and it was never voted on; it was but one single senator's opinion and there was no standing nominee at the time (see Emery 2016). Of course, in organizational behavior, norms can rise to the level of institutional rules without a formal vote. The invocation of the "Biden Rule" was a rhetorical tactic by Senate Republicans to justify their Garland blockade. An impending election had never stopped the Senate from considering a nominee for the Supreme Court before.[11] While Republicans were using the election as an excuse to deny the President one more appointment to the Supreme Court, they were within their constitutional right to do so under Article 2, Section 2 of the U.S. Constitution, but it was constitutionally unwise and highly problematic.

It seems obvious that Republicans in the Senate used the presidential election as a ploy to deny Obama a third appointment to the Supreme Court. The Appointment Clause of the Constitution states, "The president ... shall nominate, and by and with the Advice and Consent of the Senate, shall appoint judges of the supreme Court." The nation has only one president at a time. The incumbent has the constitutional authority under Section 2 to nominate an individual to fill a vacancy in any federal court. The Constitution did not require that during an election the Senate must or should suspend consideration of judicial nominees for any reason, let alone convenience. Obama nominated Merrick Garland in March of 2016, eight months before the presidential election vote was to be held on November 8. Historically, it takes about two weeks for the Senate to confirm nominees to the Supreme Court, although in recent years it has taken much longer as the loss of comity has become the currency of Capitol Hill (Shipan and Shannon 2003). If the Republican majority in the Senate had even a modicum of desire to consider Garland's nomination, there was ample time to hold hearings and an up or down vote on the nomination before senators returned to their districts to campaign for reelection.

The last time any Supreme Court nominee was considered for confirmation during a presidential election campaign was 1988 when then Vice President George H.W. Bush ran against Massachusetts Governor Michael Dukakis. President Ronald Reagan successfully appointed Anthony Kennedy that year after two earlier nomination attempts failed (Robert Bork and Douglas Ginsburg). Kennedy's nomination was confirmed by a Democratic-controlled Senate. However, in the intensely polarized Obama Era, Republicans were in charge and in no mood to return the favor. Indeed, the index of obstruction and delay in Senate processing of federal judicial nominees reached the maximum score of 1.00 (or complete obstruction) in Slotnick, Schiavoni, and Goldman's obstruction and delay scale (2017, 379).

While the stakes for any Supreme Court nomination are always high, in the case of Judge Garland they were even more so; it was a critical nomination (Ruckman 1993). Replacing Scalia with a Democratic appointee would shift the ideological center of gravity in the Supreme Court from conservative to liberal. Not a single hearing was convened to consider Garland's nomination, and the nomination expired when Donald J. Trump won in the Electoral College and was sworn in as President despite losing the popular vote by close to 3 million votes (CNN 2016). Trump would go on to nominate Tenth Circuit Appellate Judge Neil Gorsuch, who faced vociferous opposition from Senate Democrats, who remained in the minority. Traditionally, Senate rules require a positive vote of 60 senators to end a filibuster and confirm a nominee for the Supreme Court, but there were only 52 Republicans in the Senate in 2017. Without this rule, only a bare majority of 51 senators would be required. Thus, Senate Republicans invoked the so-called nuclear option[12] to confirm Gorsuch, meaning they had to suspend indefinitely the rule requiring 60 senators to confirm a Supreme Court nominee. This represents a significant structural change in the confirmation process that both parties may come to regret because it will be easier for all future Supreme Court nominees, including ideological extremists, to be confirmed by the Senate (provided the Senate is ideologically aligned with the president).

The Influence of Obama Justices in the Supreme Court

Since the Supreme Court sits atop the American judicial system, justices review cases involving all aspects of the Constitution and federal laws. In this section, we evaluate whether and how Obama's two appointees, Sotomayor and Kagan, are shaping the direction of the Court and, if so, in which policy areas the influence is most prominent. We proceed by comparing the liberalism of these justices with that of their immediate predecessors. For Sotomayor, we examine a period of eight terms; for Kagan, we analyze seven terms, starting from when the justices joined the Court. For their predecessors, Souter and Stevens, we examine their last eight and seven terms, respectively, to determine their patterns of liberalism.

Figure 4 shows the voting patterns of Obama's appointees compared to their immediate predecessors. The data are from the Supreme Court Database (Spaeth et al. 2017). The pie charts suggest that Obama Justices and their predecessors are remarkably alike in their overall voting patterns. Both Sotomayor and Souter voted in a liberal direction approximately

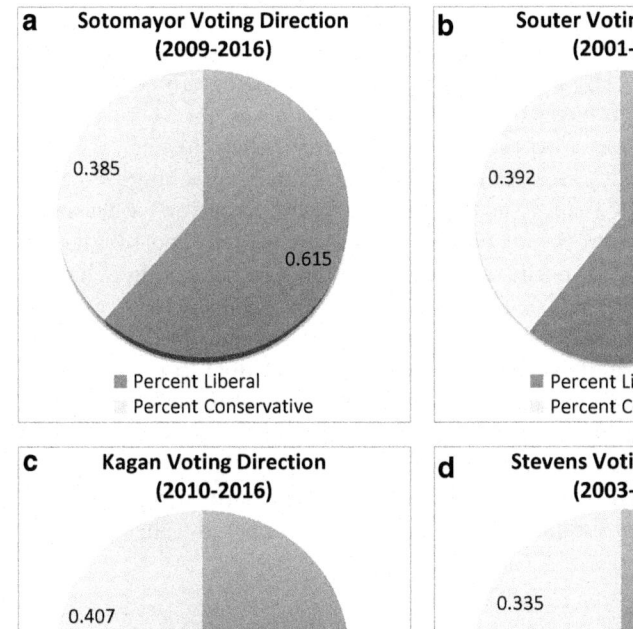

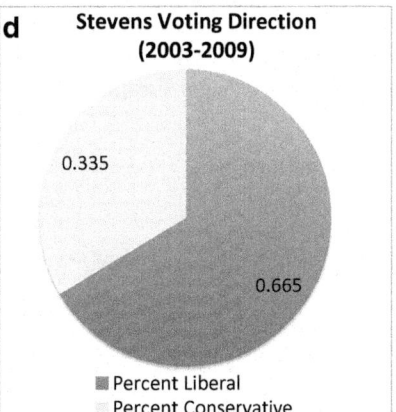

Fig. 4 Comparing Obama justices to their immediate predecessors. (a) Percentage of total votes-Sotomayor (**b**) Percentage of total votes-Souter (**c**) Percentage of total votes-Kagan (**d**) Percentage of total votes-Stevens

61 percent of the time. Thus, these justices are virtually carbon copies of each other for the period examined, even though they were appointed by ideologically dissimilar presidents.[13] A two-sample difference of proportions test reveals that the liberal voting percentages of the two justices are not statistically distinct. However, we found a small but statistically significant difference in the liberalism of Justices Kagan and Stevens. Justice Kagan voted liberally 59 percent of the time whereas Justice Stevens voted

liberally 66 percent of the time. This statistically significant difference suggests that Justice Stevens was moving the Court in a more progressive direction during his last seven terms on the Court than was Justice Kagan during her first seven terms on the Court.[14]

We now dig deeper into the voting patterns of these justices across a range of specific policy areas to unmask any potentially meaningful differences. We follow the main issue designations in the Supreme Court database. As shown in Fig. 5, out of the 11 issue areas identified by Harold Spaeth, we find no statistically significant difference in the voting behavior of Justices Sotomayor and Souter in any substantive issue area.[15] In many of these issue areas, Sotomayor and Souter demonstrate similar levels of liberalism. The largest difference occurs in individual privacy, where Sotomayor appears much more conservative than Souter. However, the difference is not significant at the conventional level.

In Fig. 6, we present a similar analysis comparing Kagan and Stevens. We find only one issues area, criminal procedure, where Justice Kagan is making a statistically significant difference when compared to her immedi-

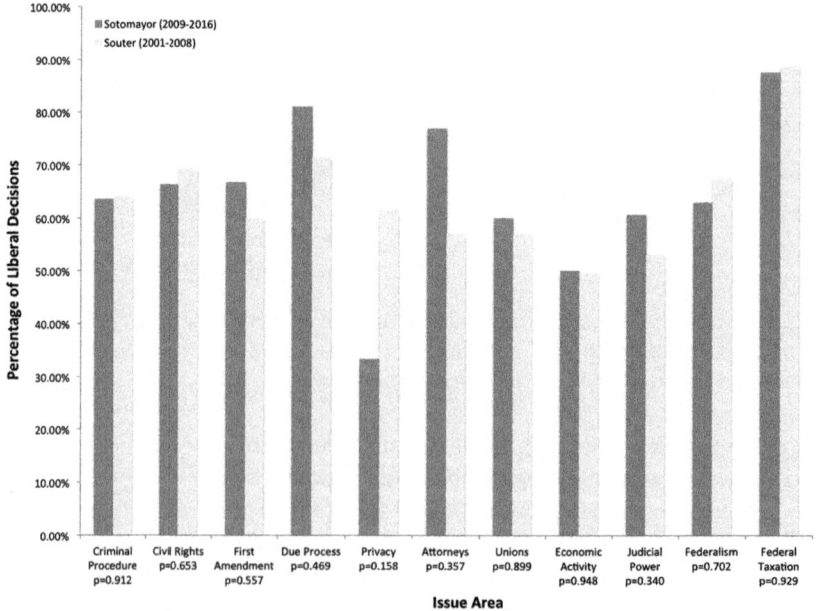

Fig. 5 Sotomayor vs. Souter – percent liberal decisions

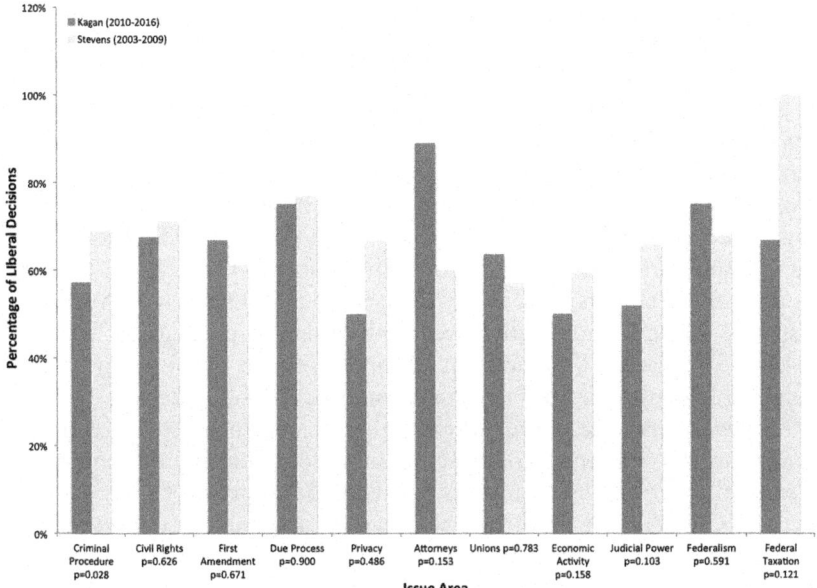

Fig. 6   Kagan vs. Stevens – percent liberal decisions

ate predecessor. In this area, Justice Kagan is voting in a more conservative fashion than did Justice Stevens. In the remaining ten issue areas, we find no difference between the two justices. We must recognize that the specific legal issues being decided are likely quite different, as is the timing. For example, privacy issues that a liberal justice might have no difficulty finding intrusive might be tougher many years later because of widespread social acceptance of technological intrusions into individual privacy.

Our analysis indicates that Justice Kagan is not as liberal or as progressive on most issues as some, including perhaps President Obama himself, might have thought. This is an interesting finding for which there are several possible interpretations. First, Obama might have misjudged the extent of Kagan's liberalism, thinking she is more liberal than she really is. The fact that she has never been a judge could have made a true assessment of her liberalism more difficult. A second possibility is that Obama is a pragmatist who understands that Kagan is not the most liberal individual he could have appointed and as such would not be surprised by her moderate voting record. Third, we can surmise that Justice Kagan is merely exercising her independent judgment and voting where the law takes her. Research on small group dynamics suggests that it is easy for group members to influence each other's thinking (Eisenstein et al. 1988). This raises the possibility that Justice Kagan is being influenced by her conservative colleagues more than her predecessor was influenced by his. After all, Kagan maintained a very strong friendship with Justice Antonin Scalia when he was alive. For instance, they went hunting together on numerous occasions and Kagan publicly expressed her admiration for Scalia's wit and persona, saying that she learned "a lot" from Scalia about how to be a judge.[16] Indeed, if such influence exists, it does not appear to have come only from Justice Scalia. As Table 1 shows, she voted with Scalia 54 percent of the time, Roberts 50 percent of the time, and Kennedy 59 percent of the time. The comparable figures for Sotomayor are less indicative of influence.

Finally, on the question of whether the Obama Justices are having an impact on the Supreme Court, we examine opinion-writing patterns.[17] The architecture of opinion assignment in the Supreme Court dictates that the Chief Justice designates who writes the majority opinion if the chief votes in the majority. Otherwise, the most senior associate justice in the majority assigns the majority opinion author. Importantly, the opinion writer exercises a great deal of agenda control over the content and structure of the opinion. Thus, we can also rely on majority opinion output in specific areas as another way of gauging the type of impact Obama's justices are having on the Court.

From the analysis presented in Fig. 7, Sotomayor wrote significantly more opinions and is therefore having a greater impact in matters concerning attorney claims compared to Souter. In Fig. 8, we show that Justice Kagan also wrote significantly more opinions than Stevens in the area of attorneys. However, no other statistically significant differences emerge from the analysis.[18]

Finally, we examine voting agreement scores to determine the extent to which Obama Justices are voting in line with the conservatives on the Court. This will also help us determine which of the two Obama appointees is more liberal overall. We look at the 2013–2014 term. We find that Justice Kagan voted with conservative justices at a proportionally higher level than Sotomayor. Therefore, we conclude that while both justices are having an impact on the Court, Sotomayor's is a more liberal impact than Kagan's. In the next section we examine some key cases decided by the Supreme Court during Obama's tenure.

Table 1 Supreme Court voting agreement scores, 2013–2014 term[a]

	Ginsburg	Sotomayor	Kagan	Breyer	Kennedy	Roberts	Alito	Thomas	Scalia
Ginsburg									
Sotomayor	71								
Kagan	83	74							
Breyer	68	67	71						
Kennedy	40	38	58	56					
Roberts	32	38	50	56	76				
Alito	25	22	35	33	63	54			
Thomas	28	25	38	36	48	64	88		
Scalia	44	33	54	36	56	72	71	84	

Entries reflect percentage of non-unanimous cases where justices agreed in full, in part, or in the judgment only. Entries in bold reflect Sotomayor and Kagan's agreement with scores of conservative justices

[a]Source: SCOTUblogStatPack. https://sblog.s3.amazonaws.com/wp-content/uploads/2014/07/SCOTUSblog_tables_OT13.pdf

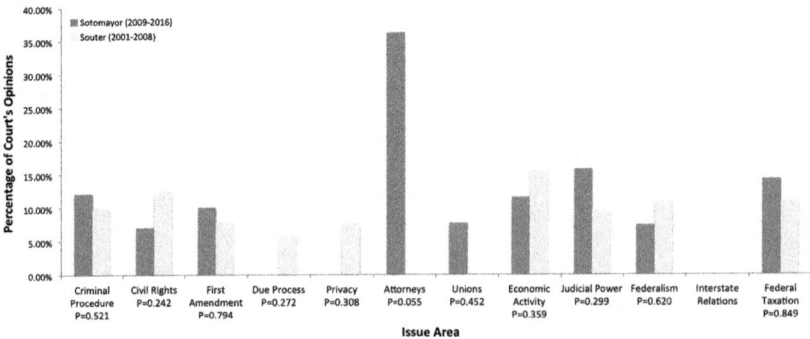

Fig. 7 Sotomayor vs. Souter – percentage of the Supreme Court's majority opinions by issue area

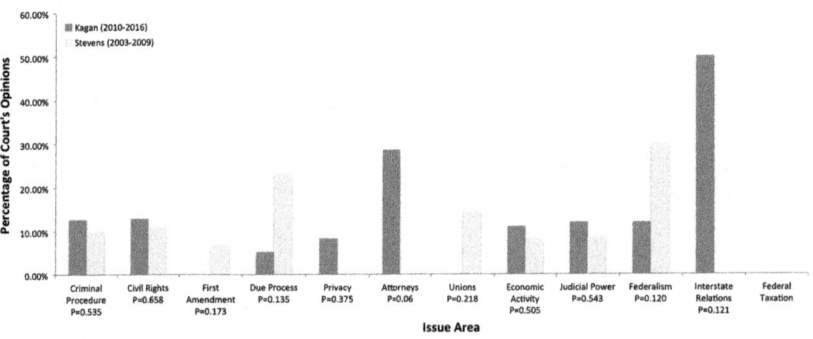

Fig. 8 Kagan vs. Stevens – percentage of the Supreme Court's majority opinions by issue area

BIG CASES, BIG ISSUES, AND THE OBAMA PRESIDENCY

The Supreme Court found itself in the thick of many prominent issues during the Obama Era. For example, Obama had bet his entire presidency on the seminal issue of healthcare reform. He sidestepped other legislative priorities, including immigration, climate change, and energy, to focus his legislative resources on reforming America's crumbling healthcare system. Whereas Democrats in Congress supported his efforts, Republicans opposed him at every step of the way, claiming that the proposed reform effort is a jobs killer, too expensive, and ineffective at slowing down healthcare costs. American presidents as far back as Teddy Roosevelt have tried to reform the healthcare system without success, with the last valiant effort launched by Bill Clinton also a failure. Many doubted that Obama would be successful, yet he persevered. *The Patient Protection and Affordable Care Act* (aka Obamacare) passed in March 2010 without a single Republican vote.

Obamacare: The Case, Legislative Legacy, and Court Legitimacy

Among the most popular provisions of the law are that: (1) no one will be denied health insurance because of a preexisting condition, (2) parents can retain their young adult children on their health insurance until age 26 unless they are married, and (3) states can rely on federal subsidies to provide expanded Medicaid coverage for their poorest citizens and the elderly. The most controversial provision was the individual mandate, which requires individuals to buy health insurance or pay a fine. It was included to overcome free-rider problems. Soon after the law's passage, attorneys general from several conservative states joined different lawsuits challenging the new law. The lead case in the Supreme Court was *National Federation of Independent Business v. Sebelius* (2012). For conservatives, the primary issue with the law was clearly the individual mandate. They argued that this provision means that the federal government is forcing people to buy a product or else pay a tax, and that this was government overreach in violation of the interstate Commerce Clause and the Necessary and Proper Clause of the Constitution. The individual mandate was a significant departure from previous actions of the federal government under the Commerce Clause. Another key issue in the case was that of severability, whether to strike down the entire law including all its good features or strike down only the unsavory individual mandate.

At conference the justices were split, with four (conservatives) to strike down and four (liberals) to affirm the law. Chief Justice John Roberts became the deciding vote. He authored the opinion upholding the law as constitutional. Specifically, the individual mandate was upheld as a tax that Congress can impose under its expressed taxing authority in Article 1 Section 8 rather than a fine under the Commerce Clause or the Necessary and Proper Clause of the Constitution. Roberts's opinion did not uphold the individual mandate under the Commerce Clause because the majority concluded it was not a valid use of Congress's power to regulate interstate commerce. Instead, Roberts located the individual mandate's constitutional authority under the congressional power to impose taxes. As such,

Congress had not contravened its constitutional authority under Article 1 of the Constitution. It was a monumental decision that salvaged Obama's major legislative victory, and the President was reelected to the chagrin of Republicans. However, while Roberts's opinion was met with widespread criticism from conservatives, particularly over his invocation of Congress's taxing and spending power,[19] Toobin (2012) argues that his vote and opinion were "acts of strategic genius" (p. 295) that limited the scope of federal authority under the Commerce Clause and effectively removed the Supreme Court from the larger Democratic agenda. We hasten to add that Roberts was likely influenced by his concern for the Court's perceived legitimacy. The Chief Justice is very protective of the Court's public image and he, perhaps more than any other justice, was no doubt aware of the social and political implications for the Court of striking down the Affordable Care Act.

Subsequent litigation on Obamacare involved federal subsidies in the form of tax credits issued to individuals who cannot afford to buy their own health insurance. In *King v. Burwell* (2015), the Court reaffirmed the Affordable Care Act, ruling that the law authorizes federal tax credits for eligible Americans living not only in states with their own exchanges but also in the 34 states with federal marketplaces. Once again, Chief Justice Roberts came to Obama's rescue and authored the majority opinion preventing millions of Americans from losing healthcare coverage.

In terms of immediate impact, healthcare was the biggest policy issue the Court tackled, but it was certainly not the only significant issue. The issue of marriage equality was also momentous, as the Court issued two landmark decisions in *Obergefell v. Hodges* (2015) and *United States v. Windsor* (2013) during the Obama presidency. While the Court's decision in *Obergefell* granted same-sex couples a fundamental right to marry, we focus on *United States v. Windsor* due to its implications for separation of powers, executive power, and the president's right not to defend a federal law.

United States v. Windsor: *Separation of Powers, Standing, and Equal Protection*

Same-sex couple Edith Windsor and Thea Spyer married in Canada but settled in New York. When Spyer died in 2009, she left her estate to Windsor. However, because Windsor did not meet the definition of spouse under Section 3 of the 1996 federal Defense of Marriage Act (DOMA), she could not claim the estate tax exemption for surviving spouses, even though her marriage was recognized by the State of New York. Thus, a federal estate tax of approximately $363,000 was levied against Windsor. After the IRS denied her request for a refund, Windsor sued on grounds that DOMA violated her right to equal protection under the law (Funk 2014).

Congress passed DOMA following a Supreme Court of Hawaii opinion that the state's prohibition on same-sex marriages might constitute a violation of the state constitution's equal protection clause (Tipler 2013).[20] In enacting the law, members of Congress argued that if Hawaii or other states legalized same-sex marriage, the Full Faith and Credit Clause of the U.S. Constitution would require other states to recognize those marriages (Singer 2005). While Section 2 of DOMA directly addressed this concern by assuring states that they need not recognize same-sex marriages from other states, it was Section 3 of the law that proved the most controversial. Section 3 specified that marriage is defined as a legal union between one man and one woman. This meant that same-sex spouses were not eligible for the same federal marriage benefits provided to married heterosexual couples.[21]

Both the George W. Bush and Clinton Administrations defended DOMA's constitutionality in court, but the Obama Administration reversed course. In a letter to House Speaker John Boehner, Attorney General Eric Holder made it crystal clear that while the executive branch would continue to enforce the law, it believed DOMA was unconstitutional on equal protection grounds and would no longer defend it from future court challenges.[22] Holder also invited any member of Congress who wished to defend the law to participate in the Windsor lawsuit,[23] prompting the House Bipartisan Legal Advisory Group (BLAG) to hire counsel to defend the law in court. The district court struck down Section 3 and ordered the Treasury to refund Windsor's tax. Both BLAG and the DOJ appealed the decision, DOJ to ask the Court of Appeals to adopt a heightened scrutiny standard for sexual orientation and BLAG to defend Section 3's constitutionality (Funk 2014). The appeals court affirmed, and the government again appealed to the Supreme Court, where the justices had to decide whether the Supreme Court has jurisdiction to hear the case since the Obama administration already agreed with the lower court that DOMA is unconstitutional. The justices agreed that they did have jurisdiction, agreed with the lower courts, and struck down Section 3 as a violation of the 5th Amendment's right to equal protection of the law.

The *Windsor* decision has many important implications for separation of powers. The Obama Administration's decision to enforce but not defend DOMA in court was met with derision by those who argued that the President ought not pick and choose which federal law to enforce and which to ignore because doing so sets a dangerous precedent for future presidents.[24] However, this choice is not unprecedented in the Obama Administration (Pepper 2013). After all, the President invoked his non-enforcement power regarding his refusal to deport individuals who are living in the United States illegally but are the parents of American-born children under Deferred Action for Parents of Americans (DAPA). His administration also engaged in lax enforcement of federal marijuana laws and lax prosecution of non-violent drug offenders (Tribe and Matz 2014). Much of this was in line with the administration's view that for many years our justice system had unfairly targeted individuals who are poor and non-white, making them a disproportionate segment of the incarcerated.

The *Windsor* saga also exposed the administration's departure from executive branch tradition. In previous administrations, it was traditional for the president to ask Congress to fix the part of a law that the administration deems unconstitutional even while refusing to enforce it because of questionable constitutionality. Faced with a more tolerant public, the inability or unwillingness of Congress to alter Section 3, and a growing number of state laws legalizing same-sex marriage, the Administration decided to seek a judicial solution by refusing to defend the law in court rather than invite Congress to remedy the law (Funk 2014).

The decision also has implications for Court procedure. While the Court did declare Section 3 of DOMA unconstitutional, the Court's ability to exercise jurisdiction was called into question by the apparently non-adversarial nature of the appeal to the Supreme Court. As Scott (2014) argues, *Windsor*, as well as the Court's decision in *Hollingsworth v. Perry*, reshaped the Court's precedents on standing to appeal. According to Article III of the U.S. Constitution, federal courts have jurisdiction over "cases or controversies." In *Windsor*, despite agreeing with the lower court decision, the federal government nonetheless did not refund Windsor's tax payment and appealed to the Supreme Court instead. Previously, the Court had consistently noted that there is "no case or controversy within the meaning of Art. III of the Constitution" when "both litigants desire precisely the same result."[25] However, in *Windsor* the Court allowed the case to proceed because BLAG's participation as an amicus ensured an adversarial case, and the government was injured by the lower court ruling for the Treasury to pay Windsor. Scott (2014) finds that the Supreme Court made a sharp break with its prior precedent on Article III standing and "represented a crucial test of the power to enforce laws while refusing to defend them from constitutional challenge" (p. 81). Moreover, the Court's standing decision largely ignored BLAG's right to defend the law in court, an action typically exercised by the executive branch (Funk 2014). Thus, *Windsor* failed to establish precedent on the right of Congress to defend its enacted laws in federal court.

Windsor was a landmark case that brought an important victory for LGBT advocates from both legal and institutional perspectives. The events leading up to the decision and the decision itself demonstrate important lessons concerning the fluidity of separation of powers, and signal interesting developments for the Court's treatment of litigant standing and its approach to equal protection cases. For presidential power, the case was important in preserving executive authority to simultaneously enforce but not defend a congressional statute. The Court also considered executive power, as well as federal authority, in its immigration decisions. In the next section, we present a broad overview of the Court's recent immigration rulings, focusing principally on federal preemption and the Court's treatment of Arizona's controversial immigration law, SB 1070, in *Arizona v. United States*.[26]

Immigration Exceptionalism and Federal Preemption

During the Obama presidency, the Supreme Court made immigration an important part of its docket (Johnson 2015).[27] This was partly in reaction to an increase in petitions filed to challenge the Administration's aggressive effort to deport illegal immigrants, especially those who committed crimes. Annually, the U.S. government removes approximately 400,000 immigrants, many of whom are permanent residents convicted of minor criminal offenses (Johnson 2015). Indeed, Ingrid V. Eagly (2013) writes that "the deportation of 'criminal aliens' is now the driving force in American immigration enforcement" and that "federal immigration enforcement has become a criminal removal system" (p. 1128). Consistent with the theme of reduced deference to executive authority expressed earlier, justices often rejected seemingly overzealous immigrant-removal policies and aggressive legal stances of the executive branch, especially efforts to deport long-term lawful permanent residents for minor criminal offenses.[28] Even though this is a center-right Court, its immigration jurisprudence, according to Johnson (2015), has "lacked ideological heavy-handedness" (p. 116), "followed generally applicable legal principles" (p. 62), and has "declined to stretch its ordinary rules to review immigration cases with decidedly political overtones" (p. 63). For example, the Court declined to review politically charged state and local immigration measures in favor of resolving conflicts among circuits.[29]

Perhaps most strikingly, the Court surprised legal commentators by moving away from its plenary power/immigration exceptionalism doctrine (Johnson 2015). For over a century, federal courts used this doctrine to insulate congressional and executive immigration decisions from judicial review, effectively allowing U.S. immigration laws to discriminate against non-citizens in ways that citizens cannot be discriminated against (Johnson 2015; Motomura 1999).[30] In this way, U.S. immigration law has departed from other areas of mainstream constitutional law. The Court has noted that immigration decisions "are frequently of a character more appropriate to either the Legislature or the Executive than to the Judiciary."[31] However, in its recent immigration decisions, the Court has consistently considered executive branch immigration decisions in a manner comparable to its review of the rulings of other administrative agencies, suggesting that the Court has put immigration law well within the jurisprudential mainstream (Johnson 2015, pp. 114–115). This is nothing but good news for those wishing to challenge seemingly unfair U.S. immigration policies.

In addition, during the Obama Era, the Court issued two important rulings concerning federal preemption of state and local immigration regulation, with implications for the ability of the executive to guide the nation's immigration policy. In *Chamber of Commerce v. Whiting* (2011) and *Arizona v. United States* (2012), the Court came to opposite conclusions on whether state and local government action was preempted by federal law.

In 1986, Congress enacted *The Immigration Reform and Control Act* (IRCA). The law provided for civil penalties on employers who hired undocumented workers and preempted state and local governments from imposing civil and criminal penalties on employers. Moreover, in 1996, Congress authorized *E-Verify*, an Internet-based system allowing employers to verify whether their employees were legally authorized to work in the United States. The *Whiting* case concerned a challenge to an Arizona law imposing state penalties on employers hiring unauthorized immigrant workers and mandating that employers use *E-Verify* to ensure their employees met eligible requirements. The Court upheld the law against a preemption challenge, ruling that the *E-Verify* provision furthered federal goals and that the IRCA preserved state authority to enact licensing laws on employers (Guttentag 2013; Johnson 2015).

The Court's second and more important preemption decision came in *Arizona v. United States* (2012) where provisions of Arizona's "Support Our Law Enforcement and Safe Neighborhoods Act," or SB 1070, were challenged. Called the "nation's toughest bill on illegal immigration,"[32] the law was part of a trend in mostly conservative states to toughen restrictions on unauthorized immigration. The challenged provisions:

- Made violating the federal alien registration law a state crime (Section 3)
- Made it a state crime for an undocumented person to look for, or be employed in, unauthorized work (Section 5c)
- Authorized police officers to make warrantless arrest of individuals they suspect of committing a removable offense (Section 6)
- Required police to detain and determine the immigration status of any person the officer had reason to believe was not legally present in the United States (Section 2b, the law's most controversial provision).

The Supreme Court struck down three of the four provisions. Section 3 was invalidated because Congress's registration scheme was complete, thus preventing states from legislating in the area even if the state legislation had the same purpose.[33] Section 5c was struck down because it conflicted with Congress's decisions in IRCA to levy penalties on employers not employees. Finally, Section 6 was struck down because it allowed Arizona its own immigration authority by granting local police greater power than trained federal immigration officers are granted under federal law (Guttentag 2013). While the bill's most notorious provision, Section 2b, was upheld, the Court's opinion expressly noted that it did not "foreclose other preemption and constitutional challenges to the law as interpreted and applied after it goes into effect."

This decision enacted a framework of two principles (Guttentag 2013, p. 13). The first is that state police require federal permission to enforce federal immigration law. Second, states cannot penalize immigration violations by creating their own crimes. At its heart, the Court's majority opinion raises foreign policy concerns as an essential reason for federal preemption in this area. The Court stressed the danger inherent in state encroachment into federal authority in a realm where foreign nations hold the federal government responsible for the treatment of its citizens. Relatedly, Guttentag (2013) argues that "the foreign affairs basis for federal immigration power is the federal government's interest in using immigration policy as an affirmative tool of foreign relations" (p. 17).

This case also considered an aspect of presidential power employed more explicitly by President Obama than under previous administrations: "the power not to enforce laws to their fullest extent" (Tribe and Matz 2014, p. 210). Judge Brett Kavanaugh of the D.C Circuit writes, "One of the great unilateral powers a President possesses under the Constitution... is the power to protect individual liberty by essentially under-enforcing federal statutes regulating private behavior."[34] In particular, and as we noted earlier, President Obama had used his non-enforcement powers to limit enforcement of anti-drug laws in states that legalized marijuana and to avoid deporting undocumented persons who entered the country before they were 16 years of age. The president's ability to use such powers has been derided by critics[35] and presents a potential separation of powers concern. Critics worry that unrestricted executive discretion to enforce or not enforce laws provides the president with a second veto, granting legislative authority to the executive by avoiding calling upon Congress to alter the law (Price 2014, p. 674). Ultimately, the Court's decision "sharply constrained permissible sub-federal authority, articulated a strong foundation for federal primacy in immigration enforcement, and rejected broad theories of state power" (Guttentag 2013, p. 3). It also endorsed "the role of Executive discretion in setting enforcement priorities" (ibid, p. 15). While the Court has declined to review lower court decisions implementing its preemption opinion in *Arizona*,[36] the justices returned to the question of presidential power in *United States v. Texas* (2016), where an equally divided Court affirmed the Fifth Circuit's injunction blocking the President's DAPA.

While we have focused on healthcare, same-sex marriage, and immigration, there are several other important decisions rendered by the Supreme Court during the Obama Era that illustrate the relationship between the 44th president and the highest court. For example, the Court expanded the meaning of money as a form of political speech under the First Amendment by ruling in *McCutcheon v. Federal Election Commission* (2014) that aggregate limits on individual campaign contributions are unconstitutional. Meanwhile, the Court struck down the constitutionality of extra taxpayer-funded support for political candidates who have been outspent by privately funded opponents or by independent political groups (*Arizona Free Enterprise Club's Freedom Club PAC v Bennett* (2011)). However, in the biggest campaign spending case during the Obama Era, the Supreme Court ruled in *Citizens United v. FEC* (2010) that there must be no limits on independent corporate or organizational spending on political campaigns, essentially opening the floodgates of money into American elections. The Court thus extended its long-standing practice of considering corporations as citizens under the equal protection clause, a practice that originated in the Waite Court through an 1886 railroad tax case called *Santa Clara County v. Southern Pacific Railroad*. The *Citizens United* decision created public conflict between the Court and the President when Justice Samuel Alito mouthed "not true" at the State of the Union address in response to President Obama's denouncement of the decision as a reversal of "a century of law that I believe will open the floodgates for special interests, including foreign corporations, to spend without limit in our elections."[37]

In the areas of race and economic inequality, the Supreme Court was relatively subdued. Historically, some Supreme Court decisions have contributed to the gap between the haves and the have-nots (*San Antonio v. Rodriguez* (1973)). As a candidate, Barack Obama campaigned to reduce the widening income and wage inequality in the United States. Before he took office, the Court's decision in *Ledbetter v. Goodyear Tire and Rubber Co* (2007) seemingly ignored, exacerbated, or at the very least failed to address the wage gap between men and women. The Court ruled that the statute of limitation had expired on Lilly Ledbetter's ability to file a sex discrimination lawsuit after she learned that, for years, her employer (Goodyear Tire) had excessively underpaid her relative to male employees with similar jobs and experience level. Obama spearheaded the *Lilly Ledbetter Fair Pay Act* (2009) to counteract the effects of the Court's decision. The act was the first bill Obama signed into law as president.

In race relations, the Court was not overly active but did release one decision severely limiting the intended beneficial effect of Section 5 of the Voting Rights Act (VRA) of 1965 in *Shelby County v. Holder* (2013). Section 5 of the Act requires certain states (primarily Southern States) and their local governments to obtain federal preclearance before implementing any changes to their voting rights laws or procedures. The justices struck down the formula used to determine which states are covered by preclearance, meaning that states no longer must seek preclearance from the Justice Department for voting rights legislation. As a result, numerous states have enacted vote-curbing legislation that, for instance, limit how many days of pre-election voting people are allowed before the actual date of the general election. Many other states have enacted voter identification laws and other restrictive requirements to make it harder for citizens to cast their ballots.

180 I. UNAH AND R. WILLIAMS

Conclusion

The Obama Administration found mixed support in the Supreme Court. At the aggregate level, the President's success rate followed contemporary trends wherein the Court is exercising less deference to the executive branch. Moreover, while the Court struck down the Defense of Marriage Act in *Windsor*, constitutionalized marriage equality in *Obergefell*, and saved the President's signature legislative achievement, the Affordable Care Act, in *National Federation of Independent Business v. Sebelius*, the Court looked less favorably on the administration's positions on campaign finance and it backpedaled on voting rights. Preclearance, an important dimension of the VRA, was left without an enforcement mechanism when the Court struck down its coverage formula in *Shelby County*, effectively disabling the VRA. Moreover, Justice Kennedy's majority opinion in *Citizens United* granted outside groups greater latitude to spend money independently of political candidates.

Ultimately, the legacy of the Obama presidency in the U.S. Supreme Court will continue to be shaped by the justices he appointed, Sonia Sotomayor and Elena Kagan, as well as by the administration's failure to seat Chief Judge Merrick Garland. Obama's selections of the first Latino justice and the first female SG were important milestones for descriptive representation. However, the results of our empirical analysis suggest that while the Obama Justices are having a substantive impact on law and specific aspects of public policy, they have not pushed the Court significantly to the left relative to their predecessors, as some observers had anticipated. We have shown that Justices Sotomayor and Kagan's voting patterns are comparable to their predecessors, Justices Souter and Stevens, and for some specific issue areas even voted more conservatively. Moreover, like Sotomayor and Kagan, Merrick Garland was a moderate pick by a president committed to seeing his nominees confirmed. That Garland, a well-respected centrist and former Oklahoma City Bombing prosecutor, did not even receive a confirmation hearing provides perhaps the best signal that American politics has reached an unprecedented level of partisan polarization. The consequences of Garland's failed nomination will, in due course, be best assessed in the jurisprudence of Justice Neil Gorsuch, who was confirmed in Garland's stead.

During his presidential campaign, Donald Trump promised to nominate a Supreme Court justice "very much in the mold of Justice Scalia."[38] Justice Scalia's conservative voting record and originalist philosophy are well documented (Biskupic 2009), and Justice Gorsuch's early voting record suggests he will be a reliable conservative voice on the Court. Conservative obstructionism in the Senate is already paying dividend. At the end of his first abbreviated term on the Court, Gorsuch had voted with fellow conservatives Clarence Thomas, Samuel Alito, and John Roberts, in 100, 94, and 88 percent of cases, respectively.[39]

Beyond the U.S. Supreme Court, Obama's legacy in the federal district and appellate courts is also mixed. Facing an ideologically opposed Senate, Obama struggled to see his nominees confirmed to the lower federal bench. However, as with the Supreme Court, Obama's legacy will be written by the judges he appointed. Obama's appointments greatly reshaped the demographic composition of the lower federal courts, significantly improving descriptive representation in the federal judiciary through his appointment of more women and minority federal judges than any other president in American history. Taken together with his appointment of Kagan and Sotomayor to the U.S. Supreme Court, this could well be Obama's most important judicial legacy given the lifetime tenures of federal judges.

NOTES

1. Bureau of Labor Statistics, U.S. Department of Labor, *The Economics Daily*, Unemployment in December 2008 on the Internet at https://www.bls.gov/opub/ted/2009/jan/wk2/art02.htm (visited May 21, 2018).
2. Barack Obama: "Keynote Address at the 2004 Democratic National Convention," July 27, 2004. Gerhard Peters and John T. Woolley, *The American Presidency Project.* http://www.washingtonpost.com/wp-dyn/articles/A19751-2004Jul27.html
3. Justice Thurgood Marshall's dissent in Rodriquez echoes Obama's sentiments about the harshness of the Court's decision:

   The majority's holding can only be seen as a retreat from our historic commitment to equality of educational opportunity. In my judgment, the right of every American to an equal start in life, so far as the provision of a state service as important as education is concerned, is far too vital to permit state discrimination of this sort. (*San Antonio School District v. Rodriguez* 1973)

4. Republicans controlled the House of Representatives for the final six years of Obama's presidency and gained majority control of the Senate following the 2014 midterm elections.
5. Information obtained from http://www.uscourts.gov/judges-judgeships/judicial-vacancies/archive-judicial-vacancies

6. The blue slip process is an institutional norm used by the Senate Judiciary Committee to solicit the preferences of a senator when a lower court federal judge is nominated in that senator's home state. Traditionally, if a home state senator did not return her blue slip signaling her support of the nominee, the nominee was not considered and the nomination was essentially dead. See Slotnick et al. (2017) and Binder and Maltzman (2009).

7. Numbers derived from Slotnick et al. (2017).

8. President Barack Obama's State of the Union Address, January 28, 2014. Online by White House Office of the Press Secretary. https://obamawhitehouse.archives.gov/the-press-office/2014/01/28/president-barack-obamas-state-union-address

9. https://opinionator.blogs.nytimes.com/2012/12/26/the-n-r-a-at-the-bench/

10. The Biden Rule is strikingly like the Thurmond Rule, named after former Senate Judiciary Committee Chair Strom Thurmond. Although not a formal rule of the Senate, it is often invoked by senators who wish to deny presidential appointments to federal courts in the months preceding a presidential election (Binder 2012).

11. Note that when Senator Joe Biden made his speech, there was no vacancy on the Court and no nominee was under consideration by the Senate.

12. For an extended discussion of the history of the nuclear option, see Smith (2014).

13. Souter was appointed by George Bush to fill the vacancy created by the retirement of Justice William Brennan.

14. Based on a two-sample test of proportions conducted using Stata 13. The p-value is 0.015.

15. Spaeth identified 14 total issue areas but only 11 had sufficient cases to permit analysis.

16. See "A Conversation with U.S. Supreme Court Justice Elena Kagan" Harvard Law School, September 16, 2016. https://www.youtube.com/watch?v=zxITcqE0orM

17. As the newest member of the Court, Justice Kagan heads the Cafeteria Committee. At a speech at Harvard Law School, she spoke about being thanked profusely by law clerks for introducing a yogurt machine to the Court. She apparently also improved the quality of the coffee (ibid).

18. The percentages pertaining to opinion writing are based on 12 issue areas of the Court's docket.

19. For example, Ponnuru (2012) wrote that Roberts "acted less like a judge than like a politician, and a slippery one."

20. *Baehr v. Lewin* 852 P.2d 44 (Haw. 1993), *Baehr v. Miike* 910 P.2d 112 (Haw. 1996).

21. Pub. L. No. 104-199, 110 Stat. 2419 (1996) (codified at 1 U.S.C. § 7 (2006); 28 U.S.C. § 1738C (2006)).
22. See Letter from Eric H. Holder, Jr., Attorney General of the United States, to Hon. John H. Boehner, Speaker of the United States House of Representatives (Feb. 23, 2011) available at http://www.justice.gov/opa/pr/2011/February/11-ag-223.html
23. See Attorney General Letter: "I have informed Members of Congress of this decision, so Members who wish to defend the statute may pursue that option." https://www.justice.gov/opa/pr/statement-attorney-general-litigation-involving-defense-marriage-act
24. Moreover, the administration's argument that there was no reasonable defense of DOMA's constitutionality was met with skepticism given that the federal government had recently been defending the law in federal court (Tipler 2013).
25. *Moore v. Charlotte-Mecklenburg Bd. of Educ.*, 402 U.S. 47, 48 (1971) (per curiam); see also *Muskrat v. United States*, 219 U.S. 346, 361 (1911).
26. *Arizona v. United States*, 567 U.S. 387 (2012).
27. In its 2009–2013 terms, the Supreme Court issued thirteen decisions on the merits concerning various aspects of immigration law (Johnson 2015). The Roberts Court considered issues of federal versus state authority, executive power, and the extension of civil rights to non-resident aliens. See *Padilla v. Kentucky*, 559 U.S. 356 (2010).
28. See *Moncrieffe v. Holder* (2013), *Vartelas v. Holder* (2012), *Carachuri-Rosendo v. Holder* (2010), *Mellouli v. Lynch* (2015).
29. See *Martinez v. Regents of the University of California* (2010). See also Rosenbloom (2013)
30. See *Chae Chan Ping v. United States* (The Chinese Exclusion Case), 130 U.S. 581 (1889).
31. *Mathews v. Diaz* et al., 426 U.S. 67, 81 (1976).
32. Randal C. Archibald, Arizona Enacts Stringent Law on Immigration, *New York Times* (April 24, 2010), http://www.nytimes.com/2010/04/24/us/politics/24immig.html?_r=0
33. The Court had previously addressed this issue in *Hines v. Davidowitz* 312 U.S. 52 (1941).
34. In re *Aiken County*, 725 F.3d 255, 264 (D.C. Cir. 2013).
35. Kris W. Kobach, "The 'DREAM' Order Isn't Legal," *New York Post*, June 22, 2012.
36. See *Lozano v. City of Hazleton*, 724 F.3d 297, 300 (3d Cir. 2013), *Villas at Parkside Partners v. City of Farmers Branch*, 726 F.3d 524 (5th Cir. 2013) (en banc), *Valle del Sol, Inc. v. Whiting* 134 S. Ct. 1876 (2014), and *Keller v. City of Fremont*.

37. President Barack Obama, State of the Union Address (January 27, 2010) (transcript available at http://millercenter.org/president/speeches/detail/5706).
38. Transcript of the Second Debate, *New York Times* (October 10, 2016).
39. Source: SCOTUSblog Stat Pack: http://www.scotusblog.com/wp-content/uploads/2017/06/SB_agreement-tables_20170628.pdf

Bibliography

Applebaum, Binyamin, and Michael D. Shear. 2016. "Once Skeptical of Executive Power, Obama Has Come to Embrace It." *The New York Times*, August 13, 2016, https://www.nytimes.com/2016/08/14/us/politics/obama-era-legacy-regulation.html

Archibald, Randal C. 2010. "Arizona Enacts Stringent Law on Immigration, *The New York Times*, April 24, 2010, http://www.nytimes.com/2010/04/24/us/politics/24immig.html?_r=0

Arizona v. United States, 567 U.S. 387 (2012).

Arizona Free Enterprise Club's Freedom Club PAC v. Bennett, 564 US 721 (2011).

Baehr v. Miike 910 P.2d 112, 116 (Haw. 1996).

Baehr v. Lewin 852 P.2d 44 (Haw. 1993).

Bailey, Michael A. 2013. "Is Today's Court the Most Conservative in Sixty Years? Challenges and Opportunities in Measuring Judicial Preferences." *Journal of Politics* 75: 821–834.

Barnes, Robert. 2010. "Justice John Paul Stevens announces his retirement from Supreme Court." *The Washington Post*, April 10, 2010, http://www.washingtonpost.com/wp-dyn/content/article/2010/04/09/AR2010040902312.html

Binder, Sarah A. 2012. "'Tis the Season for the Thurmond Rule." *Brookings*, June 14, 2012, https://www.brookings.edu/opinions/tis-the-season-for-the-thurmond-rule/

Binder, Sarah A., and Forrest Maltzman. 2009. Advice and Dissent: The Struggle to Shape the Federal Judiciary. Washington, D.C.: Brookings Institution Press.

Biskupic, Joan. 2009. *American Original: The Life and Constitution of Supreme Court Justice Antonin Scalia*. New York: Sarah Crichton Books.

Biskupic, Joan, Janet Roberts, and John Shiffman. 2014. "At America's Court of Last Resort, A Handful of Lawyers Now Dominate the Docket. *Reuters*, December 8, 2014 https://www.reuters.com/investigates/special-report/scotus/#sidebar-analysis

Black, Ryan C., and Ryan J. Owens. 2011. "Solicitor General Influence and Agenda Setting on the U.S. Supreme Court." *Political Research Quarterly* 64(4): 765–778.

Breyer, Stephen. 2016. *The Court and the World: American Law and the New Global Realities.* New York: Vintage Books.

Bullock, Charles S. and M.V. Hood. 2012 "The Tea Party, Sarah Palin, and the 2010 Congressional Elections: The Aftermath of the Election of Barack Obama." *Social Science Quarterly,* 93: 1424–1435.

Canon, Bradley C., and Michael Giles. 1972. "Recurring Litigants: Federal Agencies before the Supreme Court." *Western Political Quarterly* 25: 183–91.

Caplan, Lincoln. 1987. *The Tenth Justice: The Solicitor General and the Rule of Law.* New York: Vintage Books.

Carachuri-Rosendo v. Holder, 560 US 563 (2010).

Carp, Robert A., and Kenneth L. Manning. 2016. "U.S. District Court Database." 2016 version n=110977. http://districtcourtdatabase.org

Chamber of Commerce v. Whiting, 563 U.S. 582 (2011).

Chae Chan Ping v. United States, 130 U.S. 581 (1889).

Citizens United v. Federal Election Commission, 558 U.S. 310 (2010).

Chevron U.S.A. Inc. v. Natural Resources Defense Council, 467 U.S. 837 (1984).

CNN. 2016. "Its Official: Clinton Swamps Trump in Popular Vote." December 22. https://www.cnn.com/2016/12/21/politics/donald-trump-hillary-clinton-popular-vote-final-count/index.html

Crowley, Donald W. 1987. "Judicial Review of Administrative Agencies: Does the Type of Agency Matter?" *Western Political Quarterly* 31: 265–83.

Dahl, Robert A. 1957. "Decision-making in a Democracy: The Supreme Court as a National Policymaker." Journal of Public Law, 6: 279.

Eagly, Ingrid V. 2013. "Criminal Justice for Noncitizens: An Analysis of Variation in Local Enforcement." *New York University Law Review.* 88: 1126–1223.

Eisenstein, James, Roy B. Flemming, and Peter F. Nardulli. 1988. *The Contours of Justice: Communities and Their Courts.* Boston: Little, Brown and Company.

Emery, Eugene C. Jr. 2016. "In Context: The 'Biden Rule' on Supreme Court nominations in an election year." *Politifact, Last visited January 13, 2018* http://www.politifact.com/truth-o-meter/article/2016/mar/17/context-biden-rule-supreme-court-nominations/

Entin, Jonathan L. 2012. "War Powers, Foreign Affairs, and the Courts: Some Institutional Considerations." *Case Western Reserve Journal of International Law,* 45(1): 443–459.

Esposito, Liugi and Laura Finley-Barry. 2009. "Barack Obama, Racial Progress, and the Future of Race Relations in the United States." *The Western Journal of Black Studies* 33:164–175

Feinstein, Dianne. 2017. "Opinion: Republicans Reversed Course on 'Blue Slips' for Judicial Nominees." *Roll Call.* Last visited May 21, 2018 https://www.rollcall.com/news/opinion/blue-slips-judicial-nominees-feinstein

Frontline, 2013. "Inside Obama's Presidency." January 15, 2013. Last accessed January 10, 2018 at: https://www.pbs.org/wgbh/frontline/film/inside-obamas-presidency/

Funk, Derek. 2014. "Checking the Balances: An Examination of Separation of Powers Issues Raised by the Windsor Case." *Arizona State Law Journal* 46: 1471–1497.

Gibson, James L., and Gregory A. Caldeira. 2011. "Has Legal Realism Damaged the Legitimacy of the U.S. Supreme Court?" *Law and Society Review* 45: 195–219.

Goldstein, Amy and Paul Kane. 2009. "Senate Votes 68 to 31 to Confirm Sonia Sotomayor to Supreme Court" *The Washington Post*, August 7, 2009, http://www.washingtonpost.com/wp-dyn/content/article/2009/08/06/AR2009080601706.html

Greenhouse, Linda. 2012. "The N.R.A. at the Bench." *New York Times*, December 26.

Guttentag, Lucas. 2013. "Immigration Preemption and the Limits of State Power: Reflections on Arizona v. United States." *Stanford Journal of Civil Rights. & Civil Liberties.* 9: 1–46.

Handberg, Roger. 1979. "The Supreme Court and Administrative Agencies: 1965-1978." *Journal of Contemporary Law* 6 (Fall): 161–76.

Hines v. Davidowitz, 312 U.S. 52 (1941).

Hirschl, Ran. 2011. "The Judicialization of Politics." In *The Oxford Handbook of Political Science*, Oxford University Press.

Hollingsworth v. Perry, 570 U.S. ___2013.

In re Aiken County, 725 F.3d 255, 264 (D.C. Cir. 2013).

Johnson, Kevin R. 2015. "Immigration in the Supreme Court, 2009-13: A New Era of Immigration Law Unexceptionalism." *Oklahoma Law Review* 68: 57–188.

Keller v. City of Fremont, 719 F.3d 931, 951 (8th Cir. 2013), cert. denied, 134 S. Ct. 2140 (2014).

King v. Burwell, 576 U.S.___(2015).

Kobach, Kris W. 2012. "The 'DREAM' Order Isn't Legal." *New York Post*, June 22, 2012, https://nypost.com/2012/06/22/the-dream-order-isnt-legal/

Ledbetter v. Goodyear Tire & Rubber Co., 550 U.S. 618 (2007).

Liptak, Adam. 2010. "Court Under Roberts is Most Conservative in Decades." *The New York Times*, July 24, 2010, http://www.nytimes.com/2010/07/25/us/25roberts.html

Lozano v. City of Hazleton, 724 F.3d 297, 300 (3d Cir. 2013), cert. denied, 134 S. Ct. 1491 (2014).

Mathews v. Diaz et al., 426 U.S. 67, 81 (1976).

Martinez v. Regents of the University of California, 241 P.3d 855, 860 (Cal. 2010), cert denied, 131 S. Ct. 2961 (2011).

Maxwell, Angie and T. Wayne Parent. *2012.* "The Obama Trigger: Presidential Approval and Tea Party Membership." *Social Science Quarterly,* 93:1384–1401.

McCutcheon v. Federal Election Commission, 572 U.S. ___(2014).

McGuire, Kevin T. 1993. *The Supreme Court Bar: Legal Elites in the Washington Community.* Charlottesville: University Press of Virginia.

McGuire, Kevin T. 1995. "Repeat Players in the Supreme Court: The Role of Experienced Lawyers in Litigation Success." *The Journal of Politics* 57(1): 187–96.

McGuire, Kevin T. 1998. "Explaining Executive Success in the U.S. Supreme Court." *Political Research Quarterly* 51(2): 505–26.

Mellouli v. Lynch, 575 U.S.___(2015).

Memoli, Michael A. and Lisa Mascaro. 2016. "Obama's Choice of Popular Centrist Merrick Garland for Supreme Court puts GOP to the Test." *Los Angeles Times,* March 16, 2016

Moncrieffe v. Holder, 569 U.S.___(2013).

Moore v. Charlotte-Mecklenburg Bd. of Educ., 402 U.S. 47, 48 (1971).

Motomura, Hiroshi. 1999. "Federalism, International Human Rights, and Immigration Exceptionalism." *University of Colorado Law Review* 70: 1361–94.

Muskrat v. United States, 219 U.S. 346, 361 (1911).

National Federation of Independent Business v. Sebelius, 567 U.S. 519 (2012).

Obama, Barack. 2006. *The Audacity of Hope: Thoughts on Reclaiming the American Dream.* New York: Penguin Random House.

Obergefell v. Hodges, 576 U.S. ___(2015).

Pacelle, Richard L. Jr. 2003. *Between Law and Politics: The Solicitor General and the Structuring of Race, Gender, and Reproductive Rights Litigation.* College Station: Texas A&M University Press.

Padilla v. Commonwealth of Kentucky, 559 U.S. 356 (2010).

Pepper, Stacy. 2013. "The Defenseless Marriage Act: The Legitimacy of President Obama's Refusal to Defend Doma § 3." *Stanford Law and Policy Review* 24:1–34.

Ponnuru, Ramesh. 2012. "In Health-Care Ruling, Roberts Writes His Own Law." *Bloomberg,* June 28, 2012.

Posner, Erik and Lee Epstein. 2018. "The Decline of Supreme Court Deference to the President. *University of Pennsylvania Law Review* 166: 829–860.

Price, Zachary S. 2014. "Enforcement Discretion and Executive Duty." *Vanderbilt Law Review* 67: 671–769.

Roeder, Oliver. 2015. "Despite this Week's Victories, Obama Has Struggled at the Supreme Court." *FiveThirtyEight,* June 26, 2015, https://fivethyeight.com/features/despite-this-weeks-victories-obama-has-struggled-at-the-supreme-court/

Rosenbloom, Rachel E. 2013. "The Citizenship Line: Rethinking Immigration Exceptionalism." *Boston College Law Review* 54: 1965–2024.

Ruckman, Peter Sturges, Jr. 1993. "The Supreme Court, Critical Nominations, and the Senate Confirmation Process." *Journal of Politics* 55:793–805

Salokar, Rebecca M. 1992. *The Solicitor General: The Politics of Law*. Philadelphia: Temple University.

San Antonio Independent School District v. Rodriguez, 411 U.S. 1 (1973).

Santa Clara County v. Southern Pacific Railroad, 118 U.S. 394 (1886).

Savage, Charlie. 2012. "Obama Lags on Judicial Picks, Limiting His Mark on Courts." *The New York Times*, August 17, 2012, http://www.nytimes.com/2012/08/18/us/politics/obama-lags-on-filling-seats-in-the-judiciary.html

Scott, Ryan W. 2014. "Standing to Appeal and Executive Non-Defense of Federal Law After the Marriage Cases." *Indiana Law Journal* 89: 5: 67–93.

Segal, Jeffrey A., and Harold J. Spaeth. 2002. *The Supreme Court and the Attitudinal Model Revisited*. New York: Cambridge University Press.

Segal, Jeffrey. 1990. "Supreme Court Support for the Solicitor General: The Effect of Presidential Appointments. *Western Political Quarterly* 43(1): 137–52.

Singer, Joseph W. 2005. "Same Sex Marriage, Full Faith and Credit, and the Evasion of Obligation." *Stanford Journal of Civil Rights and Civil Liberties* 1: 1–50.

Shapiro, Ilya. 2016. "Obama has Lost in the Supreme Court More than Any Modern President." *The Federalist*, July 16, 2016, at http://thefederalist.com/2016/07/06/obama-has-lost-in-the-supreme-court-more-than-any-modern-president/

Shelby County v. Holder, 570 US___(2013).

Sheehan, Reginald S. 1992. "Federal Agencies and the Supreme Court: An Analysis of Litigation Outcomes, 1953-1988." *American Politics Quarterly* 20 (October): 478–500.

Shipan, Charles R., and Morgan Shannon. 2003. "Delaying Justice(s): A Duration Analysis of Supreme Court Confirmations. *American Journal of Political Science* 47:654–668.

Slotnick, Elliot, Sara Schiavoni, and Sheldon Goldman. 2017. "Obama's Judicial Legacy: The Final Chapter." *Journal of Law and Courts*, 5:363–422.

Smith, Steven S. 2014. *The Senate Syndrome: The Evolution of Procedural Warfare in the Modern U.S. Senate*. Norman: University of Oklahoma Press.

Spaeth, Harold J., Lee Epstein, et al. 2017 Supreme Court Database, Version 2017 Release 1. URL: http://Supremecourtdatabase.org

Spaeth, Harold J., and Stuart Teger. 1982. "Activism and Restraint: A Cloak for the Justices' Policy Preferences." In *Supreme Court Activism and Restraint*, ed. Halpern and Lamb, 277–302. Lexington, MA: Lexington Books.

Sotomayor, Sonia. 2002. "A Latina Judge's Voice." *Berkeley La Raza Law Journal* 13: 87–94.

Stone, Geoffrey R. n.d. "How a 1973 Supreme Court Decision Has Contributed to Our Inequality." *The Daily Beast*. Accessed 1/18/18. https://www.thedailybeast.com/how-a-1973-supreme-court-decision-has-contributed-to-our-inequality

Tate, C. Neal. 1995. *The Global Expansion of Judicial Power*. New York: New York University Press.

Tipler, Kathleen. 2013. "Obama Administration's Non-Defense of DOMA and Executive Duty to Represent." *Maryland Law Review* 73: 287–311.

Toobin, Jeffrey C. 2012. *The Oath: The Obama White House and the Supreme Court*. New York: DoubleDay.

Tribe, Laurence, and Joshua Matz. 2014. *Uncertain Justice: The Roberts Court and the Constitution*. New York: Henry Holt and Company.

Unah, Isaac and Ange-Marie Hancock. 2006. "Supreme Court Decision Making, Case Salience, and the Attitudinal Model." *Law & Policy* 28: 298–320.

United States v. Curtiss-Wright Export Corp., 299 U.S. 304 (1936).

United States v. Windsor, 570 U.S. 744 (2013).

United States v. Texas, 579 U.S. ___(2016).

Valle del Sol, Inc. v. Whiting 732 F.3d 1006 (9th Cir. 2013), cert denied, 134 S. Ct. 1876 (2014).

Vartelas v. Holder, 566 U.S.____(2012).

Villas at Parkside Partners v. City of Farmers Branch, 726 F.3d 524 (5th Cir. 2013) (en banc), cert denied, 134 S. Ct. 1491 (2014).

Washington Post. 2009. "NRA's Target: Sonia Sotomayor." Editorial, July 28.

Wheeler, Russell. 2017. "Senate GOP used "Blue Slips" to Block Obama Judicial Nominees, But Now Wants to Trash the Practice." *Brookings*. Accessed May 15, 2018.

Whitehouse, Sheldon. 2015. "Conservative Judicial Activism: The Politicization of the Supreme Court Under Chief Justice Roberts." *Harvard Law & Policy Review* 9: 195–210.

Youngstown Sheet & Tube Co. v. Sawyer, 343 U.S. 579 (1952).

The Obama Administration's Global Warming Legacy: Going with the Flow and the Politics of Failure

George A. Gonzalez

The *New York Times* in responding to President Donald J. Trump's global warming policies issued an editorial titled "Nailing the Coffin on Climate Relief."[1] If President Trump has nailed the coffin on climate relief, was the Obama administration complicit in building the coffin? Since the 1970 establishment of the Environmental Protection Agency, the lead federal agency in environment policy, its role has been controversial. In 1990, the law was amended (PL 101-549) to impose stricter federal standards on urban smog, automobile exhaust and other air pollutions. Nevertheless, in regulating emission controls, the United States, for several administrations, has not impeded the trend toward world climate catastrophe.

Part of this chapter was published as "Is Obama's 2014 Greenhouse Gas Reduction Plan Symbolic?: The Creation of the US EPA and a Reliance on the States," *Capitalism Nature Socialism* Vol. 26, No. 2 (January 2015) pp. 92–104.

G. A. Gonzalez (✉)
University of Miami, Coral Gables, FL, USA
e-mail: george.gonzalez@miami.edu

© The Author(s) 2019   191
W. C. Rich (ed.), *Looking Back on President Barack Obama's Legacy*,
https://doi.org/10.1007/978-3-030-01545-9_9

Although the Obama years were considered climate control-friendly, this chapter reconsiders this image as it relates to automobile emissions.

Beginning in the 1920s, the automobile revolution was centered in, even monopolized, by the United States—with 85 percent of all automobiles built in America during this period. After World War II, many Americans were able to purchase an automobile. In 1956, the Eisenhower administration enacted the Defense Highway Act. Americans are able to live further away from their workplace and the city center. This subsequently resulted in the federal government promoting urban sprawl (suburban development), with state and local governments playing important, key supporting roles. Urban sprawl fostered automobile dependency (longer commuters and traffic jams) and relatively large homes in low-density neighborhood, which would be filled with copious amounts of consumer durables (retail items expected to last three years—furniture, appliances, electronics, etc.). In addition to excelling in the production of automobiles, the US industrial base also led the world in the manufacturing of consumer durables. Urban sprawl in the U S led to the massive consumption of fossil fuels (oil, coal, natural gas)—as automobile dependency and the large homes in suburban zones creates an energy ineffective transportation and housing infrastructure. The end result being that the U S for much of the twentieth century was the prime source of greenhouse gas emissions, and the global warming phenomenon.[2]

While China has in the 2000s surpassed the U S as the world's leading greenhouse gas emitter, US emissions still remain high, and most glaring it holds by far the lead in per capita (per person) emissions among countries with populations over 40 million. US high per capita emissions are mostly, if not entirely, the result of proliferation of automobiles and expanding urban sprawl. Thus, American global warming emissions are decisively about luxury—huge automobiles (SUVs), driving long distances on a daily basis to huge homes that consume lots of energy to heat, cool and electrify. (Homes in the US are at least twice as energy intensive as those in Europe and Japan.)[3]

While these policies and emission patterns were set long before Barack Obama was elected president in 2008, his administration deepened the nation's dependency on fossil fuels—at a time when the signs of global warming were clearly evident (most significantly, the research explaining the collapse of the Arctic ice sheets) and there was the hope and an expectation that the world could negotiate an effective climate change treaty. (Indeed, in 2013, the Obama White House was promising that the 2015

Paris global warming conference would result in a substantive treaty.[4] Under President Obama's leadership, both the 2009 Copenhagen and 2015 Paris climate change meetings of world leaders failed to produce a treaty.) Also, in 2008 the global price of oil hit the all-time high of $147 a barrel.

Thus, with broad concerns that global oil shortfalls made the US liberal petroleum consumption policies unfeasible (i.e., urban sprawl and the SUV craze), and fears about global warming being high on the agenda, the Obama presidency (2008–2017) seemed to be on the cusp of a much-needed reset on American energy policies—a reset that would put the US and the world on a climate and energy sustainable path. Instead, however, the Obama administration oversaw the hydro-fracking revolution and the expansion of production from the Canadian oil sands. These actions conveyed the true energy, climate policies of the Obama administration. In other words, President Obama supported pro-fossil fuels as did his predecessors.[5] Significantly, the Obama State Department created in 2011 a Bureau of Energy Resources, "for the purpose of channeling the domestic energy boom [from gas and oil shale] into a geopolitical tool to advance American interests around the world."[6] This new agency ostensibly paved the way for the global exporting of large amounts of US liquefied natural gas.[7]

PRESIDENT OBAMA'S ENVIRONMENTAL PROFILE

Under President Obama the EPA begin to impose new regulations on automobile emission, utility power plants and other emission of carbon pollution. In 2009, the president appointed Lisa Jackson as EPA Administrator, the first chemical engineer to hold the job. The EPA issued a regulation that stated that carbon dioxide and other greenhouse gases were inimical to public health and welfare. During her tenure (2009–2013), there were several high-profile clashes over global warming with the Congress and state governments. According to Reuters writer Ayesha Roscoe, "Some speculated Jackson would step down in 2011, when Obama decided to delay rules to restrict emissions of smog forming chemicals from power plants."[8] Despite the sometime partisan nature of Congressional review (or oversight), the automobile industry pushbacks and the interactions between the White House and the EPA administrator, President Obama, generally speaking, received favorable coverage from the media regarding his environmental policies. He was considered by the public as a pro-environment president. What set President Obama apart from predecessors is that he did not question the science and reality of global warming. Nevertheless, Obama responded like his predecessors to the public's broad concerns about the environment—through symbols. This is consistent with Murray Edelman's *Symbolic Uses of Politics*, that is, some policies have more symbolic effects rather than solving problems.[9] Except Obama's environmental symbols sought to assuage fears about climate change. The Obama administration's $70 billion allocated to clean energy in 2009, for instance, was a one-off expenditure.[10] Perhaps more significantly, the administration did not use this money to finance government research, but instead utilized it to issue loan guarantees for entrepreneurial projects. It was reported that $500,000,000 of this money was dispensed in an irregular manner and the result was that a Barack Obama campaign finance donor was reimbursed on a bad investment.[11] The Obama administration 2012 rule to strengthen automotive fuel efficiency standards was predominately about the future—with the most significant increases set to occur beyond 2016.[12]

A case can be made that the Obama administration's 2009 allocation to clean renewables served to obscure the hydro-fracking revolution, and the Obama White House rejection of the Keystone XL pipeline served to obscure the fact that source material from the Canadian oil sands had increased. When the pipeline was rejected, oil exports from Canada (including oil sands dilbit [diluted bitumen]) to the US had already increased to 3.8 million barrels per day from 2.5 million barrels in 2008, while imports from OPEC countries had significantly declined.[13]

Seemingly, the most significant effort to curb global warming emissions during the Obama presidency was the February 2014 plan (under Section 111 of the 1970 Clean Air Act) to directly address US greenhouse gas emissions from its fleet of power plants—about 600 of which are coal-fired.[14] Critics have noted that the administration's goal of reducing emissions by 30 percent from 2005 levels by 2030 is a minimal goal since emissions are already down by 15 percent due to the expanded usage of natural gas as a replacement for carbon intense coal.[15] However, there was a more serious flaw at the core of the Obama greenhouse gas plan—namely, that the plan was predicated on being implemented by the US subnational governments (i.e., the individual states). In outlining the Obama greenhouse gas plan, the *New York Times* observed, in an article titled "Taking Page from Health Care Act, Obama Climate Plan Relies on

States," that "rather than imposing a uniform standard for reducing power plant carbon emissions, the regulation unveiled on Monday offers the states flexibility to pick from a menu of policy options."[16]

The decision by the Obama administration not to challenge Clean Air Act policy of devolving environment policies implementation to the states rendered the plan essentially symbolic, as there is a disparate capacity among individual states. In addition, some state leaders are openly pro-business. They seek to attract more manufacturing corporations and jobs to their states. As such, many states will prioritize economic growth over environmental protection, and emissions may increase in response to states' growth strategies.[17] This is because depending on the price of natural gas, states may shift back to coal. Already, investment is moving toward the US precisely because of its comparatively low energy prices.[18] Historically speaking, a reliance on the states to develop and implement national environmental regulatory policies has been a way to weaken/undermine said policies. This was evident in the founding of the Environmental Protection Agency (EPA). The EPA was specifically created by President Nixon as a symbol of the government response to nascent environmental concerns—intended to pacify the environmental social movement of the late 1960s. The origins of the EPA enforcement structure and powers can be traced to an economic elite policy discussion group—the President's Advisory Council on Executive Organization (aka the Ash Council).

Matthew Cahn in his book, *Environmental Deceptions,*[19] is the first to apply Murray Edelman's notion of symbolic politics to the US environmental policy realm. Here I extend Cahn's analysis and argue that the institutional configuration of US environmental regulatory policies (i.e., a reliance on the individual states) is a key reason why these federal policies are symbolic. Moreover, I show the role that economic (or business) elites had in establishing this flawed institutional configuration.

BUSINESS LEADERS AND PUBLIC POLICYMAKING

The US economic elite is composed of decision makers within large corporations and of other persons of substantial wealth. These actors are integrated into a cohesive elite or class through social clubs, interlocking directorates of both private and public organizations,[20] policy discussion groups (e.g., the Business Roundtable, Council on Foreign Relations and the Committee on Economic Development), and inter-marriage.[21] Altogether, the economic elite compose roughly 0.5–1 percent of the total US population; it has a disproportional impact on policy. This elite is a dominant factor in the development of public policy because it possesses large amounts of the most important political resources in the United States—wealth and income.[22] The wealth and income of the economic elite allow it to accumulate superior amounts of other valuable resources, such as *social status, organization, campaign finance, lobbying,* and *political access to legal scientific expertise.* The theoretical approach that emphasizes the political behavior and political influence of economic elites is entitled economic elite theory. Economic elites develop policy goals and political consensus through policy discussion groups, which are largely made up of these elites.

In 1969, President Nixon appointed Roy L. Ash president of Litton Industries to head a discussion group, known as the Ash Council. The Council was convened to deal with the environmental movement that was sweeping the nation at the time. The Council proposed establishing a new regulatory agency (i.e., the creation of the EPA) in response to a growing activist environmental movement.

The Ash Council

The six-person Ash Council (appointed by President Richard M. Nixon) was made up entirely of economic elites and directly responsible for the creation of the Environmental Protection Agency in December of 1970. The chair of the council was (1) Roy L. Ash—co-founder and president of Litton Industries:

> Through a series of acquisitions, Beverly Hills-based Litton Industries became one of the fastest-growing conglomerates of the 1950s and '60s, a highly diversified and multinational company whose products ranged from manufacturing electronic typewriters and industrial microwave ovens to producing electronic guidance systems for aircraft and building ships.[23]

(2) George P. Baker was a leading consultant to major airlines, railroads and government. He served as a director of numerous major corporations, including the Mobil Oil and Lockheed Aircraft Corporations;[24] (3) John B. Connelly, prior to becoming Governor of Texas, was the lawyer for the oil magnates Sid W. Richardson and Perry Bass. When Richardson died in

1959, Connelly was his co-executor;[25] (4) Frederick R. Kappel was a former chairman of the AT&T Corporation;[26] (5) Richard M. Paget was a director of many companies, including the Liggett & Myers Tobacco Company, the Washington Post Company and Union Dime Savings Bank. Paget had also been a trustee of the Metropolitan Museum of Art and had been president of the Association of Consulting Management Engineers;[27] (6) Walter N. Thayer was for more than 30 years a close associate of the late financier John Hay Whitney, on whose behalf he arranged the acquisition of the financially troubled [New York] *Herald Tribune* in 1958—of which he became president.[28]

What prompted the organization of the Ash Council and the subsequent overhaul of federal environmental legislation and the creation of the Environmental Protection Agency? Rachel Carson's book *Silent Spring* (1962) alerted Americans to the harmful and toxic effects of pollutants. In addition, it was broadly understood that the environmental social movement of the 1960s and early 1970s brought about an acknowledgment of the environmental crisis by the Nixon administration—a crisis that would only get worse with the passing decades (i.e., global warming). Historian J. Brooks Flippen's book *Nixon and the Environment* documents how the environmental movement moved the environment as a political issue to the forefront of the administration's agenda.[29] John Quarles, who was a leading official in the EPA from its inception, explains the political factors that brought about the creation of this agency. Quarles observes that:

> The environmental movement has been one of America's most effective protests... It gained power from the rebellion of youth, which dominated the civil rights and antiwar movements of the 1960s. At its peak it attracted vocal support from nearly all groups within the nation. It became a crusade.[30]

Quarles, who notes that he "never planned to be either a bureaucrat or an environmentalist,"[31] describes the political milieu in 1970: "...the eruption of citizen protest, the demand that government do something to save the environment."[32]

The Ash Council issued its memo on April 29, 1970.[33] In it the council takes note of the profound environmental problems facing the country (something heretofore Washington, D.C. [especially the executive branch[34]] didn't express much concern about):

The Environmental Crisis. Pollution is essentially a by-product of our vastly increased per capita consumption, intensified by population growth, urbanization, and changing industrial processes. In the coming years, problems of environmental degradation will rise exponentially.

While our population will increase from 200 to 260 million by the year 2000, pollution will increase much more rapidly. Even if 50 percent of the nation's electric generating capacity is nuclear-powered by the year 2000, pollutants resulting from fossil-fuel generation will double by 1980 and redouble by 2000.

Similarly, a seven-fold increase is expected in industrial wastes produced by the large water-using industries. These wastes are also expected to become more variable, more difficult to decompose, and more toxic. At the same time, our demand for fresh water will increase from 350 to 800 billion gallons a day—considerably exceeding the dependable supply of fresh water now available, some 650 billion gallons daily. More and more clean water will have to be retrieved from progressively dirtier waterways.

Even the fact that Americans annually junk 7 million cars, 100 million tires, 20 million tons of paper, 28 billion bottles, and 48 billion cans, does not reveal the dimensions of the problem. The 7 million cars, for example, represent less than 15 percent of the annual solid waste load. Each year we create 400 to 500 new chemicals. Many are toxic, but their exact ecological effects are not fully understood. We cannot even reliably forecast where or how they will turn up in our environment after they are used.

The enormous future needs for land, minerals, and energy require that the protection of our environment receive a powerful new impetus. In this, the nation will be on the "horns of a dilemma." The economic progress that we have come to expect, or even demand, has almost invariably been at some cost to the environment.

Pesticides have increased the yield of our crops and made it possible for less land to produce more food. They have also polluted the streams and lakes. Automobiles have broadened our economic and social opportunities, even as they have dirtied the air and jammed our highways. Some means must be found by which our economic and social aspirations are balanced against the finite capacity of the environment to absorb society's wastes.

The Ash Council's recommendation of how to deal with the "Environmental Crisis" was institutional reorganization:

Inadequacy of Present Organization. Our National Government is neither structured nor oriented to sustain a well-articulated attack on the practices that debase the air we breathe, the water we drink and the land that grows our food. Indeed, the present departmental structure for dealing with environmental protection defies effective and concerted action.

The environment, despite its infinite complexity, must be perceived as a unified, interrelated system. Present assignments of departmental responsibilities do not reflect this primary characteristic.

One of the institutional reforms proposed by the Ash Council was to place all the ongoing environmental protection activities under a new agency, the Environmental Protection Administration (EPA).

In arguing for the concentration of federal regulatory responsibilities (air, water, pesticides) in one agency[35] the Council was not positing a "confrontational" environmental politics. This is evident in the fact that "The Council also believes that an independent EPA would offer distinct advantages to the business community and to state and local governments."[36]

The Federal Government is not equipped solely or even primarily to effect a turnabout in our environmental situation through its own powers and resources. The business community is an indispensable partner in this process, even though enforcement is needed so that a business which cooperates will not be placed at a competitive disadvantage. The single agency would simplify the relationship of the private sector whose cooperation and ingenuity are essential if any real progress is to be made.

Federal anti-pollution programs must rely heavily on state and local efforts. The trend toward merger and coordination of environmental efforts at the state and local level is often inhibited by present Federal fragmentation. The EPA will simplify relationships with state and local governments and reduce the need to shop around for grant programs and other assistance.

Thus, the Council was not arguing for a fundamental reordering of institutions to effect environmental protection. With an emphasis that the EPA operate through business and states/localities, its creation does not amount to meaningful reformism but rather a limited regulatory agency.

The limits were for two reasons. Firstly, a key "role and function of the EPA" (according to the Council) is "to coordinate pollution control activities with state and local agencies and with the private sector." The *New York Times* reported in an article commemorating the 40th anniversary of the creation of the EPA that from its initial creation it "work[ed] with industries to set pollution standards."[37] Secondly, federal law already stipulated that states/localities report to the federal government on air and water pollution matters. Federal clean air and clean water legislation of the early 1970s maintained the structure whereby states/localities remain as the main focus of environmental regulatory policymaking and enforcement—with the EPA exercising oversight of states' regulatory goals and enforcement efforts.

STATES AS GROWTH MACHINES

It is a widely accepted axiom among those who study urban/regional politics that cities/states, broadly speaking, can be most aptly regarded as "growth machines."[38] City and state political and business leaders form pro-growth coalitions to recruit businesses and to create jobs. In other words, many state and local government scholars acknowledge that the desire for economic investment is a central political agenda item for almost every locality.

Given the importance assigned to local investment, state and local governments are aggressive with regards to attracting potential capital investment. These government entities also provide certain economic and political enticements to attract such investment. Schools, roads, and airports, for example, can be seen as overall efforts to attract capital to an area. In the most abstract sense, these government-provided amenities are subsidized inputs into the production process. Additionally, state and local governments assure potential investors that their investments were welcome and will be afforded political priority.

The Competition for Capital and Clean Air Regulations

Thus, in the first instance the Ash Council, and subsequently federal environmental regulatory laws, continued to rely on states/localities in shaping government pollution abatement efforts. The main institutional reform of the early 1970s was the centralization of federal oversight over state/local pollution policies—that is, the EPA. A key reason why government policies into the late 1960s allowed for the environmental crisis identified by the Ash Council is precisely because states/localities in the US were predominately growth machines. Put differently, the prime goal of these leaders is local/regional economic growth. In *the Politics of Air Pollution* and "The Politics of U.S. Water Pollution Policy",[39] I argue that clean air and clean water are simply means to attracting capital investment and increasing regional property values. Owen Temby finds the same political dynamic surrounding the policies of air pollution abatement in Toronto.[40]

While Temby and I point to outcomes when local growth politics led to cleaner air and water, Matthew A. Crenson (1971) in his landmark study, *The Un-Politics of Air Pollution*, shows that in Gary, Indiana, during the post-World War II period the severe air pollution from the local US Steel factory was kept off of the political agenda. Similarly, my research documented the case of Chicago in the early twentieth century when in the face of railroad opposition regional economic elites (operating through the Chicago Association of Commerce), the city leaders backed down from efforts to prompt the electrification of the lines running into the city. Such electrification would have significantly reduced air pollution. Moreover, during this period, Chicago continued its heavy reliance on the region's highly polluting (but low priced) bituminous (or soft) coal. Cheap coal, coupled with the fact that Chicago was the major railroad hub of the Midwest, were key factors in making the city a global center of industrial production and the Second Industrial Revolution. Precisely because local and regional governments in the US prioritized economic growth, going into the 1970s American cities were significantly polluted.

The US continues to have an uneven clean air and clean water regime. Some sub-governments have relatively exemplary environment policies, while others have shortcomings. Some regions actively pursue policies to abate pollution, while others seemingly sacrifice air and water quality in an effort to attract/maintain business investment. The current context of global neoliberalism may serve to create/intensify a race to the bottom by these governments.

Prior to 1970, the most significant instance of air pollution abatement efforts occurred in Los Angeles, and California, more broadly. During the 1940s and 1950s, Southern California's lucrative real estate market was threatened by the severe air pollution (smog) that was brought on by its somewhat unique topography and meteorology, along with its expanded industrial base and bourgeoning automobile population. In response, the *Los Angeles Times* and its owners (the Chandler family)—in conjunction with other economic elites—instituted the strongest air pollution regime in the country.[41] California continues to be the national leader in airborne emissions control.

The California case, however, still shows that states are essentially unreliable in terms of pollution abatement. This is outlined in Douglas S. Eisinger's 2010 book *Smog Check: Science, Federalism, and the Politics of Clean*

Air. Eisinger documents how in the 1990s California undermined federal efforts to establish an effective automobile inspection regime—whereby all automobiles would be individually inspected to ensure compliance with emission rules. Beginning in 1992, the EPA sought to create an inspection regime that was centralized and directly overseen by state governments. California instead argued for a system that allowed private garages to conduct automobile emissions testing. The EPA viewed the California proposal as having two key flaws: first, allowing private garages to conduct inspections meant greater possibilities for fraud (with the concern being that private mechanics would be more likely to "pass" cars that were in fact non-compliant); second, private garages could not afford the most effective/sensitive emission detection technologies, whereas centralized test-only facilities could recoup the costs of the best technology available. The EPA held that "garage-based" inspection programs "were only half as effective at reducing emissions as centralized test systems."[42]

More was at stake in this EPA/State political face-off than California's automotive inspection regime. At the time that California was seeking "flexibility" from the EPA to incorporate private garages into its inspection regime, the EPA was pressing other states to adopt its centralized inspection scheme. EPA's concern was that if it acceded to California's request to bring private garages into the automotive emission inspection process, other states would demand similar variances, and, worse, states that had already agreed to EPA's centralization plan would renege from such agreements (which did occur—most glaringly, Texas). In April 2001, the federal government ended its effort to mandate tailpipe emission inspections.

CONCLUSION

This chapter reviewed EPA automobile emission policies during the Obama administration. As we suggested, the EPA is authorized to make environmental regulations based on the laws passed by the Congress. We also accepted the fact that throughout the history of the EPA regulations, they have been challenged in the courts. Yet, this review of the leadership of the EPA and president's environmental legacy with regard to tackling global warming emissions tragically was found superficial and symbolic. This is why the Trump administration has so easily undone it[43]—including reversing the Obama decision on the Keystone XL pipeline.[44] The Obama administration did not challenge unrelenting urban sprawl or curb US fossil fuel dependency. Arguably, as a result Obama failed to produce a global climate change treaty. Thus, Obama left no treaty or even legislative legacy to combat global warming.

Despite the careful nurturing of a positive environmental image for President Obama, his administration oversaw the hydro-fracking revolution and encouraged viewing the gas and oil shale as an international hegemonic device. This policy helped open the door to the exportation of liquefied natural gas, which will serve as a barrier to the global use of clean renewable energy.

Returning to the issue of domestic policy, the Obama administration did not seek to reform the institutional configuration of US environmental policies. Indeed, he designed his signature global warming policy to adhere to the history of relying on the states to design and institute this policy. It was far from certain that the states (collectively) would have achieved even the modest goal set in the Obama policy to reduce emissions from power plants, as their economic growth agenda will take priority over this and all other goals. Even California, which has a strong reputation on addressing airborne emissions, has in the contemporary era undermined the country's clean air regime (i.e., the automobile smog program).

In the modern era, reliance on the states to regulate pollution has been a way to evade federal regulatory responsibilities. The assignment of implementation of environmental policy to states by the Ash Council and the creation of the EPA has proven to have undermined the overall effort to prevent air pollution. Unfortunately, this policy of a continued dependence on the states—thereby avoiding the kind of organizational and policy reform that could have come from centralizing governmental regulatory power in a single agency has apparently been endorsed by the Trump administration.

NOTES

1. "Nailing the Coffin on Climate Relief," *New York Times*, October 11, 2017, A22.
2. George A. Gonzalez, *Urban Sprawl, Global Warming, and the Empire of Capital* (Albany: State University of New York Press, 2009), *Energy and Empire: The U.S. Politics of Nuclear and Solar Power in the United States* (Albany: State University of New York Press, 2012), and *Energy, the Modern State, and the American World System* (Albany: State University of New York Press, 2018).

3. George A. Gonzalez, *Energy and the Politics of the North Atlantic* (Albany: State University of New York Press, 2013).

4. Till Neeff, "How Many will Attend Paris? UNFCCC COP Participation Patterns 1995–2015," *Environmental Science & Policy* 31 (August 2013): 157–159; David Jolly and Chris Buckley, "U.S. and China Find Convergence on Climate Issue," *New York Times*, Nov. 22, 2013, A3; David Jolly,"Deals at Climate Meeting Advance Global Effort," *New York Times*, Nov. 24, 2013, A14.

5. George A. Gonzalez, *American Empire and the Canadian Oil Sands* (New York: Palgrave Macmillan, 2016).

6. Coral Davenport, and Steven Erlanger, "U.S. Hopes Boom in Natural Gas Can Curb Putin," *New York Times*, March 6, 2014, A1. Also see "Natural Gas as a Diplomatic Tool," *New York Times*, March 7, 2014, A24; Clifford Krauss, "U.S. Gas Tantalizes Europe, but It's Not a Quick Fix," *New York Times*, April 8, 2014, B1; Stanley Reed and James Kanter, "For a European Energy Chief, a Difficult Alliance," *New York Times*, April 28, 2014, B1; Rick Gladstone, "Russia and Iran Reported in Talks on Energy Deal Worth Billions," *New York Times*, April 29, 2014, A12; Jim Yardley, and Jo Becker, "How Putin Forged a Pipeline Deal That Derailed," *New York Times*, December 31, 2014, A1.

7. Clifford Krauss, "U.S. Boom in Natural Gas Could Ripple From the Arctic to Africa," *New York Times*, October 18, 2017, B3.

8. Ayesha Roscoe, "Jackson to Step Down as Obama's Environmental Chief," Reuters, December 27, 2012. Web.

9. See Murray Edelman, *The Symbolic Uses of Politics*, 2nd ed. (Champaign: University of Illinois Press, 1985).

10. Harvey Blatt, *America's Environmental Report Card: Are We Making the Grade?* 2nd ed. (Cambridge, MA: MIT Press, 2011), 180–181; "The End of Clean Energy Subsidies?" *New York Times*, May 6, 2012, SR12.

11. Rachel Weiner, "Solyndra, explained," *Washingon Post*, June 1, 2012. Web.

12. Bill Vlasic, "U.S. Sets High Long-Term Fuel Efficiency Rules for Automakers," *New York Times*, August 29, 2012, B1. The current Trump administration is revising the Obama automotive fuel efficiency rule downward. Hiroko Tabuchi, Brad Plumer and Coral Davenport, "Plan to Loosen Emission Limits Disputes California's Right to Set Its Own," *New York Times*, April 28, 2018, A15.

13. Clifford Krauss, "Pipeline Plan was Begun Amid Dim U.S. Forecasts," *New York Times*, November 7, 2015, A12.

14. George A. Gonzalez, "Is Obama's 2014 Greenhouse Gas Reduction Plan Symbolic?: The Creation of the U.S. EPA and a Reliance on the States," *Capitalism Nature Socialism* 26, no. 2 (2015): 92–104.

15. Justin Gillis, and Henry Fountain, "Trying to Reclaim Leadership on Climate Change." *New York Times*, June 2, 2014, A14; Clifford Krauss, and Diane Cardwell, "Hopes Modest for Carbon Rules." *New York Times*, June 3, 2014, B1; Porter, Eduardo. 2014. "A Paltry Start in Curbing Global Warming." The New York Times, June 4, B1.
16. Coral Davenport, and Peter Baker. 2014. "Taking Page From Health Care Act, Obama Climate Plan Relies on States." New York Times, June 3, A16.
17. Ibid.
18. Stanley Reed, "High Energy Costs Plaguing Europe," *International Herald Tribune*, December 27, 2012. Web; Nelson D. Schwartz, "Boom in Energy Spurs Industry in the Rust Belt," *New York Times*, September 9, 2014, A1.
19. Matthew A. Cahn.1995. *Environmental Deceptions: The Tension between Liberalism and Environmental Policymaking in the United States*. Albany: State University of New York Press.
20. Michael Useem. 1984. *The Inner Circle: Large Corporations and the Rise of Business Political Activity in the U.S. and U.K.* Oxford: Oxford University Press.
21. Clyde W. Barrow. 1993. *Critical Theories of the State* (Madison: Wisconsin University Press), Chap. 1, and *Toward a Critical Theory of States: The Poulantzas-Miliband Debate After Globalization* (Albany: State University of New York Press, 2016) G. William Domhoff. 2014. *Who Rules America?* 7th ed. New York: McGraw-Hill.
22. See "The Democrats Stand Up to the Kochs." *New York Times*, March 11, 2014, A20; Martin Gilens, and Benjamin I. Page, "Testing Theories of American Politics: Elites, Interest Groups, and Average Citizens." *Perspectives on Politics* 12, no. 3 (2014): 564–581. doi: https://doi.org/10.1017/S1537592714001595; Jacques Leslie. 2014. "The True Cost of Hidden Money." *New York Times*, June 16, A19; Gordon Lafer, *The One Percent Solution: How Corporations Are Remaking America One State at a Time* (Ithaca: Cornell University Press, 2017).
23. Dennis McLellan. 2012. "Roy L. Ash Dies at 93; Former Litton President, Budget Director." *Los Angeles Times*, January 12. Web.
24. Ronald Sullivan. 1995. "George Baker, Harvard Dean and U.S. Adviser, Dies at 91." *The New York Times*, January 28. Web.
25. Charles Ashman. 1974. *Connally: The Adventures of Big Bad John*. New York: William Morrow & Company, 70–71.
26. Kenneth N. Gilpin. 1994. "Frederick Kappel, 92, Ex-Chief of AT&T and Former U.S. Aide." *New York Times*, November 12. Web.
27. "Richart Paget, 78; Helped Reorganize Federal Government," *New York Times*, January 9, 1991. Web.

28. Albin Krebs, "Walter Thayer, 78, Herald Tribune President, Dies." *New York Times*, March 5, 1989. Web; E.J. Kahn. *Jock: The Life and Times of John Hay Whitney* (New York: Doubleday, 1981).
29. Brooks J. Flippen. *Nixon and the Environment* (Albuquerque: University of New Mexico Press, 2000 [2012]).
30. John Quarles, *Cleaning Up America: An Insider's View of the Environmental Protection Agency* (Boston: Houghton Mifflin, 1976), xiv.
31. Ibid., xii.
32. Ibid., 13.
33. The Ash Council Memo can be found: http://www2.epa.gov/aboutepa/ash-council-memo
34. Dennis L. Soden, *The Environmental Presidency* (Albany: State University of New York Press 1999); Tarla Rai Peterson, *Green Talk in the White House: The Rhetorical Presidency Encounters Ecology* (College Station: Texas A&M University Press, 2004).
35. According to one historian, by the late 1960s "over eighty federal agencies dealt with pollution." Flippen. *Nixon and the Environment*, 85.
36. The Ash Council Memo can be found: http://www2.epa.gov/aboutepa/ash-council-memo
37. Emily Yehle, "Drastic Enforcement Cases' Heralded Arrival of EPA 40 Years Ago," *The New York Times*, December 2, 2010. Web.
38. John C. Mollenkopf. 1983. *The Contested City*. Princeton, NJ: Princeton University Press.; Jonas, Andrew E. G., and David Wilson, eds. 1999. *The Urban Growth Machine: Critical Perspectives Two Decades Later*. Albany: State University of New York Press.; Logan, John R., and Harvey L. Molotch, *Urban Fortunes: The Political Economy of Place*. Berkeley: University of California Press, 2007 [1987]).
39. George A. Gonzalez, *The Politics of Air Pollution: Urban Growth, Ecological Modernization, and Symbolic Inclusion* (Albany: State University of New York Press, 2005); George A. Gonzalez, "The U.S. Politics of Water Pollution Policy: Urban Growth, Ecological Modernization, and the Vending of Technology." *Capitalism Nature Socialism* 24, no. 4 (2013): 105–121.
40. Owen Temby. 2013. "Trouble in Smogville: The Politics of Toronto's Air Pollution during the 1950s." *Journal of Urban History* 39 (4): 669–689. doi: https://doi.org/10.1177/0096144212441710
41. Scott H. Dewey, *"Don't Breathe the Air": Air Pollution and U.S. Environmental Politics, 1945–1970* (College Station: Texas A& M University Press, 2000).
42. Douglas S. Eisinger, *Smog Check: Science, Federalism, and the Politics of Clean Air* (Washington, DC: Resources of the Future, 2010), 11.

43. Lisa Friedman and Brad Plumer, "E.P.A. Announces Bid to Roll Back Emissions Policy," *New York Times*, October 10, 2017, A1; "Nailing the Coffin on Climate Relief"; Lisa Friedmen, "Carbon Dioxide Is Harmless, Says Trump Pick for Environmental Adviser," *New York Times*, October 14, 2017, A9, and "For U.S., Climate Talks Are Awkward Moment," *New York Times*, October 19, 2017, A10; "Mr. Trump's Conflicted Regulators," *New York Times*, October 18, 2017, A26.
44. Peter Baker and Coral Davenport, "President Revives Two Oil Pipelines Thwarted Under Obama," *New York Times*, January 25, 2017, A1.

BIBLIOGRAPHY

Ashman, Charles. 1974. *Connally: The Adventures of Big Bad John*. New York: William Morrow & Company.

Bacot, A.H. and R.A. Dawes. 1997. "State Expenditures and Policy Outcomes in Environmental Program Management." *Policy Studies Journal* 25 (3): 355–370.

Baker, Peter, and Coral Davenport. 2017. "President Revives Two Oil Pipelines Thwarted Under Obama," *New York Times*, January 25, A1.

Barrow, Clyde W. 1993. *Critical Theories of the State*. Madison, WI: Wisconsin University Press.

———. 2016. *Toward a Critical Theory of States: The Poulantzas-Miliband Debate AfterGlobalization*. Albany: State University of New York Press.

Blatt, Harvey. 2011. *America's Environmental Report Card: Are We Making the Grade?* 2nd ed. Cambridge, MA: MIT Press.

Cahn, Matthew A. 1995. *Environmental Deceptions: The Tension Between Liberalism and Environmental Policymaking in the United States*. Albany, NY: State University of New York Press.

Crenson, Mathew A. 1971. *The Un-Politics of Air Pollution*. Baltimore: Johns Hopkins University Press.

Davenport, Coral, and Peter Baker. 2014. "Taking Page From Health Care Act, Obama Climate Plan Relies on States." *New York Times*, June 3, A16.

Davenport, Coral, and Steven Erlanger. 2014. "U.S. Hopes Boom in Natural Gas Can Curb Putin." *New York Times*, March 6, A1.

Dewey, Scott H. 2000. *"Don't Breathe the Air": Air Pollution and U.S. Environmental Politics, 1945–1970*. College Station, TX: Texas A&M University Press.

Domhoff, G. William. 2014. *Who Rules America?*, 7th ed. New York: McGraw-Hill.

Edelman, Murray. 1985. *The Symbolic Uses of Politics*, 2nd ed. Urbana: University of Illinois Press.

Eisinger, Douglas S. 2010. *Smog Check: Science, Federalism, and the Politics of Clean Air*. Washington, D.C.: Resources of the Future.

Flippen, Brooks J. 2000 [2012]. *Nixon and the Environment*. Albuquerque: University of New Mexico Press.

Friedman, Lisa. 2017. "Carbon Dioxide Is Harmless, Says Trump Pick for Environmental Adviser." *New York Times*, October 14, A9.

———. 2017. "For U.S., Climate Talks Are Awkward Moment." *New York Times*, October 19, A10.

Friedman, Lisa, and Brad Plumer. 2017. "E.P.A. Announces Bid to Roll Back Emissions Policy." *New York Times*, October 10, A1.

Gladstone, Rick. 2014. "Russia and Iran Reported in Talks on Energy Deal Worth Billions." *New York Times*, April 29, A12.

Gilens, Martin, and Benjamin I. Page. 2014. "Testing Theories of American Politics: Elites, Interest Groups, and Average Citizens." *Perspectives on Politics* 12, no. 3: 564–581.

Gillis, Justin, and Henry Fountain. 2014. "Trying to Reclaim Leadership on Climate Change." *New York Times*, June 2, A14.

Gilpin, Kenneth N. 1994. "Frederick Kappel, 92, Ex-Chief Of AT&T and Former U.S. Aide," *New York Times*, November 12. Web.

Gonzalez, George A. 2005. *The Politics of Air Pollution: Urban Growth, Ecological Modernization, and Symbolic Inclusion*. Albany: State University of New York Press.

———. 2012. *Energy and Empire: The Politics of Nuclear and Solar Power in the United States*. Albany: State University of New York Press.

———. 2013a. *Energy and the Politics of the North Atlantic*. Albany: State University of New York Press.

———. 2013b. "The U.S. Politics of Water Pollution Policy: Urban Growth, Ecological Modernization, and the Vending of Technology." *Capitalism Nature Socialism* 24 (4): 105–121.

———. 2015. "Is Obama's 2014 Greenhouse Gas Reduction Plan Symbolic?: The Creation of the U.S. EPA and a Reliance on the States," *Capitalism Nature Socialism* 26, no. 2: 92–104.

———. 2016. *American Empire and the Canadian Oil Sands*. New York: Palgrave Macmillan.

———. 2018. *Energy, the Modern State, and the American World System*. Albany: State University of New York Press.

Hulse, C., and Ashley Parker. 2014. "Koch Group, Spending Freely, Hones Attack on Government." *New York Times*, March 21, A1.

Jonas, Andrew E.G., and David. Wilson, eds. 1999. *The Urban Growth Machine: Critical Perspectives Two Decades Later*. Albany: State University of New York Press.

Jolly, David. 2013. "Deals at Climate Meeting Advance Global Effort." *New York Times*, Nov. 24, A14.

Jolly, David and C. Buckley. 2013. "U.S. and China Find Convergence on Climate Issue." *New York Times*, Nov. 22, A3.

Kahn, E.J. 1981. *Jock: The Life and Times of John Hay Whitney*. New York: Doubleday.

Krebs, Albin. 1989. "Walter Thayer, 78, Herald Tribune President, Dies," *New York Times*, March 5. Web.

Krauss, Clifford. 2014. "U.S. Gas Tantalizes Europe, but It's Not a Quick Fix." *New York Times*, April 8, B1.

———. 2015. "Pipeline Plan was Begun Amid Dim U.S. Forecasts." *New York Times*, November 7, A12.

———. 2017. "U.S. Boom in Natural Gas Could Ripple From the Arctic to Africa." *New York Times*, October 18, B3.

Krauss, Clifford, and Diane Cardwell. 2014. "Hopes Modest for Carbon Rules." *New York Times*, June 3, B1.

———. 2014. "Paranoia of the Plutocrats." *New York Times*, Jan. 27, A19.

Lafer, Gordon. 2017. *The One Percent Solution: How Corporations Are Remaking America One State at a Time*. Ithaca, NY: Cornell University Press, 2017.

Logan, John R., and Harvey L. Molotch. 2007[1987]. *Urban Fortunes: The Political Economy of Place*. Berkeley: University of California Press.

McLellan, Dennis. 2012. "Roy L. Ash Dies at 93; Former Litton President, Budget Director." *Los Angeles Times*, Jan. 12. Web.

"Mr. Trump's Conflicted Regulators." 2017. *New York Times*, October 18, A26.

Neeff, Till. 2013. "How Many will Attend Paris? UNFCCC COP Participation Patterns 1995–2015." *Environmental Science & Policy* 31 (August): 157–159.

"Nailing the Coffin on Climate Relief." 2017. *New York Times*, October 11, A22.

"Natural Gas as a Diplomatic Tool." 2014. *New York Times*, March 7, A24.

Peterson, Tarla Rai. 2004. *Green Talk in the White House: The Rhetorical Presidency Encounters Ecology*. College Station: Texas A&M University Press.

Porter, Eduardo. 2014. "A Paltry Start in Curbing Global Warming." *New York Times*, June 4, B1.

Quarles, John. 1976. *Cleaning Up America: An Insider's View of the Environmental Protection Agency*. Boston: Houghton Mifflin.

Reed, Stanley. 2012. "High Energy Costs Plaguing Europe." *International Herald Tribune*, Dec. 27. Web.

Reed, Stanley, and James Kanter. 2014. "For a European Energy Chief, a Difficult Alliance," *New York Times*, April 28, B1.

"Richart Paget, 78; Helped Reorganize Federal Government." 1991. *New York Times*, January 9. Web.

Rome, Adam. 2013. *The Genius of Earth Day: How a 1970 Teach-In Unexpectedly Made the First Green Generation*. New York: Hill and Wang.

Roscoe, Ayesha. 2012. "Jackson to Step Down as Obama's Environmental Chief." Reuters, December 27. Web.

Schwartz, Nelson D. 2014. "Boom in Energy Spurs Industry in the Rust Belt." *New York Times*, Sept. 9, A1.

Soden, Dennis L. *The Environmental Presidency*. Albany: State University of New York Press 1999.

Sullivan, Ronald. 1995. "George Baker, Harvard Dean And U.S. Adviser, Dies at 91." *New York Times*, January 28. Web.

Tabuchi, Hiroko, Brad Plumer, and Coral Davenport. 2018. "Plan to Loosen Emission Limits Disputes California's Right to Set Its Own." *New York Times*, April 28, A15.

Temby, Owen. 2013. "Trouble in Smogville: The Politics of Toronto's Air Pollution during the 1950s." *Journal of Urban History* 39 (4): 669–689.

"The Democrats Stand Up to the Kochs." 2014. *New York Times*, March 11, 2014, A20.

"The End of Clean Energy Subsidies?" 2012. *New York Times*, May 6, SR12.

Useem, Michael. 1984. *The Inner Circle: Large Corporations and the Rise of Business Political Activity in the U.S. and U.K.* Oxford: Oxford University Press.

Vlasic, Bill. 2012. "U.S. Sets High Long-Term Fuel Efficiency Rules for Automakers." *New York Times*, August 29, B1.

Weiner, Rachel. 2012. "Solyndra, explained," *Washingon Post*, June 1. Web.

Yardley, Jim, and Jo Becker. 2014. "How Putin Forged a Pipeline Deal That Derailed." *New York Times*, December 31, A1.

Yehle, Emily. 2010. "Drastic Enforcement Cases' Heralded Arrival of EPA 40 Years Ago." *New York Times*, Dec. 2. Web.

Unfulfilled Hopes: President Obama's Legacy

Stanley Renshon

Presidential legacies are strange political creatures. They are born in the deepest recesses of presidential ambition and purpose. They are then subject to modification by the innumerable vicissitudes of any presidents' term/s of office. And finally, they are refined by historical perspective and comparison. If presidential legacies represent ambition's dreams, real-world circumstances deflect their intentions with the often-unforgiving political reality principle. Such is the fate of the legacy of Barack Obama.[1]

President Obama came into office with a large reservoir of good will even from those who did not vote for him. He was after all, the first American of African descent to gain the presidency, and that fact marked a political, cultural, and racial milestone. Americans of all political views could be, and most were, proud of this historic accomplishment.

The election of Barack Obama to the presidency, however, promised more than the historic accomplishment of breaking the highest political level color ceiling in American politics and a base on which to make further progress in American race relations. His low-key demeanor, seemingly thoughtful reflective perspectives on the issues that divided

S. Renshon (✉)
City University of New York Graduate Center, New York, NY, USA
e-mail: srenshon@gc.cuny.edu

© The Author(s) 2019   211
W. C. Rich (ed.), *Looking Back on President Barack Obama's Legacy*,
https://doi.org/10.1007/978-3-030-01545-9_10

Americans, and his clarion call for a vision of presidential leadership for all Americans,[2] represented a political promise that proved incompatible with the president's transformational ambitions.

UNDERSTANDING PRESIDENTIAL LEGACIES

The origins of presidential legacies are found in the choices presidents make. Yet, their legacies also require some accounting of those choices— their purposes, their successes, their effectiveness, their limits, and their failures. Determining which categories into which to place presidential efforts, however, is no easy matter.

Any such effort must immediately address the issue of the metrics by which to sort the evidence. Every modern president's calendar is filled to the brim with meetings, speeches, travel, planning, analysis, and policy declarations. If activity equaled success, every modern president would be a candidate for having his face carved on Mt. Rushmore.

There is also the "full accounting" issue of presidential choices and their consequences. The debates that lead up to most presidential choices are made out of public view. In the past, the conventional wisdom was that a fuller accounting of a president's legacy would have to await the work of historians, and the passage of time, to allow the development of "perspective," removed the partisan conflicts of the day. In that view presidential legacies and reputation, two terms that are obviously related but not necessarily synonymous, are provisional until historians complete their work. In reality, that promise of that certainty was never more than a hope. Historians still debate the nature and consequences of presidential actions and their effects, offering their interpretations. These too are unresolved debates, not unanimous conclusions.[3]

Similar problems arise in the assumption that the passage of time provides "perspective" removed from the partisan battles of the day. In truth, those battles rarely fade and are simply carried on in other forms. Consider the historical reputations of presidents assessed by the periodic presidential rating polls. Reputation questions are asked either of the general public or those with academic credentials.[4] Unfortunately, for the idea of neutral presidential ratings, assessments of presidential "success" are tied to the evaluator's view of just what that term means. If they favor "activist" presidents, their judgment will lean one way. If they favor presidents of restraint, they will lean another way.[5]

There is of course, some consensus agreement about the "greats,"[6] George Washington, Thomas Jefferson, Andrew Jackson, Abraham Lincoln, and Franklin D. Roosevelt. Yet tellingly, there is no consensus about what makes them great. Landy and Milkis conceptualize great presidencies by their having "the opportunity and capacity to engage the nation in a struggle for its constitutional soul." That involves "civic education" and the use of political party to have a lasting impact. And such presidents accomplish these markers of greatness "…in a democratic spirit by taking the people to school and explaining why great changes had to be accomplished in a manner compatible with constitutionally prescribed liberties and republican forbearance."[7] Whatever else one may think of these particular metrics, they are more conceptual than empirical—more theoretical than practical.

Of course, most presidents are not "great." A few have been judged to be mediocre, for example, James Buchanan, Franklin Pierce and Warren G. Harding. Some are just ordinary. Indeed "Ordinary" presidents are the historical norm. Ordinary here means that most presidencies are mixture of accomplishments and disappointments. As a result, it would be useful to have a set of metrics that help us to gauge the impact of typical presidents—their level of "success" and the consequences of their political and policy choices in order to better understand and evaluate their presidencies and their legacies.

PRESIDENTIAL LEGACIES IN POLITICAL TIME

Presidential legacies have a dual time focus. They have their roots firmly planted in both the present and the future. Their present reflects a president's choices and their consequences—for better or worse, while he is in office. Legacies in that time frame are an effort to develop an accounting of his efforts to forge policies, exert leadership, and respond to the events and circumstances that define "his watch."

Yet, presidents are also expected to have an eye on the future—often before they officially step through the Oval Office doors. Running for the presidency requires a rationale. And that in turn assumes a purpose—a reason that people would vote for you, an understanding of the real issues the country faces, and a sense of what you wish to accomplish and be known for.

Presidential legacies also require some assessment of policy consequences over time. Inherent in the idea of a president's legacy is that he acted in way or put policies into place that had some staying power beyond his administration or that shaped or informed those administrations that followed. Accordingly, political and policy staying power is an element of "success" both during and after a president's term/s of office. This is especially true if the president who continues a policy differs in partisan outlook from the one who initiated it.

In such cases, successful staying power suggests that the policy or choice did successfully address to some degree the rationale for the initiative. The national security architecture that George W. Bush put in place after the 9/11 attacks was built on, not discarded by President Obama. That is an indication that Bush's policies not only served a continuing purpose but also provided some value while doing so. Dwight D. Eisenhower did the same with Truman's containment policy. And FDR's alphabet agencies may not have ended the Great Depression, but they did address the public's desire to have the government use its powers to stimulate a well-functioning economy. That expectation is now taken for granted.

Although the word "legacy" denotes something that follows a presidency, its origins begin with the president's choices while in office. And paradoxically, a case can be made that there has never been more information available to assess a president while he is still in office. This includes a great deal of "behind-the-scenes" information about an ongoing presidential administration available to researchers at the time it is taking place. Those trends have reached their apogee with the Trump presidency, but its elements—more and diverse reporting, a 24/7 news cycle, a hunger for scoops whether accurate or not, leaks motivated by partisan and/or policy differences, and a clearly partisan national press that has spawned a conservative leaning alter-ego press in response have been increasingly evident for some time.

Even the publications of tell-all books no longer wait until the president is out of office. The first one on the Trump administration came out shortly before he was in office one year.[8] This tsunami of in-time information makes possible potentially deeper understanding of the dynamics of a presidency at the time while the president is still in office. Yet caution in using such sources is not only prudent but mandatory. Any serious scholarship must still develop and apply metrics that help separate fact from fiction and develop theories that make useful sense of the data.[9]

Clearly, assessments of the most recent presidents must contend with the increasingly strong emotional and political currents that are part of the modern presidency. Presidents Clinton, (G.W.) Bush, Obama, and Trump would, taken individually over time, represent an increasing level of emotion and partisanship, into which any assessment of success must step with caution and humility.

Presidential Success: A Modest Proposal

If the first place to begin assessing a president's legacy is his actual time in office, then we clearly need some set of metrics that allows us to step away from the president's daily activities to focus on the things that usefully capture the ingredients of a legacy. This chapter proposes three general psychological and political elements shape a president's legacy, and they are the ones that will be applied to analyzing the Obama legacy. They include: (1) the president's purposes or ambitions in becoming president; (2) his major policy and political accomplishments while serving in that office; and (3) his major political or policy mistakes.

OBAMA'S PRESIDENTIAL AMBITION: GREATNESS

Ambition would seem, at first, to provide little leverage to assess a president's legacy. After all, every modern president could be accurately said to be ambitious, thus presenting little variation through which to make judgments about presidential legacies. A further complication is that all presidents want to do a good job, not make any catastrophic mistakes (or even major errors), get the bills passed that they think the country needs, respond effectively and productively to the circumstances that arise, and leave the country in better shape than it was when they came into office. So, strong ambitions and good intentions can be considered givens for every modern president.

Yet, the general rule of good intentions masks a little realized psychological fact. All presidents want to do well, but some want to be great. The difference is important and not well recognized because we assume, correctly, that all presidents have very high levels of ambitions and end our analyses there.

Again, some presidents, few in number as they may be, aspire to be more than adequate. These presidents want to do more than fulfill their responsibilities well; they want their leadership and policies to catapult them into the ranks of the greats or at least the tier just short of it. They not only want to leave the country a better place than they found it, they want to leave it a very different country. They want to politically transform the nation that elected them.

Some presidents, and Obama is one of them, see themselves not only as American presidents but world figures of historical magnitude.

President Obama as a Transforming President

There can be little doubt about President Obama's desire to "transform the country." Announcing his candidacy in Springfield, Illinois, he said, "let us transform this nation."[10] Campaigning in Iowa he said directly, "I want to transform this country."[11] Campaigning in New Hampshire he told those assembled, "we're going to change the country and change the world."[12] In his inaugural address, he called on his fellow citizens to help "remake America"—not change mind you, but remake.[13] On his 100th day in office at a town meeting he said, "So today, on my 100th day in office, I've come to report to you, the American people, that we have begun to pick ourselves up and dust ourselves off, and we've begun the work of remaking America. We're working to remake America."[14]

Asked in an interview about his personal list of heroes that include Lincoln, FDR, Gandhi, and Martin Luther King he replied, "When I think of what makes them together, I'm enamored of people who change the framework, who don't take something as a given, but scramble it."[15] Discussing Obama's role as commander in chief and having two wars to contend with, one report noted, "Mr. Obama sees them as 'problems that need managing,' " as one adviser put it, "while he pursues his mission of transforming America."[16]

The evidence for President Obama's "great man" theory of his own presidential aspiration seems quite clear.

President Obama as a Great President

There is also little doubt about President Obama's view of himself as an unusual, even uniquely consequential leader. Ryan Lizza, who covered Obama on the campaign trail, wrote that he is "keenly aware that presidential politics is about timing, and that at this extremely low moment in American political life, there is a need for someone—*and he firmly believes that someone is him*—to lift up the nation *in a way no politician has in nearly half a century.*"[17] In an early interview, Obama himself said directly that he wished to be a "great president."[18]

He was then asked about what he meant during a *Meet the Press* interview[19]:

MR. RUSSERT: You told *Men's Vogue Magazine*, that if you wanted to be president, you shouldn't just think about being

SEN. OBAMA: president, that you should want to be a great presi-
                 dent. So you've clearly given this some thought.

SEN. OBAMA: Yes.

MR. RUSSERT: And what would, in your mind, define a great
                 president?

SEN. OBAMA: But I think, when I think about great presidents, I
                 think about those *who transform how we think about
                 ourselves as a country* in fundamental ways so that,
                 that, at the end of their tenure, we have looked and
                 said to ours—that's who we are. And, and our, our—
                 and for me at least, that means that we have a more
                 expansive view of our democracy, that we've included
                 more people into the bounty of this country.... *And
                 they transformed the culture* and not simply promoted
                 one or two particular issues.

It should be noted that President's Obama view of what constitutes
greatness differs from ordinary understanding. Many presidential scholars
associate greatness with a president's response to dire and monumental
political circumstances. Lincoln had to respond to the breakup of the
Union. FDR had to respond to a severe economic dislocation that threatened to destroy the economic foundations of American democracy and a
world war that threatened its national security.

President Obama is not making this kind of argument. His contention
is that great presidents succeed in changing the cultural and political foundations of the country—not as a result of dire circumstances like world
wars or depressions but by force for policy initiatives. His model, and
apparently the president whom he wished to compare himself with, and be
compared to, was Ronald Reagan.[20]

In one interview Obama said, "I think Ronald Reagan changed the
trajectory of America in a way that, you know, Richard Nixon did not and
in a way that Bill Clinton did not."[21] One title of a news analysis captured
this thinking precisely, "How Barack Obama wants to be the Ronald
Reagan of the left."[22] How was this to be accomplished with no major
wars in sight and a severe economic liquidity crisis that had already
occurred and been directly and successfully addressed during the last
months of his predecessor's administration?[23] The answer is to be found in
Political Scientist Stephen Skowronek's theory of presidents in political
time.[24]

President Obama as a Reconstructive *President*

Skowronek's theory of presidential time locates presidents in the following typology: preemption, articulation, disjuncture, and reconstruction. It is the last of these four, reconstructive presidents that we focus on here because it so clearly parallels President Obama's ambitions.

That kind of presidency can take place when the "established regime and pre-established commitments of ideology and interest have, in the course of events, become vulnerable to direct repudiation as failed or irrelevant responses to the problems of the day."[25] A reconstructive presidency further occurs when "there is a general political consensus that something fundamentally has gone wrong in the high affairs of state."[26] In these political circumstances, "the order-creating capacities of the presidency were realized full vent in the wholesale reconstruction of the standards of legitimate national government."[27] In short, "'reconstructive politics' presidents like Franklin Roosevelt and Ronald Reagan (to take only the last two cycles) transform American politics in their own image, clearing the field of viable competition and setting the terms of political debate."[28] More importantly, reconstruction presidencies are episodic and require certain social, economic and political conditions.

Now compare Skowronek's theory of reconstructive presidencies with Obama's view regarding the nature of his presidency. Speaking of Ronald Reagan, Obama said[29]:

> He put us on a fundamentally different path because the country was ready for it. I think they felt like, you know, with all the excesses of the 60s and the 70s, and government had grown and grown, but there wasn't much sense of accountability in terms of how it was operating. I think people just tapped into—he tapped into what people were already feeling, which was, we want clarity, we want optimism, we want a return to that sense of dynamism and entrepreneurship that had been missing. I think Kennedy, 20 years earlier, moved the country in a fundamentally different direction. So I think a lot of it just has to do with the times. *I think we are in one of those times right now, where people feel like things as they are going, aren't working, that we're bogged down in the same arguments that we've been having and they're not useful. And the Republican approach I think has played itself out.*

Obama's Dilemma: Transformational Ambitions, but Not Transformational Circumstances

Ronald Reagan's two terms (1981–1989) as a governing conservative were noticeably successful on many grounds—economic, foreign policy, and public support for his leadership. Interestingly, Reagan's public approval ratings rose to their highest levels only after his terms of office.[30] Still, that status and the view that he had been, overall, a very successful president is why President Obama adapted him as a transformative model.

Reagan was followed by his chosen successor, a president of *articulation*, George H.W. Bush who was not able to earn a second term to further consolidate Reagan's *reconstructive* presidency. George (H.W.) Bush was then followed by Bill Clinton, a two-term liberal centrist. He seems to fit most comfortably in Skowronek's category of *articulation*, though of a liberal vision that still commanded the support of roughly half of a more or less evenly divided electorate. He was followed by George W. Bush, another two-term president, but his was a presidency of *articulation* reflected in a decided right-center point on the still divided political continuum. The 9/11 attacks made President Bush into a wartime president whose focus was on preventing another, worse terrorist attack. His articulation of his right-center governing stance had neither the political time or space to gain much traction.

It was into those historical circumstances that President Obama stepped with his historic victory in 2008. He assumed office with the country generally split between moderately liberal and moderately conservative views and no imminent or operative crises to address. However, there had been decades and a decades long period of decline in public faith in government, its leadership, and their policy solutions. This was a crisis that few took as one because it had been "hidden in plain sight" for so long.

That long-term decline in public trust seems to accord with Obama's observation, noted above, that "...*I think we are in one of those times right now, where people feel like things as they are going, aren't working.*" In addition to the growing partisan sorting of the American electorate, the past five decades had seen a relentless decline in the public's faith in the honesty, integrity, and competence of national leaders of both parties, and the country's major political and civic institutions.

At the time of the 2008 presidential election, Americans' satisfaction with the "way things are going in this country today" was 11%![31] Trust in government, to "do the right thing" "almost all" or "most of the time" had declined from 73% in 1958 to about 22% in January 2007—a year before Obama's election.[32] Confidence in the American presidency stood at 25% the year before Obama ran for and won the presidency. In 2017 at the conclusion of his two terms that figure stood at 32% and the number of Americans who had little or no faith in that office was 47%.[33]

There are no Gallup data available for confidence in the presidency before and after Reagan's terms of office (1981–1989). However, a rough surrogate measure, Trust in Government, provides evidence relevant to our interests here. In 1981, the year that Reagan took office, the public's view that you could trust government to "do what's right" all or most of the time stood at about 23%—well below the high of 73% in 1958.[34] Two major reasons for the level of distrust were ratings of government performance and opinion of political leaders.[35] In other words, the public's distrust was related to cynicism about the performance of political leaders and their policies, neither of which measured up to expectations—which were primarily driven by leaders themselves.

During the Reagan terms that trust measure reached a high of over 40%—again, well below the former high, but a substantial improvement. One plausible reason for this uptick is that Reagan both ran and governed as a conservative. That is, he ran on a platform that directly reflected his conservative views, campaigned on this authentic political identity, and then governed on it as well. Aside from whatever success he had as a president in domestic and foreign policy, and they were substantial in many respects, he presented himself honestly to the public and when elected governed the same way. A person might not agree with his political philosophy, and many didn't, but the basic integrity of his political identity allowed Americans to accurately know where he stood, agree or not.

CAMPAIGNING AND GOVERNING: TWO DIFFERENT OBAMAS

During the 2008 Democratic presidential nomination campaign, Senator Barack Obama ran as a pragmatic realist with populist overtones. He presented himself as a moderate centrist, willing to take strong international stands when necessary but not before exhausting the virtues of international cooperation and engagement.

He presented himself not so much as a liberal, but as a "pragmatist" who looked for practical not ideological solutions. He also presented himself as someone who could "move beyond the divisive politics of Washington and bring Democrats, independents and Republicans together to get things done."[36] His attempt to discard the liberal label was aided by a persona that came across as radiating reasonableness and fair-mindedness, traits that are viewed as being inconsistent with ideological zealotry.[37]

Yet, while Obama presented himself to the American public as a political moderate, his voting record as a state senator and then US senator told a different story. A *Washington Post* reporter covering Obama's years in Springfield as a state senator wrote that he arrived there as "a committed liberal."[38] Another *Washington Post* reporter covering his tenure there wrote that "Obama and three other members who made up a faction known in Springfield as 'liberal row,'" that "his record learned more liberal than other senators," and that he "stayed true to his liberal principles."[39] One of Obama's biographers, who covered him for the *Chicago Tribune*, called him "aggressively liberal."[40]

His U.S. Senate voting record was equally, if not more liberal.[41] *National Journal* rated Obama as the most liberal member of the Senate in 2007,[42] and that he voted with his party 97% of the time in 2007.[43] David Remnick concluded in his Obama biography that his votes in the Senate "were more predictably liberal than he advertised."[44]

After winning the Democratic nomination, Barack Obama moved decisively to the political center.[45] Among the many positions he modified were those dealing with his support for restrictive gun laws,[46] national security-related wiretapping laws (FISA),[47] NAFTA,[48] debating his opponent in a series of town hall meetings,[49] his policy on Iraq[50] and on Iran,[51] his policy about talking to dictators without preconditions,[52] Social Security tax hikes,[53] and refusing public financing for his campaign when he vowed to use it.[54] The number and importance of these shifts led to charges of "flip-flopping,"[55] but movements to the center from either the left or right, depending on the candidate, are politically *de rigueur*.

After he won election, but before he entered office, President Obama said of himself that he was a "progressive pragmatist." Introducing Governor Tim Kaine as his choice to head the Democratic National Committee, Obama said, "Tim and I share a philosophy. It's a pragmatic progressive philosophy that was at the heart of my campaign and will be at the heart of this administration."[56]

What is a progressive pragmatist? "Populist," "moderate," "pragmatic," "centrist" and "progressive pragmatist"—are words and phrases that cover a lot of political territory. They do not come with established policy benchmarks that would allow Obama to be placed in conventionally understood ideological space. Indeed, Gallup found that "large segments of all three ideological groups are unsure what 'progressive' means," which may be precisely its virtue and therefore its point.[57] The mystery of Obama's real political views before he revealed them in his presidential policy choices owed much to Obama's own efforts.

Having run as centrist, Obama tracked strongly to the left upon entering office. His major health care legislation and spending initiatives were used to fund policy goals were all in the service of the president's progressive agenda. He used his executive powers at major executive agencies—DHS [immigration], Justice, Education and the EPA to name several, to further strongly liberal or as he preferred, "progressive" positions.

His foreign policy of engagement reflected a policy perspective of "liberal internationalism"[58] and "progressive realism."[59] He emphasized support for and working with multilateral organizations, signing international agreements (but not necessarily sending them to the Senate for ratification), committing to international collaboration, and often binding American sovereignty to international institutions. His support for the Paris Climate Accords and the very large gamble on the Iran nuclear agreement are two cases in point.

Like many other modern presidential candidates, Barack Obama was forced to address the issue of reconciling his own progressive political views with an electorate that was increasing divided along partisan and ideological lines. Bill Clinton had tried to square that circle by proclaiming himself a "New Democrat," implicitly distancing himself from the old ones. George W. Bush, before 9/11, presented himself as a "compassionate conservative," implying that the GOP had not been sufficiently empathetic. Only Ronald Reagan ran and governed on the political identity that truly reflected his views as an unabashed conservative.

Obama's resolution of this dilemma was to declare himself a "pragmatist." Obama's candidacy was premised in part on his promise to bridge political divides and pragmatism was his stated means of doing so. He said he was a leader who was interested in what worked, not in hewing to any particular ideological line.[60] We will, shortly, examine Obama's characterization of his views.

OBAMA'S TWO GOVERNING MISTAKES

In 1968, the Hungarian psychoanalyst Michael Balint published his seminal book, *The Basic Fault*.[61] His insight was that for all structural and dynamic psychological complexities that characterized most adult functioning, the real roots of peoples' troubles lay in an early mismatch between their needs and their experiences. In Balint's view this "basic fault" represented the starting point of an emotional fault line that often carried over into later life. Even among successful people, the right circumstances could trigger this "basic fault" and undermine them.

I'd like to borrow that innovative and useful idea and apply it to the political arena in this analysis. In this context a *Basic Political Fault* is an unsupported, unsustainable difference between a basic political narrative and the basic reality in conflict with it. A narrative of course, is an explanation, often built on selected facts and interpretations, constructed to covey a preferred political position or stance. It is more or less true, but rarely is "the truth," since its purpose is persuasion not accuracy.

President Obama committed a basic political error, setting up a *Basic Political Fault* line at the core of his presidency. That basic political fault diminished President Obama's ability to have a successful presidency. Worse from his perspective, and ironically, it set into motion the political dynamics that have led to the likely undoing of the major policy parts of his legacy.

President Obama's Basic Political Fault

The presidency of Barack Obama had many of the characteristics that favor presidential success. He was reasonably smart and conveyed a sense of thoughtfulness that he had clearly applied to his career and political positions. He had had some political experience and was a smooth articulator of his own and his party's political and policy positions. He had an engaging life story and presented the opportunity for Americans to break an important racial barrier.

Moreover, he was well liked by the public and his campaign slogan of "Hope and Change" seemed to encapsulate what many Americans hoped for in their new president. Had he governed as he had campaigned—as a real moderate, his presidency, his legacy and contemporary American politics would have been much different. That really wasn't likely however for one simple but basic reason.

President Obama's ambition to be a transformational, great president was, at its core, incompatible with being a political moderate. Mr. Obama's transformational ambitions led him to favor bold audacious precedent-breaking policies meant to establish a new political order. President Obama clearly saw himself and his administration that way, while the public wanted the moderate president Obama he had presented himself as being.

Real political moderation could have led to real bi-partisanship, but according to William Galston, a liberal Democrat on the senior staff of the Brookings Institution analyzing Obama's first two years in office this was not really possible because[62]:

> In reality, the divide between the parties and between red and blue America went well beyond incivility to embrace disagreements on core principles and conceptions of how the world works. Bridging this divide...would have required, ...a policy agenda that breached traditional partisan bounds. But there was little in Obama's agenda that corresponded to Bill Clinton's heterodox positions on crime, welfare, trade, and fiscal restraint. Instead, Obama synthesized and advocated policies representing the consensus within the Democratic Party. Republicans rejected that agenda as a basis for reaching common ground.

As a result, the public came to see Obama's real political views and identity relatively quickly. By November 4, 2009, a majority of Americans thought that Obama's policies were "mostly liberal."[63] Polls taken a year apart showed a similar trajectory. In late November 2008, 24% of the public saw Obama as "very liberal" and 19% as "liberal." One year later, those figures were 34% and 20% respectively.[64] By June of 2010, "More Americans continue to say that Obama is listening more to liberals in his party than to moderates (46% vs. 34%)."[65] Whatever terms Obama and his supports might choose to call his philosophy and worldview, the public increasingly seemed to be settling on its own characterizations of his politics and policies. And they were correct.

As noted, Obama believed there was an opening for transformational leadership, and perhaps there was. At one point during the campaign he said "I think there's the possibility of a significant realignment politically in this election."[66] And perhaps that was possible too.

However, Obama's basic mistake—his *Basic Political Fault*, was to hide his true ambitions and intentions behind a moderate façade. As Galston points out,[67] "There was indeed a tension at the heart of the Obama campaign between the rhetoric of post-partisanship and the substance of the agenda."

It is possible that Obama truly believed what he said: "I think what people are looking for right now is somebody who can bring the country together and maybe *shape the kind of majority that will actually deliver on health care, that will actually deliver on a bold energy strategy, that can actually do something about serious education reform.*"[68]

Perhaps the president's political strategy was to dazzle the American public with the audacity and boldness of his transformative plans. If so, he failed to sufficiently consider that a president whose ambitions are major transformative change, the kind of change that to use Obama's words, quoted above, "*transform how we think about ourselves as a country* in fundamental ways" needs to prepare the public for what he wants to do. Not just simply do it, and hope Americans will applaud, approve, or accept it.

There was another problem with this view as well. Passing major legislation that the public does not support or is ambivalent about is not the same as passing legislation that the public has been calling for, has seen the need for and therefore supports. Gallup found that of the five major initiatives in his first two years of office, only one (financial regulatory reform) received a majority of public approval.[69] All of this is quite aside from the larger long-term question of whether the legislation, desired or not, would actually work as promised.

Obama's hiding of his true ambitions behind the façade of a reasonable persona and odes to his moderation, and then governing as an unabashed progressive did nothing to alleviate the decades long decline in Americans' trust in government. His initiatives ran into trouble on the trust dimension in another way as well. Obama's progressive agenda "required a significant expansion of the scope, power, and cost of the federal government, [while] public trust in that government stood near a record low throughout his campaign, a reality his election did nothing to alter."[70]

For all his substantial political talents, Obama's quest for greatness undermined the opportunities that would have helped him have a successful presidency and a robust and positive legacy.

OBAMA'S SECOND POLITICAL MISTAKE: POLICY MODERATION OR TRANSFORMATION

Obama's second basic political mistake followed his original *Basic Political Fault*. It is related to his policy choices in the first part of his administration. There was a disconnect between how Obama defined himself and what the electorate wanted him to do. The public wanted the president to focus on the economy and jobs.[71] The president wanted to focus on his transformative ambitions and his legacy as a great president.

Since the president had no immediate crisis comparable in magnitude to those that Lincoln or FDR faced, President Obama was forced to discuss other events like a Gulf oil spill in dramatic terms ("it will jeopardize our national security. It will smother our planet") or the problems of health care coverage for some Americans in order to elevate public concern to crisis levels.

There was a purpose in escalating the rhetoric. Obama's chief of staff had famously said in an interview with the *Wall Street Journal* that "You never want a serious crisis to go to waste…Things that we had postponed for too long, that were long-term, are now immediate and must be dealt with. This crisis provides the opportunity for us to do things that you could not do before."[72] Among the areas he mentioned were "energy, health, education, tax policy, (and) regulatory reforms."[73]

In exaggerating these events as severe crises requiring immediate fixing and major government programs, President Obama ran several large risks. The first was that a gap might be created between what Obama saw as important issues to address and what the public thought. A second related issue was the mismatch between Obama's dire language and public views about the severity of these crises and the rationale for using them to insist on large new government programs about which many Americans were already skeptical. These in turn, risked the most precious leadership commodity of all, the perception of Obama's leadership integrity.

Health Care, Not the Economy or Immigration

In Obama's first two years of office he had a Democratic majority in both houses of Congress and for a time a filibuster proof majority in the Senate. It was during one of the filibuster proof majority periods that the president pushed through his transformative health care initiative.

It is true that a determined minority can delay or kill legislation through the use of filibusters that can't be stopped by a closure vote. And it is true that Democrats had a veto proof majority for only limited periods of the president's first two years of office. Still, the president could have chosen and passed a variety of measures. He could have spent more of his time on the economy. For example, the administration was able to pass its stimulus legislation with the help of three Republican Senators (Collins, Snowe, and Specter) who helped Democrats break a Republican filibuster.

Passing comprehensive immigration reform presented an even greater opportunity. A 2016 comprehensive immigration bill had passed the Senate and a year later another bill came very close to passage. Certainly, there were enough moderate and liberal Republicans in Congress during

Obama's first two years of office to have made that effort likely to be successful. President Obama however chose not to try.

In an interview with Hispanic news anchor and activist Jorge Ramos, the president had specifically promised to do that. He said, "I cannot guarantee that it is going to be in the first 100 days... But what I can guarantee is that we will have in the first year an immigration bill that I strongly support and that I'm promoting. And I want to move that forward as quickly as possible."[74]

He didn't. In another subsequent interview in 2012, Mr. Ramos brought up the president's earlier promise. The president rejected the criticism, responding that he had made the promise "before the economy was on the verge of collapse. ... And so my first priority was making sure that we prevented us from going into a Great Depression."[75]

That wasn't accurate. The actual economic "verge of collapse" took place in the last months of the G.W. Bush presidency and was averted when he signed the TARP legislation. President Obama did face a recession, and in response he passed the Economic Stimulus Act of 2008 that was enacted on February 13, 2008, shortly after he took office.[76] Another major stimulus bill was passed by Congress on February 11, 2019,[77] and signed into law on February 17—one week later. Both pieces of legislation had been drafted during the last months of the G.W. Bush administration.

Having passed two major stimulus bills directed toward helping a limping economy by February 2009, Mr. Obama had ten months ahead of him before the midterm elections to pass further legislation in a Democratic-controlled Congress. Obama's stimulus policies did help result in a level of stabilization after a traumatic recession, albeit at a modest level of overall economic performance.[78] The 2008 recession officially ended in 2010,[79] but economists in the Obama administration saw the economy stuck in a "new normal" of high unemployment, low growth, and lower wages.[80]

THE LEGACY COSTS OF CHOOSING "GREATNESS"

The president faced a choice. He could have devoted himself and his administration to new economic policies[81] and a sharp rhetorical focus[82] on them that might have helped lift the economy out of its slow performance doldrums, as Trump's efforts in both these areas appear to have done.[83] Or, he could have tried to pass "comprehensive immigration" reform and gone into the midterm election period with a very solid record of major legislative accomplishment and a more centrist presidential persona.

Instead Obama chose to focus much of his energy, his political capital and the fate of his party to an enormous and complex legislative effort—remaking the American health care system. It was a fraught and emblematic decision that proved in retrospect to be a grave political error. It passed and was signed into law, but its subsequent fate suggests in passing this clearly historic legislation, Obama achieved a pyrrhic victory.

The Affordable Care Act: A Pyrrhic Presidential Success

The Affordable Care Act was introduced into the Senate in August 2009, and eventually passed on a straight party line vote,[84] during one of the periods when the Democrats enjoyed a veto proof majority. The president signed the bill, and his political circumstances, standing and legacy were substantially damaged as a result.

The president's successful effort to push through his health care legislation came with a price. He now had almost every member of the Republican Party and their supporters opposed to his health care legislation and dedicated to getting rid of it. The lack of any bipartisan support for this bill guaranteed continual opposition.

And after the 2010 midterm elections, President Obama no longer had a Democratic majority in the House. Here again is William Galston[85]:

> ...there is more to the losses that President Obama and the Democratic Party suffered in November 2010: the public punished them, not only for high unemployment and slow growth, but also for what it regarded as sins of both commission and omission. The White House and congressional leaders pursued an agenda that the people mostly rejected while overlooking measures that might well have improved the economy more, and almost certainly would have been more popular, than what they did instead. In short, while Obama was dealt a bad hand, he proceeded to misplay it, making the political backlash even worse than it had to be.

Jonathan Alter reports in his book that Rahm Emanuel, Obama's then Chief of Staff, said of the health care legislation, "I begged him not to do this," but Obama overrode that advice, privately taking a bit of shot at President Clinton by telling advisers that he hadn't been sent to the White House to do 'school uniforms.'"[86] Fundamentally, Obama thought that restructuring American health care was a transformational project worthy of a great president.

The Affordable Care Act was an enormous and complicated piece of policy legislation and passing that kind of bill ordinarily counts as a major presidential achievement. However, as noted, the legislation was sold to the public on the basis of inaccurate claims. This is true of many pieces of legislation, but health care is a particularly sensitive area since it involves life and death issues and people's personal relationships with their doctors. President Obama claimed numerous times that if you like your doctors, your insurance or your health care, you can keep them. This was not true and the administration knew it.[87] That famous claim garnered the infamous "lie of the year" award from one fact-check organization.[88]

There definitely were issues with American health care including, but not limited to portability, being turned down because of previous conditions, its cost (for some people), and also gaining insurance coverage. However, most Americans were satisfied with their health care, liked their doctors and wanted to keep them. In short, heath care reform was needed, but wholesale transformation of the American health care system wasn't necessary to accomplish those reforms.

Recall that transforming the American health care system was not what Americans wanted President Obama to do. They remained focused on the economy and jobs. It was a classic mismatch of presidential ambition, in this case "great man" transformational ambition and ordinary public concern with more basic prosaic, but nonetheless important concerns.

The public supported President Obama and his promise of "Hope and Change" but were disappointed with the results. His soothing articulate rhetoric of moderation was undercut by his actual policies domestically and abroad where he governed as what he was—a dedicated and determined liberal/progressive. Half the country was thrilled; the other half of the country was appalled.

In governing as if he had mandate for his transformational ambitions, Obama opened the door to the undoing, not only of his presidency but also of his legacy.

TRADITIONAL METRICS OF PRESIDENTIAL SUCCESS

There are several obvious performance markers that help us to gage presidential "success." One is re-election. A president that isn't re-elected fails a primary test of presidential leadership. He has failed to accomplish enough over his term of office, or has not led or governed in a way that instilled enough confidence going forward, to justify his return to office. President Obama decisively surmounted that hurdle.

Another frequently used metric to judge presidential success is the passage of substantial amounts of legislation. There is, however, more to this metric than is commonly understood. The underlying assumption about the amount of legislation passed metric is clearly stated by Ken Duberstein former chief of staff for Republican President Ronald Reagan. He noted, "To be viewed as an effective president, you have to be viewed as winning on Capitol Hill."[89]

That metric is clearly on display in this analysis[90]:

> By sheer numbers, Congress was less productive in 2017 than in 2009, the first year of Mr. Obama's presidency. In 2009, Mr. Obama signed 125 bills into law, including a huge economic stimulus package, the expansion of the Children's Health Insurance Program and legislation to regulate tobacco.

It's true that the passage of legislation is one key way through which the president enacts his preferred policies. Yet it is not the only way—or even necessarily, as we will argue shortly, the most important way. Such a metric is heavily influenced by which party controls the House and/or Senate and, the internal cohesion of each party.[91]

There is also the hugely important question of the substantive importance of the legislation passed. Some legislation is anodyne; others extremely consequential. So, for example, when President Trump claimed that he had signed more bills into law in his first hundred days than any other president, critics responded that he has signed fewer significant bills into law after one year in office than any presidency since Dwight D. Eisenhower.[92] And they had a point.

On numbers alone President Obama clearly won the legislation passed competition[93]:

> In 2009, Mr. Obama signed 125 bills into law, including a huge economic stimulus package, the expansion of the Children's Health Insurance Program and legislation to regulate tobacco. This year, Mr. Trump signed 93 measures into law, but of those, 15 were joint resolutions of disapproval which rolled back pending Obama-era regulations.

However, the Obama-Trump legislative record comparison underscores the point that substance counts as much as size. It is not only passing legislation that counts but also passing "significant" legislation that matters. What that adjective actually means matters, but at minimum it means that it contains provisions that make a serious attempt to address a substantial policy problem, even if its premises and assumptions are rooted in the president's policy thinking, which may or not be correct. And of course, passage of even "significant" legislation does not guarantee that it will work as promised or planned.

On these more robust, but still narrow grounds of absolute numbers of "significant" legislation, President Obama's record is one of very solid accomplishment. It includes a number of significant bills—two stimulus bills, a child health care bill, financial sector reform, and of course health care legislation. It is this substantial record of legislative accomplished that led Trump critics to argue early in his term that "Even if the tax bill passes he isn't much of a doer."[94]

Trump's tax reform bill did pass, and it is legitimately considered a major piece of legislation. It will, like Obama's legislative record, be part of Trump's legacy. Yet, like Obama's legislative record, as large and successful by many measures as it was, it is unlikely to be definitive. The reason is that there is much more to a legacy of presidential success than the number of legislative laws passed on your watch.

Comparing the two legislative records underscores a number of critical features about presidential success that are rarely mentioned much less analyzed. These are their legislation record's relationship to the overall efforts to fulfill presidential purpose and their success in doing so.

Presidential Success, and Failure, by Other Metrics

We proposed at the beginning of this analysis that one of the three essential elements for assessing a president's legacy was the president's purposes or ambitions in becoming president. Of Obama's core presidential purposes, there can be little doubt. He saw himself a great man in history.[95]

Furthermore, in keeping with this view, he aspired to "transform" the nature of American political life, and with it what he hoped would be deep, transformative and long-lasting accompanying social and cultural changes. Obama was absolutely a president who had the courage of his convictions. He believed in his transformative vision and acted on it. His most basic problem however was that many Americans were not supportive of what he had in mind, and he had taken care not to clearly spell them out. And when Obama's real purposes become clear beyond any doubt, resistance to them dramatically increased.

In the 2010 midterm elections, the president not only lost his filibuster proof Democratic majority in Congress, but his party lost majority control of the House. The Republican Party gained 63 seats in the US House of Representatives recapturing the majority. That was the largest seat change since 1948 and the largest for any midterm election since the 1938 midterm elections. The Republicans also gained six seats in the US Senate, expanding their minority position.

Also, importantly, Republicans gained 680 seats in state legislative races. That put them in control of 26 state legislatures, compared to the 15 still controlled by Democrats. In addition, as a result of this election Republicans took control of 29 of the 50 State governorships. By any reasonable interpretation these results were both a rebuke and a warning.

Jacobson attributes the striking loses to several factors among them the seemingly paradoxical idea that[96]:

> ...the results reflected the failure of Obama and his allies to persuade most Americans—most importantly, political independents—that his policies, including his landmark legislative victories, were to their or the nation's benefit. That is, Obama's legislative successes were, on the whole, political failures.

That seeming paradox is not hard to resolve. Voters wanted the moderate president they were led to believe would sit in the oval office. Here again the president had a choice. The public was signaling in the strongest most direct way that it did not approve of the president's governing purposes and direction. They wanted him to govern as he had promised. Instead they got a transformational president who doubled down, determined to remake the US in his own progressive vision.

One reason for the president's decision to double down on his transformational purposes was that he thought, seriously, that the public just didn't recognize his successes, or their importance. Reflecting back on his loss of the House in the 2008 elections followed by his party's subsequent loss of the senate to Republicans in 2012,[97] he said: "I mean, the truth of the matter is that if we had been able to more effectively communicate all the steps we had taken to the swing voter, then we might have maintained a majority in the House or the Senate."[98]

The president concluded that interview by saying:

> If we can't puncture some of the mythology around austerity, politics or tax cuts or the mythology that's been built up around the Reagan revolution, where somehow people genuinely think that he slashed government and slashed the deficit and that the recovery was because of all these massive tax cuts, as opposed to a shift in interest-rate policy—if we can't describe that effectively, then we're doomed to keep on making more and more mistakes.

The essential understanding contained in these quotes is that the president felt there was nothing wrong or necessary to change about his policies. Their correctness and success only needed to be explained better. Moreover, if he turned away from his guiding policy premises and preferences, the result would be that the country would be "doomed to keep on making more and more mistakes."

OBAMA'S EXECUTIVE ORDER PRESIDENCY: DOUBLING DOWN ON HIS TRANSFORMATIONAL PURPOSES

No longer able to pass legislation through a filibuster proof Congress, no longer in political control of the House and then the Senate, President Obama chose to bypass them in favor of executive actions. Those actions, utilizing a variety of instruments, allow the president to make and implement policy on his own.[99] They are legally the law of the land until they are reversed by other president.

A 2015 news analysis entitled "Obama's executive action rollouts increasing in pace" reflected his strategy.[100] Obama first used the term "executive action" in a "We Can't Wait Tour" in 2011 after his party's 2010 midterm steep losses. In an October 2011 speech in Las Vegas, Obama said, "I've told my administration to keep looking every single day for actions we can take without Congress, steps that can save consumers money, make government more efficient and responsive, and help heal the economy...And we're going to be announcing these executive actions on a regular basis."[101] And he did.

In 2014, a year that Obama termed the "Year of Action," he took controversial actions on Climate, Immigration, and Cuba. In 2014, he reminded his cabinet and the country that "I've got a pen, and I've got a phone." And that's all I need "Because with a pen, I can take executive actions."[102] And he did.

As the news analysis noted, the announcement of Obama's executive actions "has now become so routine that new announcements come several times a week." That same analysis went on to note that

> But by one measure, such policy rollouts are actually increasing in pace. The White House often announces executive actions with a fact sheet from the press office, and those spiked last year during what Obama called the "Year of Action." The White House issued 228 fact sheets in 2014, more than the first three years of his presidency combined. This year, the White House has already issued three more fact sheets than last year at the same time.[103]

Another analysis noted that

> Obama has made prolific use of memoranda despite his own claims that he's used his executive power less than other presidents. ...Obama has issued 195 executive orders as of Tuesday [2014]. Published alongside them in the *Federal Register* are 198 presidential memoranda—all of which carry the same legal force as executive orders.[104]

The clear fact that emerges from the above analyses is that President Obama chose to double down on his purpose of progressive transformation of the country and its domestic and foreign policies. It is not only the number of these executive actions but the fact that all of them put into place policies that were consistent with the president's transformational purposes and progressive direction. And it is not only their number and their progressive direction but also the powerful policy and political impact many of them had.

SOME CONSEQUENCES OF OBAMA'S DOMESTIC POLICY UNILATERALISM

Many of Obama's executive actions were not small matters. In 2014, the president by executive order provided renewable legal status to those who had lived in the US since 2010 and had children who were either American citizens or lawful permanent residents [DAPA]. The *New York Times* put it this way: "President Obama chose confrontation over conciliation on Thursday as he asserted the powers of the Oval Office to reshape the nation's immigration system and all but dared members of next year's Republican-controlled Congress to reverse his actions on behalf of millions of immigrants."[105] That Executive Order could have resulted in the legalization of five million new persons.[106]

That action resulted in a suit by 26 states against the decision that led to the president's action being stopped by the courts from implementation.[107] Obama then appealed that decision to the Supreme Court.[108] That court deadlocked on the decision leaving in place the lower court stay.[109]

In June of 2012, the Obama administration also put into place by Executive Order a legalization program for approximately 800,000 undocumented immigrations who had been brought to this country by their parents when they were children or adolescents (DACA).[110] In November 2014, the president indicated that he was going to expand this program to include illegal immigrants who entered the country prior to 2010, eliminate the requirement that applicants be younger than 31 years old, and lengthen the renewable deferral period to two years.

Several states sued to stop the implementation of this executive action too and an adverse decision against the Obama administration was upheld by the same appellate court ruling, which was also kept in place by the Supreme Court 4-4 tie on its merits. When Trump came into office, he rescinded Obama's DACA executive order.[111] And again, a lawsuit was filed, this time by supporters of DACA and a federal judge in San Francisco issued an injunction against stopping the program.[112] The Trump administration has asked the Supreme Court for an expedited hearing in this matter and they have agreed.[113] In the meantime, President Trump has asked Congress to provide legislation to resolve the status of DACA recipients as part of an overall package of immigration reform.[114]

The above focus on immigration underscores a point made earlier. The president had an opportunity to propose and pass substantial immigration legislation, as he had promised to do. That would have addressed and possibly resolved the DAPA and DACA population issues, but he did not. That choice and the vocal demands of one part of his base led him to reverse his repeated public stance that he had no authority to fashion immigration law by executive fiat.[115]

President Obama's Foreign Policy Unilateralism

President Obama's executive actions did just cover domestic issues. They covered important foreign policy issues as well. The president committed the US to drastic reductions in greenhouse-gas pollution.[116] President Obama joined the UN Climate treaty[117] but did not submit it to the

Senate for ratification. Republicans warned that Obama's UN climate plan could be undone, and it was.[118] President Trump withdrew the US from that treaty shortly after taking office.[119]

And finally, there is the president's path breaking and extremely controversial nuclear deal with Iran (JCPOA). In the administration's view, "the Iran deal that will ensure Iran's nuclear program is and remains exclusively peaceful."[120] The objections to the deal are many and varied.[121] They have to do with its temporary duration, its verification difficulties, its failure to reign in Iran's nuclear missile program, its failure to address Iran's support for terrorism across the Middle East and elsewhere, and the assumption that like Russia, Iran will eventually moderate and become a status quo power.

That agreement too was not submitted to the Senate to debate and ratify as a treaty. And again, President Trump, after two reluctant certifications of Iran's compliance, did not certify their compliance with the provisions of the treaty the third time[122] and asked Congress to take up measures as a response.[123] It is now in diplomatic and political limbo as the Trump administration has taken up a new more aggressive set of policies toward Iran.[124]

The patterns detailed above are very clear. They begin with President Obama's core presidential purposes of transformation and his wish to be a great man as president. That led him to win election by emphasizing the moderate leader he presented himself to be, not the transformation president he wished to become. Once in office, he governed as he wished to be, and as a result, was politically repudiated by voters in 2010 by losing his Democratic House majorities, and again in 2012 by losing his Senate Democratic majority. Voters liked President Obama and he did win re-election. However, they voted for a Republican House and then a Republican Senate in the hopes of reigning in his transformational policies. That failed.

Stymied in Congress, Obama doubled down on his transformational purposes and governed by executive actions. This led to the obvious and minimalist understanding that he had "overreached."[125] He did much more than that.

Obama came to office by disguising his real purposes. When they became clear and the public sent him strong messages, he ignored them. Americans were put on a political path to transformation that they neither agreed to nor supported. When they asked the president via their votes to stop, he doubled down though executive actions. They were powerless.

Obama became another president who caused Trust in Government to drop, during his time in office precipitously to 17%. He became another president who misled the public to gain office. And he became another president whose large political promise did not live up to its performance.

Many, though clearly not all Americans, had given up on the politics, policies, and leaders of both parties that had led to a constant stream of disappointments. They had tried establishment leaders with all the right political credentials. They had tried leaders from both political parties. They had repeatedly placed their hopes in policy narratives that establishment figures of both parties had championed that rarely, if ever, brought the promised results. And still, after all these disappointed expectations, the country still seemed headed in the wrong direction.

Many, though not all, Americans had, after many years of repeated disappointments with establishment leaders, institutions, and policy narratives just about given up on finding any political leader who would be honest about their views, skilled and courageous enough to act on them, and actually begin to make headway in successfully addressing the many problems the country faced.

Many of these Americans were willing to try almost anything to get the country moving in a different direction. And in 2017 they did. Enter Donald Trump.

OBAMA'S IRONIC LEGACY: THE TRUMP PRESIDENCY

It is not hard to miss the fact that President Trump is trying to dismantle substantial parts of President Obama's *policy* legacy. Some see this as essentially a wrecking operation with no further vision of what is to take its place. One presidential academic notes that "other presidents have proactive ideas about what to erect in place of their predecessor's programs," and is quoted as saying, "I have not seen any constructive bills in this vein that Trump has put forth...As far as I can tell, he has no independent legislative agenda other than tearing down. Perhaps tax reform."[126]

Another academic critic is quoted as saying that Trump's reversal of Obama's policies are done "with a vehemence and an order of magnitude that is different" from previous modern administrations..."more importantly, there doesn't seem to be a construction of an ideology so much as a deconstruction of the predecessor's legacy."[127]

These criticisms seem plausible, but they miss an important point. Mr. Trump's dismantling is not primarily personal. It is aimed at Mr. Obama's policies, not primarily at him personally.

Trump's presidential purposes are encapsulated in what I call the *Politics of Restoration*. Trump is not an articulate theorist of his own policy visions, but that vision is there. And it lies at a much deeper level than ordinary ideology. It is an attempt to revise, reform and modernize the policy assumptions that have guided establishment leaders from both parties for decades and whose failures are a large part of the reason that Donald Trump is president.

The Politics of Restoration

The Obama legacy has to be understood within the context of his political time. It could be argued the election of Donald Trump was a decision by the American people to move away from liberal Democratic policies and try another approach. We can see hints of this possibility in the resonance of Trump's campaign slogan.

Campaign slogans, if they are effective as Trump's "Make America Great Again" was, capture an essential feature of presidential purpose that the public can easily grasp, though not necessarily fully appreciate. And what are Trump's presidential purposes?

His most basic and important purpose in becoming a candidate was to reverse the policies and assumptions that have resulted in decades of Americans feeling the country is moving in the wrong direction. To do so, he wants to pivot away from the failed conventional policy "wisdom" of the last five decades. He also wants to pivot away from those establishment figures in both political parties who have assured the American public that, for example, unlimited immigration and limited enforcement of immigration laws has no downside, that low economic growth is the new normal and Americans should get used to it, that free trade is always a "win-win" for everyone, and that it is better not to insist on greater reciprocity abroad with American allies, or take a strong stance against adversaries.

It is clear that the vehicle for *Making American Great Again* is the *Politics of Restoration*. Yet, the question remains: what exactly does President Trump want to restore? The answer in general terms is this.

Mr. Trump wants to restore an America where ordinary people are heard and respected, where the premises of policies that have not worked as promised, or have become outdated, are reviewed, revised and if necessary, discarded. He wants to restore the "can do" spirit in the country that America gets things done. He wants to identify and act on its common and not its parochial identity-driven interests domestically and internationally. And above all, he wants to restore an America whose political leadership acts at all levels, but starting first with the president, to re-earn the trust of Americans that has been steadily lost over the last five decades, by doing what he promised.

From this perspective, Trump's presidency is not most accurately viewed primarily or solely as an anti-Obama legacy crusade. Mr. Obama's domestic and foreign policies are emblematic of a policy paradigm that President Trump wished to revise and where necessary replace. They can be viewed as the apogee of the progressive/liberal policy paradigm that began with Lyndon Johnson's "Great Society."

It is Mr. Obama's policies and their underlying paradigms, not Mr. Obama personally that are the focus of Mr. Trump's ambitions. President Obama's choice to pursue political transformation and his determination to push wide range of very liberal policies by every means possible simply magnified conflicts and difficulties that were already well in evidence.

President Obama's pursuit of "great man" status among presidents paradoxically exemplified the very traits that had disappointed many Americans in the past and led many of them to take the very large risk of electing a man with Mr. Trump's background, temperament, and psychology.

Many of President Obama's policy legacies are not likely to survive the Trump presidency, if he is successful. That will be because if he is, he will have demonstrated that policies based on his alternative premises can work, or at least represent a viable alternative to past paradigms.

If that happens, President Obama's policy legacy will be that of a relic of what policy thinking used to be. If it doesn't, Mr. Obama's legacy will be less an exemplar of antiquated and ineffective policy thinking than of one more president whose promise did not survive his performance.

There is some evidence that the president himself, while in office, was reaching the poignant realization that his quest for greatness might prove elusive. In a segment with comedian Jerry Seinfeld meant to cement the president's status as a cool cultural icon, this revealing exchange occurred[128]:

Jerry Seinfeld:	What's the coolest president commemoration [legacy].
President Obama:	Ah, ok.
Jerry Seinfeld:	to get…because you're in line to get something great.
President Obama:	*The Rushmore thing.*
Jerry Seinfeld:	Rushmore.
President Obama:	*would be interesting… but that's pretty exclusive real-estate.*

What draws one's attention here is the president's immediate association to greatness ("the Rushmore thing") followed quickly by an acknowledgment of its elusiveness. That segment was filmed in 2015 at a time when the president was in the process of gambling on his transformational rather than more incremental policies. Had Mr. Obama listened more closely to his own voice of hesitation, his presidency and his legacy would have been very different.

In the end, however, President Obama's quest for greatness proved decisive, much to the detriment of his legacy.

NOTES

1. Some portions of this analysis draw on the author's book on President Obama. See Stanley Renshon. 2012. *Barack Obama and the Politics of Redemption.* New York: Routledge Press.

   There are now a small number of books that purport to assess the legacy of the Obama presidency. They can be divided into two distinct groups. The first of these include books with strong and a priori political views.

   On one side of the political divide are Obama legacy books by progressive pundit Jonathan Chait. 2017. *Audacity: How Barack Obama Defied His Critics and Created a Legacy That Will Prevail.* New York: Custom House, whose title reflects his wish. Another of this kind is by Trump biographer and stridently anti-Trumper Michael D'Antonio. 2017 *A Consequential President: The Legacy of Barack Obama.* New York: Thomas Duane. That book contains chapters with somewhat hyperbolic titles like "Environment: Saving the Planet" and "Education: Racing to the Top" that reflect both the book's starting stance and its conclusions.

   On the other side of the political fence are several another books whose titles also reflect their emphasis on conclusions that match opening political assumptions. See Matt Margolis and Mark Noonan. *The Worst President in History: The Legacy of Barack Obama.* Victory Books, 2016 and Matt Margolis. 2018. *The Scandalous Presidency of Barack Obama.* Bombardier Books.

There are also another group of more academic Obama legacy books now reaching publication. These include Julian Zelizer (ed). 2017. *The Presidency of Barack Obama.* Princeton: Princeton University Press.

Elaine Kagan of the Brookings Institution in her 2018 review of this book in the *Boston Review* wrote:

> It becomes clearer every day that Barack Obama, a historic president, presided over a somewhat less than historic presidency. With only one major legislative achievement (Obamacare)—and a fragile one at that—the legacy of Obama's presidency mainly rests on its tremendous symbolic importance and the fate of a patchwork of executive actions.

Further, she writes, the historians included in the volume, ".. by and large, approve of Obama's policies (although some find them too timid)." Gathering all like-minded people for a volume is a recipe for hagiology, not analysis.

A more even-handed scholarly appraisal can be found in Steven E. Schier (ed). 2017. *Debating the Obama Presidency.* Rowman & Littlefield, and the current volume as well.

2. Cf., "Now even as we speak, there are those who are preparing to divide us, the spin masters and negative ad peddlers who embrace the politics of anything goes. Well, I say to them tonight, there's not a liberal America and a conservative America; there's the United States of America. There's not a black America and white America and Latino America and Asian America; there's the United States of America." Transcript: "Illinois Senate Candidate Barack Obama," *Washington Post*, July 27, 2004.

3. Cf., Galbraith, John Kenneth. 1961. *The Great Crash*, Cambridge, MA: Riverside Press and Gene Smiley. 2002. *Rethinking the Great Depression*, Chicago: Ivan R. Dee.

4. Brandon Rottinghaus and Justin Vaughn, "New ranking of U.S. presidents puts Lincoln at No. 1, Obama at 18; Kennedy judged most overrated," *Washington Post*, February16, 2015.

5. Cf. "Conservatives have complained, with merit, that presidential rankings reflect a liberal bias among historians. Our profession tends to admire activist, reform-minded presidents in the mold of FDR. Indeed, when in 2005 the Wall Street Journal conducted an ostensibly ideologically balanced survey, there were marked differences in how Democratic and

Republican historians viewed recent figures such as Ronald Reagan and George W. Bush." See Eric Foner, "Where They Stand: The American Presidents in the Eyes of Voters and Historians," *Washington Post*, July 13, 2015. Foner, a historian is reviewing a book by Robert W. Merry. 2012. *Where They Stand: The American Presidents in the Eyes of Voters and Historians*. New York: Simon & Schuster.

6. Marc Landy and Sidney M. Milkus. 2000. *Presidential Greatness: New Edition*. Lawrence, KS; University Press of Kansas; see also Thomas Bailey. 1966. *Presidential Greatness*. New York: Appleton-Century.

7. Marc Landy and Sidney M. Milkus. *Passim*.

8. "What is different about Mr. Bannon's stark assessments in Michael Wolff's new book… is not that a former aide would speak out, but that it would happen so early in a presidency." See Peter Baker, "For Trump, Book Raises Familiar Questions of Loyalty and Candor," *New York Times*, January 5, 2018. The book Baker is discussing is Michael Wolff. 2018. *Fire and Fury: Inside the Trump White House*. New York: Little Brown.

9. Matt Flegenheimer, "The Year the News Accelerated to Trump Speed," *New York Times*, December 29, 2017.

10. "Senator Barack Obama's Announcement for President," Springfield, IL, February 10, 2007. Available at: http://www.barackobama.com/2007/02/10/remarks_of_senator_barack_obam_11.php (Accessed July 14, 2010).

11. Quoted in Richard Wolffe.2009. *Renegade: The Making of a President*. New York: Crown, p. 67.

12. Toby Harden, "Barack Obama vows to 'change the world,'" *Telegraph*, October 17, 2008.

13. President Barack Obama's Inaugural Address, January 21, 2009. Available at: (https://obamawhitehouse.archives.gov/blog/2009/01/21/president-barack-obamas-inaugural-address) (Accessed January 21, 2018).

14. "Remarks by the President in Arnold, Missouri Town Hall," April 29, 2009. Available at: (http://whitehousepressbriefings.com/speeches-and-remarks/remarks-president-arnold-missouri-town-hall/) (accessed January 21, 2018).

15. Obama quoted in Wolffe, *Renegade…*, p. 188.

16. Peter Baker, "For Obama, Steep Learning Curve as Chief in War," *New York Times*, August 28, 2010.

17. Ryan Lizza, "Above the Fray," *GQ*, September, 2007 (emphasis added).

18. Obama quoted in Robin Givhan, "Mussed for Success: Barack Obama's Smooth Wrinkles," *Washington Post*, August 11, 2006.

19. Transcript, Meet the Press, *NBC*, October 22, 2008. Available at: http://www.msnbc.msn.com/id/15304689/# (accessed January 20, 2018).

20. David Paul Kuhn, "Obama models campaign on Reagan revolt," *Politico*, July 24, 2017.

21. Barack Obama quoted in Ben Smith, "Transformation, like Reagan," *Politico*, January 16, 2008.

22. Jon Ward, "How Barack Obama wants to be the Ronald Reagan of the left," *Yahoo*, February 6, 2015.

23. Andrew Glass, "Bush signs bank bailout," *Politico*, October 3, 2008.

24. Stephen Skowronek. 1977. *The Politics that Presidents Make. Leadership from John Adams to Bill Clinton, Revised Edition.* Cambridge, MA: Belknap Press.

25. Ibid., p. 36.

26. Ibid., p. 37.

27. Ibid.

28. Richard Kreitner, "What Time Is It? Here's What the 2016 Election Tells Us About Obama, Trump, and What Comes Next," *The Nation*, November 22, 2016.

29. "In Their Own Words: Obama on Reagan," *New York Times*. (emphasis added).

30. Cf., "Ronald Reagan, the nation's 40th president, became one of the nation's most revered public figures in recent years, a distinct turnabout from the more routinely average ratings he received while he served in office between 1981 and 1989." See Frank Newport, Jeffrey M. Jones, and Lydia Saad, "Ronald Reagan from the People's Perspective: A Gallup Poll Review," *Gallup*, June 7, 2004.

31. PEW RESEARCH CENTER 2015 GOVERNANCE SURVEY FINAL TOPLINE, p. 1. (http://assets.pewresearch.org/wp-content/uploads/sites/5/2015/11/11-23-2015-Governance-topline-for-release.pdf).

32. Pew Research Center, "Public Trust in Government: 1958–2017," May 3, 2017.

33. Jim Norman, "Americans' Confidence in Institutions Stays Low,' *Gallup*, June 3, 2016.

34. "DECONSTRUCTING DISTRUST: How Americans View Government," Pew Research Foundation for the People and the Press, March 10, 1998, p. 6.

35. Ibid., p. 8. For example, Pew found that "Looking at a comprehensive analysis based on the results of many questions, we also find that *criticism of political leaders is a principal driver of distrust in government.* The Pew survey found that criticism of political leaders is as important an element in the distrust equation *as the view that government does a poor job in running its programs. Cynicism about political leaders and the political system is more crucial to distrust than concerns about the proper role of government, worries about its power and intrusiveness, misgivings about its priorities or resentment about taxes.*" (emphasis added).

36. Robin Toner, "Obama's Test: Can a Liberal Be a Unifier?" *New York Times*, March 25, 2008.

37. Alec MacGillis, "In Obama's New Message, Some Foes See Old Liberalism," *Washington Post*, March 26, 2008, A01.
38. Peter Slevin, "Obama Forged Political Mettle in Illinois Capitol," *Washington Post*, February 9, 2007.
39. Eli Saslow, "From Outsider to Politician," *Washington Post*, October 9, 2008.
40. David Mendell. 2007. *From Promise to Power*. New York: Amistad, p. 7.
41. Brian Freil, Richard E. Cohen and Kirk Victor, "Obama: Most Liberal Senator in 2007," *National Journal*, January 31, 2008.
42. The composite reflects 99 key votes and assigned scores in three areas: economic issues, social issues, and foreign policy. See Brian Friel, Richard E. Cohen and Kirk Victor, "Obama: Most Liberal Senator in 2007," *National Journal*, 31 January 2008.
43. Toner, "Obama's Test: Can a Liberal Be a Unifier?…
44. David Remnick. 2010. *The Bridge: The Life and Rise of Barack Obama*. New York: Knopf, p. 433.
45. Michael Powell, "For Obama, a Pragmatist's Shift toward the Center," *New York Times*, June 27, 2008.
46. Howard Kurtz, "Pretzel Logic," *Washington Post*, June 27, 2008; see also Liz Sidoti, "McCain Backs Gun Decision, Obama Straddles Issue," *Associated Press*, June 26, 2008.
47. Jose Antonio Vargas, "Obama Defends Compromise on New FISA Bill," *Washington Post*, July 4, 2008.
48. Nina Easton, "Obama: NAFTA Not so Bad After All," *Fortune*, June 18, 2008.
49. David S. Broder, "Getting to Know Obama," *Washington Post*, June 22, 2000.
50. Jonathan Weisman, "Obama May Consider Slowing Iraq Withdrawal," *Washington Post*, July 4, 2008.
51. Daniel Dombey and Edward Luce, "Obama Camp Signals Robust Approach on Iran," *Financial Times*, July 1, 2008.
52. Jonathan Karl, "Obama's Evolving Position on Iran," *ABC News*, June 4, 2008.
53. Teddy Davis, Sunlen Miller, and Gregory Wallace, "Obama Kisses Millions Goodbye," *ABC News*, June 18, 2008.
54. Ruth Marcus, "Patriot Games," *Washington Post*, June 25, 2008.
55. Jonathan Weisman, "In Campaign, One Man's Pragmatism Is Another's Flip-Flopping," *Washington Post*, June 28, 2008.
56. Teddy Davis, "Obama Dubs Himself a 'Pragmatic Progressive,'" *ABC News*, January 8, 2009.
57. Lydia Saad, "Americans Unsure About 'Progressive' Political Label," *Gallup*, July 10, 2010. Available at: http://www.gallup.com/

poll/141218/americans-unsure-progressive-political-label. aspx?version=print (accessed January 21, 2018).

58. Walter Russell Mead, "Liberal Internationalism: The Twilight of a Dream," *The American Interest*, April 1, 2010.

59. Robin Wright, "'Progressive realism:' In search of a foreign policy," *New York Times*, July 18, 2006.

60. C-Span Interview, "President Barack Obama," May 22, 2009.

61. Michael Balint. (1968) 1992. *The Basic Fault: Therapeutic Aspects of Regression* (3rd Edition). Evanston, IL: Northwestern University Press.

62. William A. Galston, "President Barack Obama's First Two Years: Policy Accomplishments, Political Difficulties," The Brookings Institution, November 4, 2010.

63. Lydia Saad, "In U.S., Majority Now Say Obama's Policies 'Mostly Liberal'," *Gallup*, November 4, 2009.

64. Susan Paige, "1-year poll shows changed view on Obama," *USA Today*, November 28, 2009.

65. Pew Research Center for the People and the Press, "Obama's Ratings Little Affected by Recent Turmoil," June 24, 2010. Available at: http://people-press.org/reports/pdf/627.pdf (accessed January 21, 2018).

66. Obama quoted in Jonathan Weisman, "Obama May Consider Slowing Iraq Withdrawal Candidate Says He Remains Committed to Ending War," *Washington Post*, July 4, 2008.

67. Galston, *Op. Cit.*

68. Obama quoted in Ron Fournier, "Essay: Obama's transcendence is beyond race," *Associated Press*, November 5, 2008 (emphasis added).

69. Gallup, "Among Recent Bills, Financial Reform a Lone Plus for Congress," September 13, 2010.

70. Galston, *Op. Cit.*

71. "VOTERS DIVIDED ON OBAMA'S FIRST YEAR, WANT FOCUS ON ECONOMY AND JOBS TONIGHT," *NPR*, January 26, 2010; Judson Berger, "Obama Gets Second Chance to Stress Jobs Focus at State of the Union," *Fox News*, January 21, 2011.

72. Gerald F. Seib, "In Crisis, Opportunity for Obama," *Wall Street Journal*, November 21, 2008.

73. "Rahm Emanuel on the Opportunities of Crisis," *Wall Street Journal*, November 19, 2008. https://www.youtube.com/watch?v=_mzcbX-il Tkk (Accessed January 22, 2018).

74. Obama quoted in Lukas Pleva, "No big push in first year," *Politifact*, August 13, 2010.

75. Office of the Press Secretary, "Remarks by the President at Univision Town Hall with Jorge Ramos and Maria Elena Salinas," September 20, 2012.

76. https://www.congress.gov/bill/110th-congress/house-bill/5140
77. David M. Herszenhorn and Carl Hulse, "Deal Reached in Congress on $789 Billion Stimulus Plan," *New York Times*, February 11, 2019.
78. Andrew Fieldhouse, "5 Years After the Great Recession, Our Economy Still Far from Recovered," *Huffington Post*, June 26, 2014.
79. Catherine Rampell, "The Recession Has (Officially) Ended," *New York Times*, September 20, 2010.
80. United States Department of Labor, "The U.S. economy to 2022: settling into a new normal," Bureau of Labor Statistics, December 2013.
81. Damien Paletta, and Jeff Stein, "Sweeping tax overhaul clears Congress," *Washington Post*, December 20, 2017.
82. "Remarks by President Trump to the World Economic Forum," Davos, Switzerland, January 26, 2018.
83. Cf., "Mr. Trump intuitively understands just how much attitudes and expectations can shape economic decisions." See Patricia Cohen. "In Tax Overhaul, Trump Tries to Defy the Economic Odds," *New York Times*, December 20, 2017; see also Terry Morgan, "Analysis: It's the 'economy, stupid'. And right now, the Trump economy is blasting off," *ABC News*, January 26, 2018.
84. History and Timeline of the Affordable Care Act (ACA), September 22, 2016.
85. Galston, *Op. Cit.*, p. 7.
86. Greg Sargent, "Book: Rahm 'begged' Obama for days not to pursue ambitious health reform," *Washington Post*, May 14, 2010.
87. Lisa Myers and Hanah Rappleye, "Obama admin. knew millions could not keep their health insurance," *NBC News*, November 2, 2015; see also Glenn Kessler, "Obama's pledge that 'no one will take away' your health plan," *Washington Post*, October 30, 2013.
88. Angie Drobnik, "Lie of the Year: 'If you like your health care plan, you can keep it'," *Politicifact*, December 12, 2013.
89. Duberson quoted in Louise Radnofsky and Kristina Peterson, "The Year for Trump and GOP Lawmakers: Rocky Start, Smooth Finish," *Wall Street Journal*, December 22, 2017.
90. Sheryl Gay Stolberg, "After a Chaotic Start, Congress Has Made a Conservative Mark," *New York Times*, December 24, 2017.
91. Cf., Sean Sullivan, Julie Eilperin and Kesley Snell, "Senate GOP effort to unwind the ACA collapses Monday," *Washington Post*, September 25, 2017; see also Jonathan Easley, "2020 Democrats vote against Schumer deal," *The Hill*, January 22, 2018.
92. Noland D. McCaskill, "Trump falsely claims he broke a legislative record," *Politico*, December 27, 2017.
93. Sheryl Gay Stolberg, "After a Chaotic Start, Congress Has Made a Conservative Mark," *New York Times*, December 24, 2017.

94. Jonathan Bernstein, "What President Trump Has Accomplished," *Bloomberg*, December 19, 2017.
95. Sidney Hook. 1950. *The Hero in History: A Study in Limitation and Possibility*. Boston, MA: Bacon Press.
96. Gary C. Jacobson, "The Republican resurgence in 2010." *Political Science Quarterly, (126:1)*, Spring, 2011, p. 28.
97. Gary C. Jacobson, "Obama and Nationalized Electoral Processes in the 2014, Midterm," *Political Science Quarterly*, (130:1), Spring, 2015.
98. Obama quoted in Andrew Ross Sorkin, "President Obama Weighs His Economic Legacy, *New York Times Magazine*, April 28, 2016.
99. Elena Kagan, "Presidential Administration," *Harvard Law Review*, 114, 2000–2001.
100. Gregory Korte, "Obama's executive action rollouts increasing in pace," *USATODAY*, April 22, 2014.
101. Obama quoted in Korte, "Obama's executive action rollouts increasing in pace."
102. "Obama on Executive Actions: 'I've Got A Pen And I've Got A Phone'," *CBS News*, January 14, 2014.
103. Korte, *Op. Cit.*, "Obama's executive action rollouts increasing in pace."
104. Gregory Korte, "Obama issues 'executive orders by another name'," *USATODAY*, December 17, 2014.
105. Micheal D. Shear, "Obama, Daring Congress, Acts to Overhaul Immigration," *New York Times*, November 20, 2014.
106. Micheal D. Shear and Robert Pear, "Obama's Immigration Plan Could Shield Five Million," *New York Times*, November 19, 2014.
107. Michael D. Shear and Julia Preston, "Appeals Court Deals Blow to Obama's Immigration Plans," *New York Times*, November 9, 2015.
108. Michael D. Shear, "Obama to Appeal Immigration Ruling to Supreme Court," *New York Times*, November 10, 2015.
109. Adam Liptak and Michael D. Shear, "Supreme Court Tie Blocks Obama Immigration Plan," *New York Times*, June 23, 2017.
110. Memorandum: Janet Napolitano, Secretary, DHS to David Aguilar, Acting Comm'r, CBP, et al., "Exercising Prosecutorial Discretion with Respect to Individuals Who Came to the United States as Children,'" Department of Homeland Security, June 15, 2012.
111. Maria Saacchetti, "Kelly revokes Obama order shielding immigrant parents of U.S. citizens," *Washington Post*, June 15, 2017; see also Elaine Duke, "Rescission" of the June 15, 2012 Memorandum Entitled "Exercising Prosecutorial Discretion with Respect to Individuals Who Came to the United States as Children," Department of Homeland Security, September 5, 2017.

112. Michael D. Shear, "Trump Must Keep DACA Protections for Now, Judge Says," *New York Times*, January 9, 2017.

113. Richard Wolff, "Supreme Court agrees to speed up 'Trump's DACA appeal," *USATODAY*, January 23, 2018.

114. Vanessa Romo, Martina Stewart, and Brian Naylor, "Trump Ends DACA, Calls on Congress to Act," *NPR*, September 5, 2017.

115. Katie Sanders, "Boehner: Obama said '22 times' that he couldn't do immigration executive action," *Politifact*, March 1, 2015.

116. Joby Warrick, "Obama administration, citing climate risks, plans steep cuts in greenhouse-gas pollution," *Washington Post*, March 31, 2015.

117. "President Obama: The United States Formally Enters the Paris Agreement," The White House, September 3, 2016.

118. Valerie Volcovici, "Republicans warn world that Obama U.N. plan could be undone," *Reuters*, March 31, 2015.

119. Michael D. Shear, "Trump Will Withdraw U.S. From Paris Climate Agreement," *New York Times*, June 1, 2017.

120. The administration's view and its narrative of why it is in the country's best interests can be found at: https://obamawhitehouse.archives.gov/node/328996

121. Carol Morello and Karen DeYoug, "Nuclear deal with Iran scrutinized by experts," *Washington Post*, July 17, 2017; see also Anthony Cordesman, "The Need for a Serious New Strategy to Deal with Iran and the Gulf," *CSIS*, October 13, 2017; and David Albright and Andrea Striker, "Analysis of the IAEA's Eighth Iran Nuclear Deal Report: The JCPOA two years after Adoption Day," *ISIS*, November 13, 2016.

122. Anne Gearan and Karen DeYoung, "Trump announce plans to pull out of Iran nuclear deal despite pleas from European leaders," *Washington Post*, May 8, 2018.

123. Mark Lander and David E. Sanger, "Trump Disavows Nuclear Deal, but Doesn't Scrap It," *New York Times*, October 13, 2017.

124. Mike Pompeo, "After the Deal: A New Iran Strategy," The Heritage Foundation Washington, DC, May 21, 2018.

125. George C. Edwards. 2015. *Overreach: Leadership in the Obama Presidency*. Princeton, NJ: Princeton University Press.

126. Shirley Anne Warshaw, director of the Fielding Center for Presidential Leadership Study at Gettysburg College quoted in Peter Baker, "Can Trump Destroy Obama's Legacy?," *New York Times*, June 23, 2017.

127. Jeffrey Engel, director of the Center for Presidential History at Southern Methodist University quoted in Victoria McGrain, "Trump's greatest mission: Erasing Obama's legacy," *Boston Globe*, December 16, 2017.

128. "Just Tell Him You're the President" *NETFLICK*, "Comedians in Cars Getting Coffee," Season 7: Episode 1, December 30, 2015 [at 10:49] [italics added] https://www.youtube.com/watch?v=UM-Q_zpuJGU

Conclusion: Who Was President Barack Obama?

Wilbur C. Rich

The chapters in this volume examined several aspects of the presidency of Barack Hussein Obama. We attempted to answer two fundamental questions. What are the apparent legacies of the Obama presidency? Did his transformational impulses prevail? In this volume, we discussed the former president's achievements, controversies and shortcomings. We wanted to define the goals Obama set for himself and how he wanted to be judged and remembered (preferential legacy). President Barack Obama's approach to governing also reveals his character and personality. How history will judge him or what he will be known for in the long term (i.e., referential legacy) is still an open question. The final assessment will be left up to future historians. They will have more data about the long-term outcomes of Obama's policies. They will, like most evaluators, bring their own interest, preferences and biases to the new assessment.

Observing an elected president work is like being in a parade. Professional presidential watchers such as historians, journalists and political scientists often find themselves in the assembled crowd. We are assured that this presidential marcher will be inimitable and we wait for an event

W. C. Rich (✉)
Department of Political Science, Wellesley College, Wellesley, MA, USA
e-mail: wrich@wellesley.edu

© The Author(s) 2019   249
W. C. Rich (ed.), *Looking Back on President Barack Obama's Legacy*,
https://doi.org/10.1007/978-3-030-01545-9_11

that can be identified as a spectacle and be all telling. Describing what occurred requires an assortment of adjectives. Words like "cautious," "bold," "risky," "courageous," "confrontational," "imperial," "defensive," "narcissist" and "engaging" are used to explain the president. When the parade is over, adjectives often change as we learn more about the president and revise first impressions. The presidency of Barack Obama was historical for a variety of reasons. His election changed the norm of presidential recruitment and swept the nation up in the possibility of "hope and change." As the volume demonstrated, there was some hope and some change. However, somethings remained the same. Some of the writers in this volume concluded that Obama was not a Reconstruction President and that he slid into a preemptive category.

This generation of presidential watchers and historians is writing the first reviews of the Obama administration. We have lived through it. Moreover, people who were adults during his presidency may have different view of him than those who will only know him as an historical figure. Some Americans will conclude that the "hope and change(s)" that Obama promised happened. Other will disagree. Obama vigorously campaigned for the job and promised real change for the nation. And like most elected presidents, he may have overestimated what can be done from the Oval Office. The difference between what the public expects and what a president can really do is called an expectation gap. Americans often have unrealistic expectations of this evolving secular and political office. Simply put, presidents, for a variety of reasons, are expected to have supernatural powers. Political scientist Bert A. Rockman recognized this at the end of Obama's first term and concluded,

> Those with hopes beyond the possible should consult a person of the cloth. That could be transformational. Those with more realistic hopes as to what our political system can produce and what our politicians can resolve will be appropriately skeptical of the "hope and change" business. Ultimately, under any circumstances, there are a limited set of things that can be more than incrementally influenced by political action. Therefore, Barack Obama has not been a transformational president. No presidents are, certainly not by themselves. Context provides the potential for decisive actions. But using a milder standard, Obama has been a reasonably successful president when the circumstances have allowed him to be.[1]

Perhaps because of Barack Obama's background and rhetorical skills, he could not avoid the British Monty Python Flying Circus comedy group's opening prologue. "Now for something really different." Beside his skills as an extemporaneous speaker and his mastery of the teleprompter, President Obama was, in some ways, "something really different" but in many ways he was quite similar to other presidential speechmakers. For whom much is given eloquence wise, much is expected. The escalating public expectations of the presidential capabilities predated Barack Obama and will afflict his successors. These expectations have changed the nature of the presidency and presidents have to spend time attempting to appease a variety of niche groups by speaking to them directly. Put even more simply, the presidency may be lurching toward what Joshua Scacco and Kevin Coe called the "ubiquitous presidency."

> [T]he presidency over the past several decades has transitioned from a rhetorical presidency to a ubiquitous presidency, the latter characterized by frequent communication in a variety of (non)traditional settings. This shift has hinged on three elements. First, presidents have prioritized specific forms of *accessibility*, such as employing interactive media and appearing in comedic and pop culture venues. Second, the presidency has become more *personal*, prioritizing disclosive and less formal forms of communication. Finally, the presidency must now increasingly engage in a more *pluralistic* nation and world, making targeted messages (of praise or attack, depending on the speaker and the context) the new normal.[2]

The new normal requires presidents to react to a variety of domestic and international actors. In addition, there are plethora of events competing for their attention. We also know that conflicts, catastrophes and mishaps sometimes just unexpectedly happen and that some solutions are beyond the control of a president. Accordingly, some aspects of presidential legacy are imposed on the occupant. The contributors in this volume based their findings and conclusions on what they saw, read and researched about the eight years of the Obama administration.

WHAT CONTRIBUTORS KNEW?

We watched Obama campaign and heard his promises. Lyn Ragsdale's chapter traced the historic 2008 campaigns and subsequent voter turnouts. After assuming office, the new president had to make several defining political decisions. We tried to explain why President Obama engaged in domestic unilateralism in order to cope with a variety of challenges. The election of Barack Obama came at a critical moment in the history of

America, a nation that had struggled with racial inequality for decades. President Obama's impact on subsequent elections explains the continuing political challenges for the American electorate. After assuming office, the new president had to make several defining political decisions. The chapters tried to explain why President Obama engaged in domestic unilateralism in order to cope with a variety of presenting social and economic problems. The Great Recession was arguably the most challenging. The Congress passed, and the president signed several laws to address the crisis. Some people may have expected fundamental changes in the nation's financial system. However, Kristoffer Smemo concluded that Obama's financial reforms were actually pro-Wall Street, banks and corporations. Ruth Milkman was disappointed that Obama economic policies were not more job producing and labor organizing friendly. Michael A. Genovese, Todd Belt and William Lammers also make a similar point. They stated, "Rather than a New Deal-style focus on creating make work jobs to combat unemployment, Obama saw the recession as an opportunity to retool the economy for new century by providing assistance to businesses investing in high technology and green energy innovations."[3]

President Obama also addressed several cultural and social trends in America. He championed the civil rights of African Americans and the LGBTQ community. Yet, Kimberley Johnson analyzed the convergence of Obama's political and racial time and explained why he did not become a transformational civil rights president. Many of these social and civil rights issues found themselves on the U.S. Supreme Court docket. Isaac Unah and Ryan Williams examined Obama relations to the Supreme Court and concluded that the two justices he appointed were reliable members of the liberal minority. Yet the Court remains very conservative on a variety of voting and political issues.

Another domestic issue that many scholars consider his signature legislative achievement was the Affordable Care Act. Jill Quadagno and Daniel Lansford delved into the origin of Affordable Care Act and its passage. The new policy had significant start-up problems, but it provided health care to many uninsured Americans. The Trump administration was able to eliminate the individual mandates which were critical to the health care financing scheme. Consequently, the law has grown in popularity and attempts by the Trump administration to repeal it have been only partially successful. Another important domestic issue was the plight of the environment. Obama embraced globalization, Paris Climate Accord, delayed the Keystone pipeline and initiated other international climate-protecting efforts. However, the Obama administration continued to rely on state governments to implement greenhouse gas emission at home. George Gonzalez found that state political leaders did not follow through on many environmental policies and were more interested in attracting business and jobs than they were in greenhouse gas emissions.

Like his predecessors, President Obama inherited a series of foreign policy issues and decisions. There were ongoing wars and other international conflicts. Obama's management of these conflicts is a critical part of his legacy. Meena Bose examined President Obama's speeches, policy doctrine, and responses to ongoing foreign policy challenges.

Finally, Stanley Renshon examined President Obama the man, his personality and his ambitions. Judging Obama by his own standards, his tenure was a mixed record. Renshon believes the source of his modest record was related to his fixation of becoming a "great president." Obama attempted to achieve triumphantly when ordinary solutions would have sufficed. Renshon examines how President Obama misinterpreted what Americans expected from him.

We, as a group, also knew that President Obama, the 44th president of the United States, left office on January 20, 2017. We knew that once an outgoing president watches the new president take the oath of office, their time in office is officially over but their legacies are now open to summaries and evaluations. We also knew the public's view of President Obama depends on their partisan affiliation, personal ideology, class position or level of a citizen's psychological identification to him.

It may be an understatement to say that Barack Obama was elected to the presidency at a critical moment in American history. The nation was at an economic and social crossroad. His arrival to the presidency was not exactly a Rooseveltian moment but it was close. Even he knew that his presidency might not have been possible if it weren't for the Black Civil Rights Movement and overall optimism and faith of the American people. Moreover, his tenure in office came at time when the nation was struggling with the demands of a post-industrial and globalized world.

Presidencies are like water in rivers and incumbents cannot step into the same water at the same place. Heraclitus, the Greek philosopher, axiom that "you could not step twice in the same river" holds here. The presidential secession from George Washington to Barack Obama was not linear progression. There were punctuations in the economic, political and social equilibriums that defined what Obama was able to do.[4] We contributors recognized the daunting expectation gap. Obama also recognized this gap when he stated, "I serve as a blank screen on which people project their own views. As such, I am bound to disappoint some, if not all, of them"[5] Some pundits thought that Obama was not progressive enough, while others thought he was way too left of the political spectrum.[6]

The contributors in this volume attempted to reflect the complexity of President Obama's governing style and how government policy was made in a separated political system. Presidential decisions are difficult to be compartmented. One issue can overlap others. Indeed, the Obama record told us much about the last eight years but not everything. We were aware that we did not have all the data on the Obama administration. However, this review matters because evaluating presidents is a comparative enterprise. Yet, the contributors in this volume strived to present a dispassionate analysis.

PRESIDENT OBAMA AND THE ISSUES

Retrospectively, there were a variety of issues on President Obama's agenda. Like his predecessors, he inherited decisions and policies made by others. Nonetheless, presidents are inundated with new policy challenges. Some issues were recurrent while others were short lived. Some received more attention than others. Obama could not safely ignore any of these policies nor could he veer off too far from accepted methods for handling them. The dynamic civil rights agenda has been on the president's desk since the Lyndon Johnson administration. Obama expanded it. The courts played a role in this equalizing effort and with other problems facing the nation. National health reform had been around since the Truman administration, but Obama enacted Affordable Care Act. The fight against foreign terrorism grew more intense with 9/11 and Obama was obligated to continue it. The conflicts in the Middle East have defied the diplomatic talent and military acuity of many presidents. Obama was no exception. Scientists debated climate change before Obama came to office. Obama attempted to move forward on that issue. The horrific Sandy Hook Elementary School shootings in Newtown (2012) and the Charleston church shooting (2015) highlighted the need for gun control but President Obama did not have enough political power to change federal policy. Obama inherited the Great Recession and his reaction to it and the overall economic challenges for the nation will always be a part of his overall legacy.

Presidents, in general, have had some influence in alleviating problems or not letting them overwhelm their presidencies. Presidents as muddling through practitioners are often the norm, that is, making decisions with limited information in order to make incremental changes.[7] Yet, some presidents have openly tried to reverse or repudiate predecessors' policies. There was a recent cartoon in *Citizen Times* (Asheville, NC) and republished in *USA Today* that depicted the current President Donald J. Trump erasing the Obama legacy off the whiteboard.[8] Belittling and undermining the legacy of one's predecessors is not uncommon. It is part of the process of clearing the deck so that a new legacy can be made. Every president knows this or is told by staff that his legacy will be compared to his predecessors.

Legacies Matters

In 2017, *The Washington Post*-ABC polls asked respondent the question: Do you approve or disapprove of the way Barack Obama has handled/is handling his job as president? He started with 68% approval rate in 2009 and went down to 48% in 2012 and finish with a 60% approval rating. His disapproval grew from 25% to 38%. The poll also asked a legacy question: How do you think Barack Obama will go down in history—as an outstanding president, above average, average, below average or poor? The net above average was 51% with 26% outstanding and 25% above average. There was a 25% average rating and net below average 24% with a 14% poor rating.[9] Barack Obama had a good approval rating in office and he left it with an above average rating.

Modern president's yearly approval ratings are now critical to the policymaking process. Congress and the media take their cues from the various polls and use them for discussing politics. Parenthetically, there are signs that President Obama intends to follow President Carter's lead by staying active in current politics. Accordingly, his overall legacy may still be in the making. Having an active post-presidency role could prove interesting.

Contributors in this volume have evaluated only what he did while in office. Some readers may use a different matrix than the one used by this editor to locate Obama's legacies. Nevertheless, whatever box one assigns to specific policies, grading them matters. Obviously not all societal issues reach the presidency. There are needed social changes in America that presidents should not be asked to act on or comment on as the resolution of these issues is clearly in province of the civil society. All presidents should respect this axiom.

Publishers and Legacies

We live in a society in which the public wants to know a lot of personal information about their presidents. Some people are interested in the president's pet names, hobbies and their diet. They expect the former president to write a disclosing book after leaving office. For this volume, we did not have the benefits of what is now the obligatory presidential book about his days in the White House. Modern presidents received large financial advances from publishers to write book about their lives in the White House (e.g., Bill Clinton, *My Life* [2004] and George W. Bush, *Decision Points* [2010]). Penguin Random House allegedly paid the former president and the First Lady (Michelle Obama) $30 million respectfully. Publishers believe that given the historical nature of their time in the White House, these books should be enlightening for the general public.

In the past, presidents used speeches and wrote diaries to reveal their thinking and motivations. Newspaper coverage was critical to defining presidential reactions to events. Today, presidents used radio, television appearances, telephone, emails and social media to consolidate their legacy. This is perhaps more democratic because it allows citizens to know almost immediately what the president does, said and wrote. Citizens should have this type of entrée into nascent presidential legacies. Indeed, the Congress has recognized the importance of presidential legacy. This is why it requires the government to preserve the papers of the presidents and provides funding for presidential libraries. Scholars and the general public alike can now visit presidential libraries.

Finally, President Barack H. Obama is an historical figure. He will always be the first African American president of the United States. His legacy may endure even after we get the second African American president or there is another first.

Notes

1. Bert A. Rockman "The Obama Presidency: Hope, Change and Reality" *Social Science Quarterly*, Vol. 93, No. 5 (December 2012) p. 1079.
2. Joshua M. Scacco and Kevin Coe "Ubiquitous Presidency and Expectations of Presidential Communication, "*American Behavior Scientist* (2017) Vol. 61 (3) p. 302.
3. Michael A. Genovese, Todd Belt and William Lammers, Op cit. p. 221.
4. See Frank R. Baumgartner and Bryan D. *Jones Agendas and Instability in American Politics* Chicago: University of Chicago Press, 2009).

5. Cited in "Explaining the Riddle" *Economist* (August 23, 2008) p. 20.
6. Theda Skocpol and Lawrence. R. Jacobs, "Accomplished and Embattled: Understanding Obama's Presidency," *Political Science Quarterly* Vol. 127, No. 1 (Spring, 2012) pp. 1–24.
7. See Charles E. Lindblom "The Science of "Muddling Through," *Public Administration Review*, Vol. 19, No. 2 (Spring, 1959) pp. 79–88.
8. David Cohen Citizen-Times.Com/voices-news 2017 Asheville (NC) *Citizen Times.*
9. *Washington Post*-ABC News January 12–15 among 1005 U.S. Adults. The *Washington Post* (January 19, 2017) www.washingtonpost.com/politics/polling/...

Index[1]

[1] Note: Page numbers followed by 'n' refer to notes.

© The Author(s) 2019
W. C. Rich (ed.), *Looking Back on President Barack Obama's Legacy*,
https://doi.org/10.1007/978-3-030-01545-9

Printed by Printforce, the Netherlands